TALKING
AFFIRMATIVE
ACTION

TALKING AFFIRMATIVE ACTION

Race, Opportunity, and Everyday Ideology

Helen D. Lipson

ROWMAN & LITTLEFIELD PUBLISHERS, INC.

Lanham • Boulder • New York • Toronto • Oxford

ROWMAN & LITTLEFIELD PUBLISHERS, INC.

Published in the United States of America
by Rowman & Littlefield Publishers, Inc.
A wholly owned subsidiary of The Rowman & Littlefield Publishing Group, Inc.
4501 Forbes Boulevard, Suite 200, Lanham, Maryland 20706
www.rowmanlittlefield.com

P.O. Box 317, Oxford OX2 9RU, UK

British Library Cataloguing in Publication Information Available

Library of Congress Cataloging-in-Publication Data
Lipson, Helen D., 1949–
  Talking affirmative action : race, opportunity, and everyday ideology / Helen D. Lipson.
  p. cm.
  Includes bibliographical references and index.
  ISBN 0-7425-3800-1 (cloth : alk. paper) — ISBN 0-7425-3801-X (pbk. : alk. paper)
  1. Affirmative action programs in education—United States. 2. Educational
equalization—United States. 3. Academic achievement—United States. 4. Minority
college students—Recruiting—United States. 5. Minorities—Education (Higher)—
United States. I. Title.
  LC213.52.L55 2005
  379.2'6'0973—dc22

                                                                        2005019918

Printed in the United States of America

∞™ The paper used in this publication meets the minimum requirements of
American National Standard for Information Sciences—Permanence of Paper
for Printed Library Materials, ANSI/NISO Z39.48-1992.

CONTENTS

ACKNOWLEDGMENTS

Talking Affirmative Action might never have been written but for the extraordinary encouragement of Cedric Herring, who was also a resilient sounding board for some of my more heterodox views on American race relations. Joe Persky, as well, was unfailingly supportive of this project—not least through his enthusiasm for a style of research quite different from his own.

Staying the course, though, took more than a little help from my friends, especially Fran Patterson, Peter Coey, and David Schroder, always ready companions and very patient listeners. So were my sisters, Ruth Brown and Joan Muellner both of whose insights on the issues this book addresses helped to strengthen my research design and enrich my analysis.

I also want to thank Robert Carr, of the Law School Admissions Council, for repeatedly taking the time to provide detailed test score data; Johnette Peyton, of the Graduate Management Admissions Council, for helping me navigate and interpret that organization's online archives; and Peter Schmidt, of the *Chronicle of Higher Education*, who pointed the way toward some pertinent studies of American Latinos.

Critical to this project early on were the fifty faculty members at the University of Illinois at Chicago whose cooperation on a preliminary survey ensured access to an ample number and variety of interview subjects. A very special thanks, moreover, to the thirty-two men I eventually interviewed, on whose thoughtful, evocative responses this book is built.

INTRODUCTION

> It sucks! I mean, it sucks either way. It sucks if you keep somebody down because of their color. And it sucks if you elevate somebody up at the expense of somebody else.
>
> —Steve Clayburgh[1]

Almost forty years after its inception, affirmative action continues to draw very mixed reviews from the American public. Public opinion research suggests that the great majority of Americans favor efforts to dismantle longstanding public and private barriers to opportunity for women and for men of color—whether with respect to jobs, education, political participation, housing, or anything else—because such barriers are viewed as inconsistent with commonplace, collective notions of economic and social justice. What has proven far more controversial, however, is the notion that the removal of *explicit* roadblocks to racial and gender equity is not nearly enough to offset lingering, covert, de facto preferences for white males, or the lingering effects of *past* discrimination against women or persons of color.

The most widely known articulation of this perspective is probably President Lyndon Johnson's commencement address to Howard University in 1965.

> You do not take a person who, for years, has been hobbled by chains and liberate him, bring him up to the starting line of a race and then say, "You are free to compete with all the others," and still justly believe that you have been completely fair. . . . Ability is stretched or stunted by the poverty or the richness of

your surroundings. . . . There is also the lacerating hurt of early collision with white hatred or prejudice, distaste or condescension.

By this reckoning, thoroughgoing efforts to equalize opportunity necessarily involve special efforts to recruit, hire, or enroll women and minorities in those organizations, institutions, and areas of endeavor in which they have traditionally been underrepresented.

In practical terms, this can mean many different things: encouraging more young women to consider careers in physics, engineering, and the building trades, for example; upgrading science laboratories in American Indian reservation high schools; making sure that low-income *barrio* teenagers have more personal contact with Latino professionals and businesspersons; or sending more recruiters from high-profile corporations to traditionally black colleges.[2] But what most people think of when affirmative action is mentioned—and what is especially likely to invite protest—is the use of race, ethnicity, or "proportionate representation" as a selection criterion in its own right. For at first glance, this seems to fly in the face of the very principle whose long-standing betrayal created the conditions affirmative action is intended to counteract: the principle that everyone should be judged on his or her own merits, without regard to social, geographic, religious, or ethnic origins.

Advocates of affirmative action argue that this principle is no longer reasonable when special barriers to academic achievement and economic advancement have hobbled fair competition between men and women or among members of different ethnic groups. Put another way, *marginal* procedural equality—that is, treating everyone in the same manner at the same point in the distribution of opportunities—must give ground to *cumulative* procedural *in*equalities that disallow fair comparisons of individual potential.[3] Opponents, however, counter that two wrongs don't make a right, and that the more aggressive forms of affirmative action do more harm than good, especially to those they are designed to benefit. And many of us, like Steve Clayburgh, are pulled in both directions, helping to fuel a decades-long controversy not only between whites and minorities or between men and women but also within both genders and inside every ethnic group.

This book explores the nature of that controversy and its wellsprings in "everyday" ideology—specifically, in the disparate beliefs of ordinary Americans concerning inequality, the dynamics of equal opportunity, and the scope of our collective obligation to enforce it.

The subjects of my thirty-two in-depth interviews were white males, the bogeymen (bogeypersons?) of the affirmative action saga. The whole thrust of affirmative action, after all, has been to reallocate to women and to men of color much of the power, advantage, and opportunity that have traditionally accrued to white men, so it has surprised no one that public opinion surveys have repeatedly found them to be more resistant to affirmative action than any other gender/ethnic category. On the other hand, their very power and influence suggest that affirmative action—like abolition, women's suffrage, an end to *de jure* segregation, or the removal of legal barriers to abortion—cannot work very well, and can never be sustained, without some critical mass of white male advocates, both within the "power elite" and among ordinary working people and students.

So by design, my interviews were split between white men who endorsed some of the most aggressive forms of affirmative action and other white men who opposed them. At the center of my exchanges with these men was race-targeted affirmative action admissions to JD, MBA, and MD programs, whose graduates thereby gain entrée to some of the most lucrative and influential spheres and strata of the American work force. The specific issues raised in these interviews reflect the character of public debate over affirmative action, as played out in our courthouses, statehouses, and mass media; by the particulars of affirmative action in the realm of college and university admissions, recruiting, and campus programs; and by some provocative prior research.

Old News: *What do we already know about public opinion regarding affirmative action?*

One consistent finding of three decades of research is that advocates and opponents tend to explain in different ways differences in economic outcomes, both in general and between blacks and whites.[4] Advocates tend to emphasize environmental influences, such as racism past or present and inferior public schools in minority-majority neighborhoods. Opponents, by contrast, are more likely to blame differences in outcomes on a lack of ability or self-discipline among blacks themselves. More generally, opponents are also more likely to believe that "this is a land of opportunity where economic advancement is possible for those at the bottom of the economic ladder who 'have the talent and make the effort.'"[5]

What remain in dispute, however, are the sources of these disparate perspectives. A considerable body of scholarship urges us to consider opposition on ideological grounds as a smoke screen for racism, reinforcing whites' unenlightened self-interest in maintaining their superior position in America's social, economic, and political hierarchies.

Certainly, policies designed to advance racial equality will tend to be opposed by those who believe that members of other races are inherently lazier, less intelligent, or more violent than whites are, or that nonwhites are simply delegated by God to inferior status. But these days, there simply isn't enough evidence of such "old-fashioned" racism among American whites to account for the degree of antipathy toward race-conscious policies they express. On the other hand, a great many whites remain very hesitant to live in mixed neighborhoods, or to send their children to schools with large black enrollments. Whites very often view minority communities as havens for drug dealers and street gangs, as a kind of parallel universe in which the norms of working for a living and two-parent families have been abandoned. If we take this as evidence of a "new racism" or "modern racism"—whereby critiques of minority cultures or lifestyles have been substituted for less politically-correct accusations of inherent inequality—then it makes much more sense to speak of a causal link between racism and widespread opposition to affirmative action.

Research evidence for this link, though, is a little shaky. For one thing, much of the statistical evidence amounts to a circular argument, to the degree that survey items used to identify "racism" actually measure responses to public policy, so that any correlation found between "racism" and policy preferences proves nothing more than the consistency of the latter.[6] Neither racism nor white self-interest, moreover, can explain why affirmative action is opposed by a good many blacks and Latinos. Can they all simply be written off as "self-hating" or "sell-outs," Uncle Toms or Tomasos, black- or brown-on-the-outside, white-on-the-inside "Oreos" or "coconuts"? And are both white and minority advocates of affirmative action simply "blaming the victim" when they promote after-school programs, mentoring networks, and other efforts designed to counter negative aspects of life in many low-income minority communities?

Opponents, of course, have their own take on the affirmative action controversy, often defending their position in relation to "traditional values" that advocates are seen as all too ready to turn their backs on. The most vocal of white advocates, certainly, have also tended to espouse a number of causes—for gay rights, against capitalist exploitation, or against "imperialistic" intrusions on the native cultures of minority children, for example—that go against the grain of a good many "cultural conservatives." But hasn't the strongest argument for affirmative action always been the need to compensate for egregious departures from the all-American ideal of equality of opportunity? It may be worth considering that this and other consensual values are nonetheless construed somewhat differently by those on opposite sides of the issue.

All in all, what we think we know raises more questions than it answers about the roots of advocacy and opposition. And while it is well established that different ways of talking about any given policy may evoke quite different responses,[7] few studies have examined in any detail the relative acceptability to whites of different models or features of affirmative action that have taken shape at American colleges and universities.

Higher Learning: *Why affirmative action admissions matters*

These days, one rarely hears about affirmative action on behalf of Asian Americans or white women, both of whom are well represented on most campuses and in almost every field of study.[8] Things have not gone nearly as well, however, for blacks, Latinos, and American Indians, who on the average earn lower grades in high school and college, earn lower scores on standardized admissions tests,[9] and are less likely to attend or to graduate from college—any college—let alone attend highly selective institutions.

Many observers have traced much of the achievement gap among undergraduates to racial tensions on campus, excessively Eurocentric curricula, and a general sense of unease or dislocation among students of color at majority-white institutions. This may be especially true, it is argued, for those from heavily-minority neighborhoods, or from minority-majority high schools lacking the will or the resources to provide an adequate foundation for college study.[10] With this in mind, American colleges and universities have introduced a variety of programs and services designed to improve morale, performance, and graduation rates among students of color, such as "theme" dormitories, ethnic-specific academic support centers, and race-targeted research internships, as well as "outreach" programs to area high schools, or in some cases, campus programs for talented high school students.

All such efforts count as "affirmative action" and in many cases are explicitly designed to give students of color a leg up on attendance at selective colleges or postgraduate education and employment. Not surprisingly, these policies have evoked some serious criticism; but both public opinion polls and the legal record suggest that race-conscious admissions in particular is far and away the least popular model of affirmative action—especially when this clearly involves quotas, set-asides, or some other form of marginal inequality.[11]

Some of the loudest protests have come from able, ambitious white high school graduates, concerned that affirmative action may keep them from attending some of the country's most selective undergraduate colleges, and hence from enjoying the sorts of long-term professional and social advantages that often accrue to those schools' graduates. Those concerns are not illegitimate; but the fact remains that for those denied admission to those *particular* schools, there remain a great many alternatives of a quality and reputation sufficient to ensure an almost unlimited range of opportunities to their graduates. The stakes may be considerably higher, however, for applicants to graduate professional schools and programs.

This is especially evident in the case of medical school, which is not only a legal requirement for the practice of medicine in this country, but also provides better entrée than a PhD to many areas of biomedical research.[12] At the same time, the high cost of medical education and the finite resources of "teaching hospitals" sharply limit admissions. Likewise, those without a law degree are barred from the practice of law and the stepping-stone this has provided to so many careers in politics. A growing number of law schools, over the past few decades, has come closer to matching the number of openings with the number of applicants; but then, a JD per se does not offer nearly the guarantee of making a living in one's chosen field that an MD does. Entree to the most highly regarded firms and the more lucrative kinds of practice have traditionally been linked not only to one's law school performance but also to *which* law school one has attended.[13]

Affirmative action admissions to MBA programs has been much less of an issue, perhaps because few highly selective programs are offered by public institutions, whose policies applicants may hold to a stricter standard vis-à-vis constitutional guarantees. Because MBA program are known to give considerable weight to applicants' prior work experience, moreover, it's harder to make the case that white applicants have lost out to "less qualified" minorities simply by comparing their grades and test scores. In contrast to law and medicine, moreover—or for that matter, to nursing, school teaching, and other occupations that require state licensure—there are no occupations, no career tracks limited to MBAs, who often find themselves in competition with those whose graduate training is in some other field, those without graduate training, and in some cases those who (like IBM founder and megamillionaire Bill Gates, for example) hold no degrees at all.

Taking into account as well the proliferation of MBA programs over the past few decades, this degree per se may add very little to one's marketability. But this just makes the competition to enroll at the most selective schools—Harvard, Northwestern, Chicago, Wharton, and so on—more intense, not only because of the quality of education they provide, but because their superior reputations and well-placed alumni help to ensure that *their* MBAs, at least, have the inside track on a great many of the best openings in business and finance.

For aspirants to top MBA programs no less than pre-laws or pre-meds, then, graduate professional school admissions would seem to have enormous consequences for one's immediate or eventual access to some of the best jobs on the planet. So it is no accident that such schools' policies were at issue in three out of the four landmark decisions on affirmative action admissions issued over the years by our federal courts.

Courtroom Drama: *Bakke, Hopwood, Gratz, and Grutter*

"No state," the Fourteenth Amendment of the U.S. Constitution reads, "shall . . . deny to any person within its jurisdiction the equal protection of the laws." The linchpin of the legal decisions that dismantled Jim Crow policies in the 1950s, this amendment has also been at the center of deliberations over affirmative action. Supreme Court majorities have found equal protection consistent with marginal inequalities only when the latter have been introduced by organizations found guilty of a deliberate pattern of exclusion or segregation, such that even the most aggressive forms of affirmative action may be viewed as a reasonable extension of customary notions of "fair redress." Just as individuals or their families are customarily compensated for what those individuals have suffered at another's hand, so members of previously disfavored groups might now receive compensation in the form of preferences in their favor. When businesses or labor unions are found to have consistently excluded nonwhites or women from certain kinds of jobs, the Court might not simply approve but demand a special effort to find construction trades apprenticeships for African Americans, for example, or to add women to telephone companies' installation and repair crews. In like manner, colleges and universities with a history of blocking black or Mexican American attendance are expected to take whatever steps were necessary to desegregate their campuses.

In the case of organizations with *no* visible record of discrimination themselves, however, long-standing racial discrimination *in general*—on the part of schools, businesses, social clubs, and so forth—has never been enough to convince a majority of the Supreme Court that marginal inequalities should be condoned. When such inequalities have nonetheless been approved by the Court, it was on the basis of "compelling state interest"—essentially, on the grounds that greater ethnic diversity would serve the common good—or on the basis of the First Amendment.

Examples of "compelling state interest" have included racial preferences on the part of some big-city police departments, which argued successfully that greater diversity among their ranks might do a better job fighting crime in a multiracial community. A different argument, however, has kept affirmative action admissions on the books: That academic freedom, and the free play of ideas on the college campuses, was a necessary extension of freedom of speech, and that in the furtherance of a free exchange of disparate points of view, institutions of higher learning were within their rights to seek a more diverse student body.

This argument first came to the fore in 1978, when the Supreme Court issued a landmark decision on *Regents of the University of California* v. *Bakke*.[14] In 1973 and again in 1974, a white male named Allan Bakke had been denied admission to the medical school of the University of California at Davis. At the time, applicants who identified themselves as members of a racial/ethnic minority, or as economically or educationally disadvantaged, were first screened by a "special admissions" committee before any were passed on to the general committee. In contrast to other applicants, moreover, "special" applicants with undergraduate grade point averages below 2.5 were not automatically excluded. There was no guarantee that any given individual referred by the special committee would be admitted. But overall, sixteen of the one hundred places in each freshman class were set aside for applicants so recommended, and the special admissions committee continued to recommend candidates to the general committee until those places had been filled.

In addition to forty-four Asian, black, Latino, and American Indian applicants admitted through the regular admissions process over a four-year period, sixty-three more had been admitted through the special admissions program. No low-income or educationally disadvantaged whites gained admission in this manner, however, even though many had applied. For all applicants, undergraduate grades and scores on the MCAT (Medical College Admissions Test) remained the most critical selection criteria; but a great many of the special admits had substantially lower grades and test scores than a great many white rejects, including Allan Bakke.

In its decision against UC Davis, the Supreme Court admonished universities against the use of numerical quotas or set asides, which barred white applicants from even competing for those places. The court insisted, moreover, that the sort of separate-and-unequal admissions protocols Davis had established must be abolished. Addressing the more general question of whether *some* form of marginal preferences could be maintained, the court rejected three of UC's principal arguments. The mere fact of historic underrepresentation was not sufficient evidence of discrimination against minority applicants, and absent such evidence, the institution had no grounds to impose a preference in their favor "at the expense of other innocent individuals" not part of the favored groups. Any justification of such preferences on the grounds of more general, societal discrimination, moreover, would simply invite similar arguments from any number of white ethnic groups, posing an intolerable challenge to the nation's judiciary, who would therefore be asked to "evaluate the extent of the prejudice and consequent harm suffered by various minority groups," and to decide which groups' "societal injury" was sufficient to entitle them to compensatory preferences. Over time,

As these preferences began to have their desired effect, and the consequences of past discrimination were undone, new judicial rankings would be necessary. The kind of variable sociological and political analysis necessary to produce such rankings simply does not lie within the judicial competence—even if they otherwise were politically feasible and socially desirable.[15]

UC had also argued that the state had a compelling interest in ensuring adequate medical care to traditionally underserved minority communities. But this would not necessarily follow, the court concluded, from an increase in the number of minority MDs; and even if it did, there were other means to the same end that would not violate the Fourteenth Amendment. Justice Lewis Powell's majority decision, however, did endorse a fourth argument put forth by the university: that racial preferences were consistent with numerous precedents upholding academic freedom.

Citing a 1957 ruling against the requirement that New Hampshire state university faculty sign "loyalty oaths," and a 1967 ruling against undue scrutiny of a New York State faculty's course lectures and political affiliations, Powell reaffirmed Justice Felix Frankfurter's opinion that, "It is the business of a university to provide that atmosphere which is most conducive to speculation, experiment and creation . . . [and] to determine for itself . . . who may teach, what may be taught, how it shall be taught, and who may be admitted to study"[16] as well as Justice William Brennan's view that, "The Nation's future depends upon leaders trained through wide exposure to [a] robust exchange of ideas."[17]

Detractors, however, remained unconvinced that such arguments justified the consideration of race in admissions decisions, and many saw a U.S. Circuit Court's decision on *Hopwood* v. *University of Texas*[18] twelve years later as the death knell for affirmative action as we had known it.

Part of the Court's problem with UT Austin's law school was that it had instituted the same sort of procedural distinctions as UC Davis had between the way white and minority applicants were treated. Once again, though, the Court also spoke to the larger question and argued that Powell's rationale for ethnic diversity in *Bakke* could not be considered a binding precedent, because that particular rationale had appeared only in a separate opinion of Powell's that had not been joined by any other justice. *Hopwood* did not challenge the desirability of diverse points of view in the classroom, but the court argued that racial preferences at the point of admission were not an appropriate means to that end. Indeed, the very equation of ethnic diversity with divergent points of view, *Hopwood* argued, would encourage just the sort of racial stereotyping that advocates of affirmative action hoped to offset. At the same time, all of *Bakke's* arguments *against* racial preferences were upheld. Giving any weight at all to an applicant's race or ethnicity was ruled unconstitutional.

The Supreme Court let the circuit court's decision on *Hopwood* stand. But on July 23, 2003, the legal landscape shifted once again when the Court issued two more landmark decisions, one in favor and one against the University of Michigan at Ann Arbor. In *Gratz* v. *Bollinger*,[19] the court rejected the admissions policies of the undergraduate College of Literature, Arts, and Sciences (LAS); while *Grutter* v. *Bollinger* [20] endorsed those of the university's law school.

On their face, at least, neither suit challenged Powell's defense of limited racial preferences in *Bakke*. Plaintiffs' attorneys were "not suggesting an absolute rule forbidding of any use of race under any circumstances." [21] But in their view, *Bakke* had never given schools the liberty to accord race as much weight as the University of Michigan had.

In the case of LAS, racial preferences were built into a points system, whereby each applicant was assigned up to 150 points, 110 on the basis of his or her test scores and academic performance in high school, [22] and the remaining 40 on other criteria. Of the latter, a full 20 were assigned to any member of an "underrepresented minority." Whites and Asians could earn the same 20 points only if they could qualify as varsity athletes at Michigan (an advantage open to minority applicants as well), or had graduated from a high school with a predominantly black, Latino, American Indian, and/or "underprivileged" student body. While students with at least 100 points were routinely admitted, those with less than 90 were almost never admitted on the admissions office's first pass through an application, and whites and Asian Americans with less than 75 points were typically rejected without further scrutiny. With their 20-point handicap, however, admission was guaranteed to any blacks, Latinos, or American Indians who qualified for at least 80 points on nonracial grounds. A majority of the Court agreed with plaintiff's counsel that this gave members of these three groups an excessive advantage over other applicants, essentially establishing an unacceptable double standard. This was, moreover, an across-the-board advantage, without any consideration for the impact of race on a given individual's life experience or achievements. Other than one's prowess on the playing field, nonacademic achievement, leadership, or public service counted for much less. Even the student whose "extraordinary artistic talent rivaled that of Monet or Picasso," the *Gratz* decision notes, "would receive, at most, five points" on that account, while Michigan residency earned just ten points. [23]

The Supreme Court found this points system—or, indeed, any system that assigned points on the basis of race or ethnicity—unconstitutional. The Court did not, however, equate the law school's concern for some "critical mass" of each racial/ethnic minority with an explicit quota or target, and it upheld that school's use of race as part of "a highly individualized, holistic review of each applicant's file . . . [and] all the ways an applicant might contribute to a diverse educational environment." [24] Even in this context, however, ethnic identity would not remain a legitimate consideration indefinitely. "We expect that 25 years from now, the use of racial preferences will no longer be necessary to further the interest approved today." [25]

The Way We Live Now: *Holistic assessment, percentage plans, and the new, improved SAT*

Gratz and *Grutter* left affirmative action admissions alive and kicking but nonetheless extremely vulnerable to attack. For one thing, there is nothing in either decision to force race-conscious policies on any state that does not want them—California and Washington State, for example, where voter referenda years earlier had banned such policies. Other states might easily follow—and those that don't are now subject to increasing scrutiny by the U.S. Department of Education, as well as several private organizations, including the American Civil Rights Institute, the Center for Equal Opportunity, the Center for Individual Rights, and the National Association of Scholars.[26] While private institutions' admissions policies remain relatively free of interference, several schools have been forced to eliminate or modify outreach and student-support programs formerly limited to members of underrepresented minority groups.

Typically, criteria for participation in these programs have been broadened to embrace whites and Asians of relatively modest socioeconomic or academic backgrounds. At MIT, for example, two summer programs formerly limited to blacks, Latinos, and American Indians—one for incoming freshmen, and another for rising seniors in high school—are now open to other students "who had to overcome significant odds to pursue their dreams of becoming an engineer or scientist."[27] Princeton's Woodrow Wilson School of Public and International Affairs no longer offers its summer program for minority undergraduates; while in 2004, Harvard's Business School announced that its Summer Venture in Management program would now consider applicants' family backgrounds and whether they are attending an institution "whose graduates do not typically attend a top-tier, urban university."[28]

At the University of Michigan, similar steps have been taken to ensure the legality of race-conscious admissions programs. Undergraduate applicants are now asked whether they live in single-family homes, what each parent's highest level of education is, the occupations or current schooling of the applicants' siblings, and about "anything you regularly do to support your family, either by working, by providing care for family members, or through other work that you do at home." Like most other schools, Michigan's financial aid office does not share information on financial aid forms with the school's admissions staff; but undergraduate applicants now have the option of providing information about their families' gross incomes on their admissions applications as well, along with the number of people dependent on those incomes. Teachers writing recommendations are asked to comment on, among other things, "any personal circumstances, unusual accomplishments, and obstacles overcome that make this student exceptional." Another form asks high school counselors and principals to describe "any socioeconomic, personal, or educational circumstance that may have affected this student's academic achievement, either positively or negatively."[29]

In some states, socioeconomic and related criteria have—on the surface, at least—replaced race and ethnicity altogether. The University of California's system of "comprehensive review" takes into account "family educational background, academic support resources available both within and outside the school environment, and barriers to academic success such as family linguistic background or the need to work" while in high school, along with any other "particularly challenging obstacles or hardships."[30] California is also one of three states to introduce so-called "percentage plans." Any Californian who graduates in the top third of his or her high school class is guaranteed admission to at least one campus of the California State Colleges and Universities system, while anyone in the top eighth (12.5 percent) is now welcomed by at least one campus of the more selective University of California. In Florida, anyone graduating in the top fifth (20 percent) of his or her high school class is guaranteed admission to at least one of the state's university campuses. And since 1997, anyone in the top 10 percent of the graduating class of a Texas high school has been free to attend *any* state university campus he or she chooses, including the University of Texas's flagship campus at Austin.[31] These states have made no secret of their expectation that percentage plans will promote ethnic as well as socioeconomic diversity, since so many high schools are populated almost entirely by black or Latino students.

Several states' schools, moreover, have eliminated so-called "legacy admissions," whereby the children of graduates from selective colleges—much more likely to be affluent and white than to be black or Latino or low-income—receive special consideration from Mom or Dad's alma mater. (One prominent beneficiary is President George W. Bush, a C student in high school but nonetheless among the third generation of Bushes to attend Yale.) Senator Edward M. Kennedy, no child of poverty himself, has proposed that disclosure of legacy admissions be required of every school that receives any federal funding—in other words, just about every college and university in the country.

To some degree, this increased emphasis on high school performance and socioeconomic indicators reflects growing distrust of standardized test scores. The most widely used, widely taken test—and not coincidentally, the biggest magnet for criticism—is what is now called the SAT Reasoning Test, the latest incarnation of what most readers will remember as the Scholastic Aptitude Test, the Scholastic Assessment Test, or simply the SAT1. Produced by the Educational Testing Service under the auspices of the College Board, this "measure of the critical thinking skills you'll need for academic success in college"[32] has for over half a century served as a common yardstick by which colleges and universities might compare the academic potential of applicants who have attended a diverse array of public and private high schools.[33] A mounting body of research, however, suggests that differences in test scores have at least as much to do with differences in race, gender, and socioeconomic status as with genuine differences in intellectual capacities, or with the likelihood of academic success.[34] In time for the 2005 administrations of the test, several significant modifications in the SAT1 had been introduced, including the elimination of the verbal analogies section, and the addition of an essay-style writing test. Results are still out on the impact of these changes; but at this point, there is no reason to think that the new SAT1 will make campus diversity any less problematic.[35]

Likewise, neither holistic assessment nor class-conscious alternatives are likely to put the controversy over race-conscious affirmative action to rest. For one thing, percentage plans have never been viewed as a serious option for graduate schools, whose applicants are several years away from high school and, in many cases, from their communities of origin. At the undergraduate level, heavy enrollments by percentage-plan admits can easily prompt complaints that other, more highly qualified applicants have been crowded out of a given state's most prestigious campuses.[36] And while a great many opponents of race-conscious admissions view percentage plans as simply more of the same, those plans have in fact rarely yielded enough ethnic diversity to satisfy affirmative action advocates.[37] This approach to campus diversity, moreover, creates what Supreme Court Justice Ruth Bader Ginsburg has aptly described as "perverse incentives . . . [for] parents to keep their children in low-performing segregated schools, and discourage students from taking challenging classes that might lower their grade point averages."[38] Certainly, it would be difficult to apply percentage plans fairly to applicants from Chicago, Philadelphia, New York City, and other cities where a handful of extremely selective high schools bring together highly talented students from every ethnic group and socioeconomic stratum. At the same time, the University of California at Berkeley's experience with comprehensive review suggests an uncertain future for holistic assessment elsewhere. While most UC campuses employ a points system—still legal, presumably, since ethnicity is not in play—to weigh applicants against each other on various criteria, Berkeley has since 2002 assigned each applicant a *single* score reflecting his or her qualifications overall. As described in *UC Berkeley Fall 2002 Preliminary Freshman Admission Scoring Guidelines*,[39] "The score assigned to each applicant should reflect the reader's thoughtful consideration of the applicant's qualifications, based on all evidence provided in the application, and viewed in the context of the applicant's educational and personal circumstances." This more flexible approach to admissions has proved, however, a little too flexible for many Californians to stomach. Within a year of its inception, complaints from rejected applicants and their parents and in the national media[40] prompted an extensive investigation by John Moores, the chairman of the UC Board of Regents.[41]

Much of the controversy surrounding this policy focused on applicants' scores on the SAT1 (now the SAT Reasoning Test). Out of a possible combined score of anywhere from 400 to 1600 on the verbal and mathematics portions of the SAT1, the average for Berkeley's 2002 freshmen was an impressive 1,337; but 641 applicants with scores of 1500 or higher had been rejected,[42] while 386 students had been admitted with SAT scores between 600 and 1000. Among the latter, the dropout rate had been two times higher than for other freshmen, probationary status about three times higher, and grade point averages half a point lower.[43] "While there can be little doubt," Board of Regents Chairman John C. Moores admitted, of "the overall quality of the freshman class of 2002. . . . It should trouble all regents that UC may not be admitting California's best students."[44] Berkeley's rejection of any explicit formula for weighting admissions criteria, Moores argued, also undermined accountability, since no one could say "how, exactly, student academic and non-academic performance measures relate to UC admissions" or to "measure the relative impact of any single criterion on [subsequent] college performance."[45]

Doubtless, similar questions will be raised as to whether Michigan's new holistic assessments of undergraduate applicants places more weight on race, ethnicity, or other nontraditional factors than it's supposed to. Three organizations long opposed to affirmative action—the Center for Equal Opportunity, the Center for Individual Rights, and the National Association of Scholars—have already launched a concerted effort to force selective public colleges to reveal precisely how—and how much—race and ethnicity are influencing admissions decisions.[46]

All in all, the legality of affirmative action admissions rests precariously on a slim Supreme Court majority that, moreover, cannot shield it from abolition in some additional states. Alternate routes to diversity may not get us there—and if they do, will likely be subject to intense scrutiny and active resistance.

In the end, a great deal depends on the American electorate, and how the most common arguments for and against various features and models of affirmative action resonate with the conscience and worldviews of ordinary American students, parents, and taxpayers. How well are grades and test scores seen to work, for example, as measures or predictors of "merit"? How do advocates and opponents assess the relative virtues of different models of race-conscious admissions and other efforts to enhance minority enrollments and success rates? Do they make more of a categorical distinction than *Bakke* seemed to between the experience of racial minorities and of "white ethnics"? How important *is* diversity, anyway? To what extent is social justice outside their walls viewed as a legitimate mission of American colleges and universities? If we are to craft equitable, workable, politically sustainable policies, it might help to take a closer look.

Up Close and Personal: *The subjects and the interview*

One of the things I wanted to look at in particular was the tension between principle and self-interest; and I wanted to make sure that my advocates' acceptance of affirmative action was strong enough to offset considerable self-interest in the opposite direction. For this reason, I focused my interviews on the especially high-stakes contests for admission to medical schools, law schools, and the country's best graduate business programs, and sought subjects whose own ambitions gave them a very personal stake in the policies under consideration.

I also kept in mind that, as economist Thomas Sowell has pointed out, affirmative action in any number of countries tends to favor the *most advantaged* members of those groups designated for marginal preferences, at the expense of the *least* advantaged members of other groups.[47] In Malaysia, for example, where an ethnic Chinese minority has long been economically dominant, the brightest and best-educated children of the wealthiest Chinese families are relatively insulated against efforts to improve the prospects of the indigenous people, while only the most gifted and advantaged Malays are unlikely to benefit. In the United States as well, the most gifted, most studious sons and daughters of wealthy and upper-middle-class whites—those who have taken full advantage of prestigious public and private high schools and undergraduate programs—may be significantly less vulnerable than other whites to competition from "less qualified" minorities and thus view affirmative action in more abstract terms, rather than as something facing *them.*

What I wanted, then, were young men likely to see themselves as a little more "at risk" in relation to whatever real or perceived costs to whites affirmative action brought with it. In Chicago, where I lived and worked in the 1990s, the best places to troll for the men I was looking for were not the leafy quadrangles and gothic towers of the University of Chicago or Northwestern, but the classrooms and laboratories of my own institution, the Chicago campus of the University of Illinois. A "Research I" institution just west of Chicago's "Loop" business district, straddling an "El" train and a six-lane highway, the University of Illinois at Chicago is accessible enough, both financially and geographically, to enroll an extremely diverse student body, in terms of age, socioeconomic stratum, job history, and family responsibilities. At the same time, it offers enough prestige, academic rigor, and curricular breadth to attract plenty of highly ambitious young men. With the help of a pencil-and-paper survey,

I could select a group of mostly juniors and seniors who looked forward to earning an MD, JD, or MBA themselves.[48]

Eventually, thirty-two men were interviewed. Two were college graduates pursuing undergraduate courses that would qualify them for medical school, and the rest were undergraduate degree candidates, including nine more pre-meds, eight prospective JDs, eleven would-be MBAs, and two men who expected to pursue both of the latter. Undergraduate majors included biology, biochemistry, chemistry, English, philosophy, political science, and economics, as well as "applied" majors in accounting, management, marketing, engineering, information and decision sciences, health professions, education, criminal justice, communications, and the arts. Three were "returning students," twenty-nine to thirty-five years of age, and the rest between twenty and twenty-six. Not unrepresentative of UIC's student body as a whole, four had served in the military before attending UIC, while two others had immigrated to this country as teenagers and three as very young children. A mix of "WASPS" and "white ethnics," the sample drew from several strata of America's working-class and middle-class families. While three-quarters of these families lived in Chicago or its suburbs, there were also men from the Northeast, the West Coast, the South, and small towns in Illinois and neighboring states. Based on volunteers' survey responses, I was also able to include an even number of advocates and opponents of the use of race as a criterion for admission to graduate professional schools.

At the heart of each one-on-one, two-to-three-hour interview was a discussion of eight policy options, three that involved admissions quotas or set-asides and five that involved alternate paths to more diverse enrollments. Since somewhat different issues surround affirmative action on behalf of different ethnic groups, and since in Illinois—as in most of the country—American Indians are too few in number to be perceived as any kind of threat to whites' opportunities, any marginal preferences these policies entailed were described and discussed in terms of blacks and Latinos. In each interview, moreover, these policies were described in relation to whichever type of graduate professional education the subject looked forward to himself.

As to the specifics of those policies, one option simply involved race-targeted recruiting: that is, special efforts to advertise graduate professional school options to black and Latino audiences, via direct mail or other mass media. Another involved various kinds of race-targeted programming at the undergraduate level, to help increase the number of well-qualified black and Latino graduate professional school applicants down the line: for example, tutoring, mentoring programs, field trips, and paid or unpaid internships. A third involved parallel programs for minority high school students. A fourth policy—along the lines of California's comprehensive review—was formally race-neutral but involved giving "more weight than it previously did to . . . personal interviews, life-history essays, employment history and volunteer experience, and letters of recommendation." A fifth policy was a hypothetical admissions lottery, open to any college graduate, or in the case of medical schools, any graduate with passing grades in the requisite pre-med courses.

Under the three remaining policies, admissions decisions would be made primarily on the basis of grades and test scores but would also involve racial/ethnic quotas or targets, which have of course been officially outlawed since 1978. It is difficult to believe, however, that Michigan doesn't have some number in mind when they talk about "critical mass"; and that other schools as well don't have some sense of what an *adequate* level of representation would be when they institute or expand even formally race-neutral policies designed to enhance enrollments of "underrepresented" minorities. The better to eliminate any ambiguity, and to contrast opponents with advocates of serious departures from marginal equality, each of my race-conscious admissions options was described as involving "a certain number of places" that the schools in question hoped to fill with blacks and Latinos.[49]

Two of these three quota policies involved what are sometimes called "modified quotas," whereby targets for black and Latino admissions would not actually be met unless enough blacks and Latinos were considered qualified in terms of some minimum test score or grade point average. Under one of these policies the minimum standards for applicants of all backgrounds were the same. The second, however, involved "race-norming," whereby the school would consider the top 10 percent or 20 percent, say, of college graduates from each racial or ethnic group, but the actual cut scores would vary from group to group, depending on the distribution of test scores and grade point averages that had been earned by members of each group. For example, if a school chose its white and Asian-American admits from among the top 10 percent on the LSAT in a given year, then blacks and Latinos would be selected from among the top 10 percent *of those groups*, respectively—even if that meant that whites would not be considered if they scored below 700, whereas all blacks who scored at least 650 would be considered minimally qualified.

A third alternative involved so-called "absolute quotas," whereby the only reason that a target would *not* be met was if not enough black or Latino college graduates applied (or in the case of pre-meds, not enough who'd completed the requisite series of pre-med courses). While this model of affirmative action has sometimes been employed to integrate public elementary and secondary schools, there's no evidence this policy has ever been adopted by a college or university. Nonetheless, it is just this kind of quota that many whites seem to have in mind whenever they talk about affirmative action; so it was included largely as a point of contrast to less extreme models of marginal preferences on the basis of race.

In each interview, the subject was asked to talk about his reactions to each policy, why he would support or oppose it, and what modifications—perhaps introducing features of some other option—might make it more attractive. Borrowing from quantitative research, part of these assessments involved rating each policy on a five-point Likert scale, ranging from "very acceptable" to "not at all acceptable." This set the stage for some interesting discussions with each man about why he had assigned higher scores to some policies than to others, or why a particular policy was assigned a score of 4 rather than a 5, a 2 rather than a 1.

At the same time, this array of eight alternatives would help to avoid false dichotomies. Responses to a single option—"the use of race along with other admissions criteria," for example—might suggest very different mindsets among opponents intent on marginal equality and advocates concerned about past inequities. A range of options, on the other hand, would allow me to test the limits of each man's tolerance for or resistance to affirmative action generally and see whether boundary lines drawn at different points on the policy spectrum were nonetheless defended on similar grounds. I was not out to smooth over the differences between advocates and opponents; but I did want a more precise grasp of what those differences really were.

Addressing these policies early in the interview, the subjects themselves raised most of the principal issues and arguments that have surrounded affirmative action from the outset. Subsequent sections of the interview, however, were designed to ensure that certain core issues would be addressed by every subject. There were questions about the nature of professional "merit" and how to measure it; about the possible benefits to minorities or society in general of a more diverse pool of professionals and business executives; and about the persistence of racism, and how white-on-black and white-on-Latino racism compared with discrimination past or present against other groups. There was also extensive discussion of inequality of academic and economic outcomes, both between different racial or ethnic groups and within each one. In terms of college grades and standardized test scores, why were black and Latino applicants to graduate professional schools *not* fully competitive with their white or Asian counterparts? How did each subject explain inequalities of outcomes *among whites*—perhaps within his own extended family? How did he feel about the *over*representation in certain professions of Jewish Americans and East Asian Americans, long-time victims of discrimination themselves?

I also sought each man's take on the college experience of blacks and Latinos, and the scope of higher education's "mission." Both to break the ice and get a fuller picture of who I was talking to, there were also a few questions at the beginning of each interview about the subject's own college studies, his personal background, and his professional ambitions. Their responses to these questions are explored in the next four chapters of this book.

The Plan of the Book

Each of the next four chapters addresses a somewhat different set of issues and examines somewhat different aspects of the gaps between advocates' and opponents' perspectives.

Chapter 1 explores the subjects' conceptions of professional/managerial "merit," the limits of conventional admissions criteria, and the difficulties associated with applying alternative criteria in a fair, consistent, and economical matter. Close to consensus regarding the nature of "merit," the men nonetheless express some serious differences of opinion regarding the value of professional/managerial diversity, whether in terms of "fair shares," of benefits to minority communities, of larger social benefits, or as a sign of equality of opportunity.

Chapter 2 explores explanations for inequality of outcomes. How are blacks and Latinos affected by racism, past or present? How much can be attributed to "institutional" racism in the public schools or the job market? How much to hereditary differences in capacity? How much to affirmative action itself?

Explored in chapter 3 is the question of just how far marginal inequalities should be taken to correct for inequalities of opportunity earlier on. Should such corrective action be limited to schoolchildren, or should it be extended to adolescents and adults as well? How far should we go to equalize access not just to undergraduate programs but to highly selective graduate professional schools? Do Latinos deserve the same degree of special consideration that blacks do? Are we obliged to counterbalance not just the direct impact of racism on opportunity, but the ways in which multigenerational inequality can constrain self-confidence, initiative, and other psychological correlates of achievement?

To the degree that special steps to enhance either equality or diversity are warranted, there is also the question of just *who* should bear that responsibility, addressed in chapter 4. To what extent is the righting of wrongs in the larger society a legitimate part of higher education's "mission"? Are some facets of affirmative action simply too costly for public universities to pay for? For that matter, does it get in the way of the sort of "intermixing" on campus that is essential to getting past this country's racial divide? Does *too much* affirmative action let blacks and Latinos off the hook as parents or as members of ethnic communities?

Advocates and opponents often express quite different views on the obligations of *non*racist whites to help correct for a history of racism. The data also suggest that a good many whites' biggest problem with affirmative action may be its insistence on a *degree* of equality of opportunity that these whites have long since learned to forgo themselves.

In chapter 5, I summarize my findings and explore further their implications for educators and policy makers. Among other things, I argue that strong resistance to affirmative action on the part of those nominally committed to equality of opportunity be viewed not simply as evidence of self-serving hypocrisy, or of a fundamental rift between "liberal" and "conservative" values, but as an expression of the difficulties of squaring conflicting impulses at the core of a *consensual* set of sociopolitical values. I also argue that a deep well of resistance to marginal inequality should be exploited more fully in the service of improved funding, resources, and curricula for "minority-majority" elementary and secondary schools.

Throughout the book, subjects' perspectives are conveyed as much as possible in the words of the men themselves, the better to capture their spin on familiar arguments as well as more idiosyncratic points of view. To protect their anonymity, each man has been assigned an alias (including a surname that does not necessarily match the subject's national origins) and is further identified by the type of major (e.g., humanities, engineering) he was pursuing rather than a specific department. Unless otherwise indicated, natural science majors were pre-med, business majors anticipated earning an MBA, and humanities and social sciences majors were aspiring law students. Readers who wish to keep close track of the relationship between individual subjects' viewpoints and their policy preferences may wish to consult table A.1, in the appendix, where each alias is listed with the corresponding subject's age and type of major, which type of graduate professional education he expected to pursue, and which varieties of affirmative action he gave a positive rating to.

To put a little more flesh on the bones of these men's arguments than a purely thematic organization of the material would allow—and to share more of the flavor of these interviews and the mix of perspectives each conveyed— I begin each of the next four chapters with a relatively lengthy introduction to each of three men who had something especially interesting to contribute to the issues addressed in that chapter.

We'll start with Joe.

NOTES

1. "Steve Clayburgh" is an alias for one of the subjects of the research on which this book is based.
2. For several decades, scholars and activists favored *Native American* to refer to the indigenous peoples of what is now the United States, and to their present-day descendants. My own

contacts with this population, however, indicate that the term *American Indian* is now employed much more widely for inter- and intra-tribal discourse, as well as for communication with non-Indians. For similar reasons, I generally employ the term *Latino* rather than *Hispanic* to denote individuals with roots in Latin America. *Black* and *African American* I use interchangeably, once again following the lead of those these terms refer to.

Following the practice of black academics and activists, I employ *black* interchangeably with the more cumbersome, seven-syllable *African American*. In line with traditional distinctions between Europeans and Asians, I employ the latter term to refer to the aboriginal peoples of Asia (as far west as Afghanistan and the Ural Mountains, but stopping short of the Armenian and Semitic populations of the Middle East) and of the islands of the Pacific. For simplicity's sake, and so as not to intrude on the cultural identities of Chechens, Circassians, Georgians, and other peoples native to the Caucasus Mountains, I refer to those of my own background not as *Caucasians* but simply as *white,* or in some cases, in terms of more specific ethnic ties or national origins.

3. An extended discussion of marginal and cumulative equality may be found in Michel Rosenfeld's *Affirmative Action and Justice: A Philosophical and Constitutional Inquiry,* New Haven: Yale University Press, 1991.

4. An overwhelming majority of the scholarship on attitudes toward affirmative action has focused on attitudes toward blacks in particular, and toward policies on their behalf. Seminal work in this area is presented in Mary R. Jackman and M. J. Muha, "Education and Intergroup Attitudes: Moral Enlightenment, Superficial Democratic Commitment, or Ideological Refinement?" *American Sociological Review* 49, 1984, 751–69; D. R. Kinder and David O. Sears, "Prejudice and Politics: Symbolic Racism versus Racial Threats to the Good Life," *Journal of Personality and Social Psychology* 40, 1981, 414–31; James R. Kluegel and Eliot R. Smith, *Beliefs About Inequality: Americans' Views of What Is and What Ought to Be,* Hawthorne, NY: Aldine de Gruyter, 1986; and Howard Schuman, Charlotte Steeh, and Lawrence Bobo, *Racial Attitudes in America: Trends and Interpretations,* Cambridge, MA: Harvard University Press, 1985.

5. E. Costantini and J. King, "Affirmative Action: The Configuration, Concomitants, and Antecedents of Student Opinion," *Youth and Society* 16:4 (1985), 499–525, p. 523.

6. One good example is John McConahay's Modern Racism Scale, which hundreds of studies have employed. (See John B. McConahay, B. B. Hardee, and V. Batts, "Has Racism Declined America? It Depends on Who Is Asking and What Is Asked," *Journal of Conflict Resolution* 25 (1981), 563–79, or McConahay's "Modern Racism, Ambivalence, and the Modern Racism Scale," pp. 91–125 in John Dovidio and Samuel Gaertner's *Prejudice, Discrimination, and Racism,* 1986.) This measure asked respondents to indicate how much they disagree with seven different statements, including, "Over the past few years, Blacks have gotten more economically than they deserve," "Blacks have more influence upon school desegregation plans than they ought to have," and "Blacks are getting too demanding in their push for equal rights."

7. A good deal of previous scholarship indicates that public attitudes toward affirmative action vary considerably depending on the specifics of the policy presented to research subjects, or in some cases, what they *think* "affirmative action" entails. For an interesting overview of such variant responses, see pp. 68–90 of Faye J. Crosby, *Affirmative Action Is Dead: Long Live Affirmative Action*, New Haven: Yale University Press, 2004.

8. There are still serious concerns that the success of Chinese, Japanese, and South-Asian Americans has not always been matched by other Asian American populations, and that not enough women in general are majoring in mathematics, the physical sciences, or engineering.

9. Differences in average scores on the SAT1, GMAT (Graduate Management Admissions Test), LSAT (Law School Admissions Test), and MCAT (Medical College Admissions Test) are illustrated in table A.2 in the appendix. The tests themselves are addressed in chapters 1 and 5.

10. See, for example, W. R. Allen, "Black Student, White Campus: Structural, Interpersonal, and Psychological Correlates of Success," *Journal of Negro Students* 54 (1985), 134–37; L. C. Attinasi, Jr., "Getting In: Mexican-Americans' Perceptions of University Attendance and the Implications for Freshman Year Persistence." *Journal of Higher Education* 60:3 (May–June 1989), 247–77; Oberlin College Deans' Research Group, Black Student Persistence to Graduation at Oberlin College: Summary and Recommendation, Oberlin, OH, 1988; Jacqueline Fleming, *Blacks in College: A Comparative Study of Students' Success in Black and White Institutions,* San Francisco: Jossey-Bass, 1984; K. E. McClelland and C. J. Auster, "Public Platitudes and Hidden Tensions: Racial Climates at Predominantly White Liberal Arts Colleges," *Journal of Higher Education* 61:6 (November/December 1990), 607–42; M. L. Oliver, C. J. Rodriguez, and R. A. Mickelson, "Brown and Black and White: The Social Adjustment and Academic Performance of Chicano and Black Students in a Predominantly White University," *Urban Review* 17 (1985), 3–23; and W. E. Sedlacek, "Black Students on White Campuses: 20 Years of Research," *Journal of College Student Personnel 28* (November 1987), 484–95.

11. This is borne out in the research literature as well as the history of legal challenges to affirmative action. See, for example, Seymour Lipset and William Schneider's "The Bakke Case: How Would It Be Decided at the Bar of Public Opinion?" *Public Opinion* March/April 1977, 38–44. They cite a *New York Times*/CBS poll which found that 59 percent of white respondents and 83 percent of blacks approved of "a college or graduate school giving special consideration to the best minority applicants, to help more of them get admitted than otherwise"; but 32 percent and 46 percent, respectively, approved of reserving "a certain number of places for qualified minority applicants . . . even if it meant that some qualified white applicants wouldn't be admitted." Several years later, E. Constantini and J. King, "Affirmative Action: The Configuration, Concomitants, and Antecedents of Student Opinion," *Youth and Society* 16:4 (1985), 499–525, got a much more positive response to affirmative action from college students themselves, surveyed at the University of California at Davis, the campus whose admissions policies were addressed in the Bakke case, leading to a landmark Supreme Court decision discussed later in this chapter. Two-thirds of 1977 and 1981 respondents, respectively, said that they "favor" affirmative action programs and policies, but less than half of them favored set-asides for the "disadvantaged," and less than a third favored graduate professional schools setting aside a certain number of places for minority students.

12. By "medical schools" I refer not only to MD programs but also to colleges of osteopathy (focusing on homeopathic rather than aleopathic medicine), which have also drawn many more applicants than they can accommodate in recent years.

13. See, for example, John P. Heinz and Edward O. Lauerman, *Chicago Lawyers: The Social Structure of the Bar,* Chicago: Russell Sage Foundation and the American Bar Association, 1983.

14. *Regents of Univ. of Cal. v. Bakke,* 438 U.S., 1978.

15. *Regents of Univ. of Cal. v. Bakke,* 438 U.S., 1978, p. 37.

16. *Sweezy v. New Hampshire,* 354 U.S., 1957, quoting from T. H. Huxley.

17. *Keyishian v. Board of Regents of Univ. of State of N.Y.,* 385 U.S., 1967.

18. *Hopwood et al. v. State of Texas et al.,* United States Court of Appeals for the Fifth Circuit, 94-50569, 1996.

19. *Gratz v. Bolinger et al.,* 516 U.S., 2003.

20. *Grutter v. Bolinger et al.,* 539 U.S., 2003.

21. *Gratz v. Bolinger et al.,* 516 U.S., 2003, Justice Stevens dissenting, Part II, quoting plaintiff's counsel.

22. This was calculated on the basis of each student's admissions test score, his or her high school GPA, the relative difficulty of courses taken, and the relative competitiveness of high school attended, in terms of the test scores earned by that school's students.

23. *Gratz* v. *Bolinger et al.*, 516 U.S., 2003, Part II, Section B, including a phrase quoted from *Regents of Univ. of Cal.* v. *Bakke*, 438 U.S., 1978.

24. *Grutter* v. *Bolinger et al.*, 539 U.S., 2003, p. 25.

25. *Grutter* v. *Bollinger et al.*, 539 U.S., 2003, p. 31.

26. The ACRI, it is worth noting, is led by Ward Connerly, an African American who was formerly a member of the University of California Board of Regents and spearheaded the drive to eliminate race-conscious admissions in that state. A compact but illuminating discussion of the role of private watchdog groups is provided by Roger Clegg, general counsel of the Center for Equal Opportunity in Sterling, Virginia, in "Time Has Not Favored Racial Preferences," *Chronicle of Higher Education* 51:19 (1/14/05), B10.

27. Cardinal Warde and Karl W. Reid, Minority Introduction to Engineering, Entrepreneurship and Science Program (MITE2S) 2003 Final Report. Cambridge, MA: Massachusetts Institute of Technology, 2003.

28. Quoted from the program's website, at www.hbs.edu/mba/experience/meet/diversity/svmp.html.

29. University of Michigan, 2004-2005 Application for Undergraduate Admission.

30. "UC Berkeley Preliminary Freshman Admission Scoring Guidelines," p. 170 of John Moores's *A Preliminary Report on University of California, Berkeley Admission Process for 2002.* Oakland, CA: University of California, Nov. 2003.

31. Following the Supreme Court's decisions on *Gratz* and *Grutter*, UT Austin takes race and ethnicity into consideration as well. Other state campuses, like Texas A&M, have maintained technically race-blind admissions, though they have taken other steps to increase minority enrollments.

32. From "About SAT," a section of the College Board's website. www.collegeboard.com/student/testing/sat/about/SATI.html, 2005.

33. For a compact and informative account of the origins of the SAT, see Allen Calvin, "Use of Standardized Tests in Admissions in Postsecondary Institutions of Higher Education," *Psychology, Public Policy, and Law* 6:1 (March 2000), 20–32. See also Hezlett et al.'s recent study, "The Effectiveness of the SAT in Predicting Success Early and Late in College: A Comprehensive Meta-Analysis," presented at the annual meeting of the National Council of Measurement in Education, Seattle, WA, 2001.

34. One of the most recent reviews of pertinent research findings is George Farkas's "The Black-White Test Score Gap," *Contexts* 3:2, Spring 2004, pp. 12–19. The issue of racial differences in standardized test scores is also addressed in the March 2000 (6:1) issue of *Psychology, Public Policy, and Law*; see especially Linda F. Wightman, "The Role of Standardized Admission Tests in the Debate about Merit, Academic Standards, and Affirmative Action," pp. 90–100, Cecil R. Reynolds, "Why Is Psychometric Research on Bias in Mental Testing So Often Ignored?" pp. 144–50, and John E. Hunter and Frank L. Schmidt, "Racial and Gender Bias in Ability and Achievement Tests: Resolving the Apparent Paradox," pp. 151–58.

35. The Educational Testing Service has indicated that no breakdown of scores in relation to race or ethnicity will be available before the fall of 2006. The SAT and standardized testing generally is discussed further in subsequent chapters.

36. This has already happened in Texas, where 75 percent of the freshman class of UT's flagship campus in Austin was made up of percentage plan admits. In the spring of 2005, efforts by members of the Texas legislature to limit that percentage, or to require percentage-plan admits to have completed a prescribed set of high school courses, were defeated.

37. A detailed discussion of percentage plans' outcomes is provided in *Beyond Percentage Plans: The Challenge of Equal Opportunity in Higher Education*, a report issued in 2002 by the U.S. Commission on Civil Rights.

38. *Gratz v. Bollinger et al.*, 539 U.S. 2003, Justice Ginsburg dissenting, note 10. See also Marta Tienda's 2003 report, *Affirmative Action and its Discontents: Lessons from the Texas Top 10% Plan* (Ann Arbor: University of Michigan), which finds that minority students attending integrated high schools were much less likely to benefit from the 10% plan than those enrolled in overwhelmingly minority-majority high schools.

39. Included in Moores's *Preliminary Report*.

40. Several examples are appended to Moore's *A Preliminary Report on University of California, Berkeley Admission Process for 2002*. These include, "Victims Hed [*sic*] Here," by John McWhorter, an African American and UC Berkeley associate professor of linguistics, in the *Washington Post*, August 4, 2002; "Extra Credit: To Get into UCLA, It Helps to Face 'Life Challenges,'" by Daniel Golden, *Wall Street Journal*, August 4, 2002; and "California Still Uses Outlawed Policy," by Linda Chavez, *Chicago Sun Times*, August 10, 2002.

41. Moores, *A Preliminary Report*.

42. To some extent, Moores admitted, the number of exceptionally high scorers turned down reflected the extraordinary degree of competition among applicants to certain undergraduate programs. Applicants tend to be reasonably "pragmatic," he recognized, in their choice of majors; so anyone choosing physics or bioengineering, for example, would likely join a sub-pool of applicants with especially high grades and test scores in the areas of math and science.

43. Moores, *A Preliminary Report*, p. 2.

44. Moores, *A Preliminary Report*, pp. 4, 24.

45. Moores, *A Preliminary Report*, p. 147.

46. Peter Schmidt, "Foes of Affirmative Action Push Colleges to Reveal Policies on Race-Conscious Admissions." *Chronicle of Higher Education*, March 26, 2004; Roger Clegg, "Time Has Not Favored Racial Preferences," *Chronicle of Higher Education* 51:19 (1/14/05), B10.

47. Thomas Sowell, *Preferential Politics: An International Perspective*. New York: William Morrow, 1990.

48. Survey respondents had the option of anonymity. They were encouraged to list their names and contact information, however, if they wished to be considered for an interview.

49. It should be noted that while I chose my "advocates" from among volunteers who had rated at least one quota option a '4' or '5' on the questionnaire, in the course of my subsequent interview with one of those advocates, he assigned none of those particular options a rating higher than '3.' But this man was still quite willing to give "some" weight to ethnicity, something no "opponent" was willing to do. It is fair to characterize the two halves of the sample, then, as advocates and opponents of race-conscious admissions generally, and not simply as advocates and opponents of quotas.

I

THE RIGHT STUFF

Merit and Diversity

JOE MURTAUGH: MIGHTY WHITE

> The [absolute quota] policy [on the questionnaire] was a joke. . . . "Oh,
> let's throw this down, to see if we can get him riled up." . . . Maybe [Jesse
> Jackson's] Operation PUSH wrote that . . . or the Klan wrote it for the
> white guys.

A twenty-three-year-old UIC senior, Joe Murtaugh was still hedging his bets
at the time of our interview, juggling one major in a business-school discipline with a second in one of UIC's several programs in the visual and performing arts. Offered a graduate assistantship, he'd already decided to stick
around for a master's degree in the latter and give himself a few years to
make it big. But if his artistic career was still catch-as-catch-can by his late
twenties, then, "I'm really getting too old to be messing around with changing [jobs] all the time. And I want to be able to have a family. And I don't
want to have to say . . . 'Well, I'm unemployed, I'm gonna have to go look for
a new job for—that's only gonna last six weeks.' . . . A [project] only runs for
so long. . . . I mean, who wants to get [laid off] every six weeks . . . [or even]
after a year and a half?"[1]

An MBA, at that point, would help secure a more permanent gig in a small
or medium-sized firm, preferably one that produced some tangible product.
Moreover, "I want something where, through the fruits of my labor, I'll be able
to see things expanding, see jobs created. And I want to know the people who

I'm working with." In the short run, he hoped to join his dad in a City of Chicago department that offered a flexible enough schedule to accommodate his artistic endeavors—that is, if affirmative action didn't get in the way. "I'm a bright guy; the only reason I haven't been hired yet is this white stuff won't rub off."

Joe had dated both black and Latino women and had roomed and hung out with blacks at another state university campus he'd attended. There, he'd been nicknamed "Mighty White" not for his politics but for his athleticism and whiter-shade-of-pale coloring. On the whole, he felt that affirmative action was a good thing. And he did not have a problem with *modified* quotas, whereby targets were set for the number of blacks and of Latinos a school *hoped* to enroll, on the condition that enough applicants in each group met the same minimum standard set for whites with respect to undergraduate grades and/or standardized test scores.

> The schools could . . . [draw] a line . . . that [was] rigid and high enough so that you're keeping the classroom standard up. As soon as you start to bring down the classroom standard, you've lost all control, and, myself as a student, I'm offended by it. . . . There's no such thing as a stupid question. But there are some really, really inappropriate questions to be asked. The teacher spends an hour and a half explaining something; last four minutes of class—it happens every time—somebody's gonna raise their hand, "Could you explain that again?" . . . I don't know why that teacher doesn't *throw* something at him and say . . . "That's why I have office hours. Come see me after class.". . . It wastes everybody else's time.

What really bothered Joe was the double standard he saw in race-norming—even though such a policy might actually work to his advantage, once he'd been accepted.

> I have coasted through some of my [general education] classes here because [grades] were all based on a curve, you know, the teacher said so many people were going to get A's, so many F's. And if I was in a row of idiots, I could care less. I'm glad you didn't drop. You're an idiot. Stay here. You're the F's. [In an MBA program,] am I gonna be able to use this black person, or this Latino next to me, as that idiot, or are there going to be exceptions *again* for them after they *are* in school? 'Cause I know, when you get to grade everything on an essay, which most of the master's is, my name's not Lomez. Is there gonna be a little mark on my paper, "He's a white guy, grade him harder, he's only competing with the white guys"? . . . This Latino who might be lower prepared for this than I am . . . is he going to get an A for turning in a paper I would get a D on? . . . I think it would be so difficult *not* to have that spill in. The school's gonna be showing the next-

semester flunk-out rate for their blacks and Latinos, [and] if they're just grading on a *straight* scale . . . they aren't gonna wanna show that.

Since MBA programs offered one of the principal training grounds for upper-level corporate managers, looser standards in business schools might have far-reaching consequences. "It's that upper tier of jobs that *creates* so many *other* jobs, and new industries. I don't want somebody incompetent up there who's gonna *blow up* a quarter of a million jobs."

Not that Joe had much faith in the GMAT (Graduate Management Admissions Test). "Most standardized testing is screwed up. I think it's an equally *bad* measure of both [whites and minorities.]" Growing up dyslexic had taught him that

> there will *always* be a penalty [for some test-takers] somewhere along the line. When I took [the Iowa Test of Basic Skills] you know what they told me? . . . I was functionally retarded. I went through a whole battery of tests. . . . Shrinks, everything. They knew I was dyslexic; I had a couple of other learning disabilities. . . . They decided I was "trainable." . . . They were wrong.

With some experience managing a fast-food outlet and some construction projects, as well as some projects at UIC, Joe had learned that some of the most critical features of effective management could never be measured by grade point averages or standardized tests as we know them.

> [A manager won't] be able to lead . . . if everybody on his floor, you know, sees this goof get out of his car, you know, fighting with his coat as he's coming through the doors . . . being a complete klutz and incompetent and losin' stuff. . . . He has to . . . have . . . a persona that people are willing to follow. . . .[If the receptionist] knocks on [his door] one day, completely unglued. . . . [And it] turns out that so-and-so has been blowin' off calls from another company because he was waitin' for another account to come through, and he's kind of hedging on something, and the secretary's turning down phone calls left, right, and sideways, I have to be willing to get hold of that problem. And if I'm not personable, nobody out there is gonna tell me that this problem's existing. And I'm gonna think everything's wonderful and, okay, so it could be an extra three weeks for this particular account to come through for *this* company, but *this* company over here's been cuttin' their throat trying to get this account. . . .There has to be competence and personableness.

Race or ethnicity could be an asset as well. Affirmative action regulations aside, as an executive Joe might seek out well-qualified minority candidates "only because I *am* going to have blacks and Latinos working for me, and they'd much rather see, you know, this black guy pull up in a Mercedes and park next to mine. . . . It offers an added benefit only out of relaxing some of my employees on certain issues." Moreover,

> There's always a way to build a better mousetrap. . . . I've traveled through Europe a couple times. Everybody has a different, you know, set of standards or morals or . . . whatever. I mean . . . you mention a problem, and everybody's gonna come in from—Didn't think of that. . . . This last [set of projects] has been a big exchange with Russians. And they love plastic garbage bags. They wanna use them as clothing and use them as scenery and use as them as this and use them as that. And then, so, by bringing in another point of view or another cultural thing, you know, you can get some positive results.

But even if there were some important things it couldn't measure, "The nicest thing . . . the standardized test has to offer is the fact the people are willing to come up and study for and take it. And by that, it gives you an idea of their commitment towards it." Grades, too, said something about "commitment," which could be just as vital as people skills or technical expertise. His biggest problem with my hypothetical admissions lottery—open to any college graduate, regardless of his or her academic record—was that "The guy who's really dyin' and bleedin' in his soul for the thing can't have it," not a good thing for American business.

But commitment and performance did not always correlate—one reason that Joe endorsed a formally race-neutral policy that gave less weight to traditional criteria like grades and test scores and more weight to life experience, job histories, reference letters, live interviews, and the like. Even better, Joe felt, was a *combination* of modified quotas and the reweighting of admissions criteria.

> I give that a six [on a five-point scale, with a high of five]. . . . I think that then you'd have a much stronger picture. Maybe, you know, the guy who's a couple steps behind me and stuff, maybe he dropped out of school to go to work because his sister had kids or something. . . . When somebody comes in that door, I can ask him, "How'd you *get* three raises in 18 months? How come your grades were so low?" "Well, I was working midnights." That explains everything. I've worked midnights. "Well, what were your expenses like at the time?" I'm gonna spend time talking to you, before I turn him away. "Are you gonna work midnights when you're here?" "No, I left that job long since." Good, you know. And if he's able to show extreme progress in work *after* leaving there, you know, he stands a good chance.

MBA programs would benefit as well—*especially* if they were trying to meet racial targets.

By having personal interviews . . . they're going to be working to maintain a standard rather than maintain a number. This would not allow the school to say, "Whoa! We need more black people; we're dropping the standard." Because with the work they're putting into the personal interviews, they're also getting the benefit back of being able to pick the image they want to portray in their school."

What about "priming the pump"—helping younger blacks and Latinos *build* commitment and performance through race-targeted support services, mentoring programs, field trips, internships, and the like? To Joe, the best thing that this kind of outreach had to offer was to help instill the kind of work ethic Joe had himself.

I did tunnel work for [the coal mines] . . . I felt like a mole. Your butt's always wet, you got mold growing on your feet, it isn't good. And, um, that's not good work, but there's always work to be had. . . . I have trouble with the fact that if I'm not working, why aren't I out looking for work? Or why aren't I walking around with a hammer and a saw, going, "Do you need anything built?" Or walking around with a shovel: "Do you need dirt moved?" . . . Something went wrong with the work ethic, somewhere. . . .We need to find a way to inspire [black] people to work.

PAT GAHEOGAN: LEGACY

As a perfect lawyer, [you] don't have much of a life, because [your] life is the law. . . . [The best lawyers and federal agents] will go the distance, I guess. . . . It's the person [who] sprints the last mile, because that's all they have left, they don't have anything left to do but just to keep going. . . . [FBI agent Elliot Ness] was . . . very invested [in his job]. . . .[and] if I find that I'm in that kind of job, I can see myself becoming that. Not exactly *liking* it all that much, but knowing that's what I am. . . . I have to do this. . . . [My girlfriend] doesn't believe it, but I tell her things like that.

At twenty-one, Pat Gaheogan bore the stamp of family legend. Back in the 1930s, Granddad had been a Chicago beat cop and spent some time working with Elliot Ness. Solidly built, intense, affable, but no-nonsense, one could easily imagine Pat as he saw himself a few years hence: a law school graduate working for the FBI, the Secret Service, or perhaps as a federal marshal. Characteristic of the most serious opponents of race-targeted affirmative action, Pat expressed an almost unswerving faith in dogged self-reliance and the American way of economic justice. A social science major, Pat had more confidence than Joe Murtaugh in standardized test scores, which could not only tell you whether applicants were "academically sound" but also whether they had "taken the time to find out everything they can on how to take the [Law School Admissions Test]." And that kind of determination was at the heart of professionalism—although Pat sounded a little more laid back than the Elliot Ness of the silver screen.

> You have to have people who know how to talk to people. You have to have people who know how to deal with people with courtesy and be polite. . . . If [admissions committees] think because [applicants have] been through their classes and they were number 1 in the class, that they know how to deal with people, those are the people who get into trouble, 'cause they just don't know how to cope. [A good lawyer or law-enforcement officer] can say, "Hi, how are you doin', can you relax, can you do me a favor, let's talk, we'll get this out with the least amount of stress," and they get the job done. . . .You want that [top student] going through your files, doing an A-number-1 job finding out everything they can, but on the streets, you wouldn't want that person.

Pat's most intriguing responses, however, had to do with racial targets. To both models—with race-neutral and race-normed standards, respectively—he assigned the same, not *totally* unacceptable rating of 2. On one hand, he did not like the idea of a double standard and did not think it appropriate to consider race in admissions decisions. But on the other hand, there was a kind of symmetry to race-norming that so appealed to Pat that it took him a while to grasp its full implications. He explained that race-norming "seemed better to me because you are taking the *top* that you can." But wouldn't the alternative policy, I asked him, also ensure admission of the best qualified blacks and Latinos?

> True, but this—to me it seemed like more of a cut-off for them also. Before . . . I don't know, maybe it seemed to me as if they were getting more of a break with the [race-neutral minimums policy] because they didn't have to deal with their own. You're dealing with everybody. But now . . . [it's] maybe just a little bit logical to me, to just seek percentages, as better than just saying, okay, this many is here because [of] this [target]. . . . You're taking the cream of the crop from each group.

Perhaps part of Pat's seeming ambivalence came from his recognition that an increasingly diverse population dictated diversity in the legal profession as well, both to ensure simpatico representation and to assuage legitimate fears of racism. "Who's gonna want what kind of lawyer? . . . I don't speak Spanish and I'm a lawyer, yet I have to defend the Latino who I have to talk to through an interpreter. . . . The black guy may not want me, 'cause he thinks, I'm a white guy, 'Oh, he doesn't know what he's talkin' about, he's just gonna set me up, he's gonna write me off, and not give a care.'"

The single deviation from tradition Pat did endorse was to broaden and reweight admissions criteria. Indeed, he felt that law schools deserved a great deal of autonomy in that regard.

> I believe that if that's what the university and their board of directors decide to do, that just means you have to meet their standards in their way. That means that I have to be better [at interviews]. . . . And if someone is more articulate than I am in an interview, more power to them. . . . You need people who can speak very well, and articulate themselves without any problem. It's just. . . . You have to conform to what [the law schools] want.

But Pat did not share Joe Murtaugh's appreciation for the degree of flexibility and subjectivity that alternate criteria might tend to introduce. If Pat were in charge of things, he would enforce a strict formula for adding up each applicant's qualifications.

> I'm the end-all-be-all, huh? . . . I would try and weight the ways that you go through. Like, your interview is so many percentage of it. Your written essay is so much. Your work experience. Your grades. Your GPA. . . . Your LSAT. . . . I would break things down into fixed percentages. . . . It would be the most obnoxious mathematical formula that I could understand.

With this kind of policy in place, however, Pat would be less uncomfortable with racial targets. Tallying up the scores achieved by whites and minorities through the use of that formula, the disparities between the rank orders of whites and minorities might well be smaller, he felt, than they are now: So *deviations* from rank order in the interests of diversity need not be as great or as frequent; and thus would not be as much of a problem. "It would almost seem like they didn't *have* set-asides. . . .What I am trying to do [is to] get your total scores at a closer if not comparable range." Clearly, Pat was of two minds.

> You need to take the best there is. And if all you do is take whites for it, then what do you do, have a whole white field? It won't work, and it's not right. And it just— if that's the way it turns out, fine, but it *shouldn't*, because there are too many other people. . . .
>
> [Setting up quotas is] saying that they can't do it on their own. But it doesn't go deep enough to say the *reason* we giving them [special consideration] and the *reason* they can't do it on their own is because we have not *let* them have the *chances* to do it on their own.

STEVE CLAYBURGH: THE GREATER GOOD

> We cannot be a society refusing to share; we cannot be a society that does
> not empower all of its people. We will continue to go down.

Twenty-three-year-old Steve Clayburgh's views on race relations had largely
been shaped by his experience as a youngster living on highly integrated U.S.
military bases. A "shitty" high school student, Steve spent a few years in the
military himself before turning down a hard-won offer of admission to one of
the service academies, having decided that he'd rather not impose on his future wife and children the inevitable separations and dislocations that had
eventually led to his parents' divorce. Once discharged, Steve had chosen UIC
largely to be near his fiancée, who was attending a Chicago law school. After
completing a business degree, the twenty-three-year-old hoped to earn an
MBA part-time while pursuing a first career in the electronics security industry. Not too many years hence, however, Steve hoped to have earned enough
to attend law school full time, after which he hoped to work as a federal pros-
ecutor, or perhaps for the FBI or the CIA.

By the end of the interview, I had no doubt he could do it all. Some obvious
ambivalence toward affirmative action notwithstanding, his was perhaps the
best articulated defense of affirmative action, and the most nuanced analysis
of the strengths and weaknesses of various options and arguments.

Much less equivocally than Pat Gaheogan, Steve urged greater diversity
among upper-tier executives and professionals, simply because, "It's a representation of how society is made up. . . . As long as you have a representation in the society of people, then that's really the . . . criterion [for] fairness.
That you don't have a disproportionate amount in any one particular area."

As for the how-to of diversity, Steve was one of just two men interviewed
who were quite willing to abandon standardized tests altogether. He himself
had benefited from the willingness of U.S. service academies to judge candidates from within the ranks on more than grades and test scores. "I would have
never received my appointment had I not been a good [serviceman] and
demonstrated things that outweighed the benefits of . . . meeting a minimum
[quantitative] standard . . . because of other faculties I possess."

Did he feel that any particular faculties characterized successful business-
men or lawyers? Leadership, he felt, was paramount. But "I don't think [in-
born] talents . . . has that much of an effect. . . . Things like quantum physics,
I think that there's certain individuals that have a certain knack for that. . . .
Some people know how to deal with other people and have more magnetism,
but . . . leadership . . . is not inborn, it's learned." But it was not necessarily

learned or demonstrated in the classroom. If Steve was in charge of a graduate professional school's admissions,

> I would look at involvement at the last level [of schooling or employment] that
> you were in . . . the not-traditional or not-required things that you were involved
> in—political action activists, environmentalists, feminism, things like that. How
> [much] you were committed to a certain particular charity or a certain particular
> organization. How much time did you put into going above and beyond what was
> required?

This could, of course, reveal more than one's experience as a leader. One of
the differences Steve saw between law school and graduate business school
admissions was that law schools ought to focus

> first and foremost [on] the benefit to society. On what contributions they can
> give, and the ideals that they bring into it, aside from just monetary compensa-
> tion. Because I think that the corruption that we see in the legal system is a per-
> fect reflection of the quality of the people [in it]. . . . [As compared with private-
> sector business and industry] I think there should be more emphasis on weeding
> [unethical] people out.

On the other hand, undergraduate grades reflected more than cognitive
skills or a relevant knowledge base. "Most . . . good students, who have developed a consistent work ethic . . . who budget their time, and who are willing
to give up [some] things for the short time to get the things [they want] in the
long run . . . they're going to do pretty well [in an MBA or JD program]."
At the same time, greater reliance on alternative criteria invited other
problems. Steve had taken advantage of opportunities for UIC students to
participate to some extent in campus governance, and sitting in on the selection of a campus chancellor and a college dean had taught him some things
about the difficulties of consensus building. "I can understand the things—
the backbiting, the infighting, the prejudices that come into things, that aren't
even connected to race *at all*. And when you take something that's such a
volatile subject as race and average it into the equation, you know, it's so difficult to get somebody who is professional enough to handle that." Serious al-
terations in admissions criteria "gives too much room for someone to discriminate in." It also

> creates more of a hostility inside . . . the graduate student community towards
> each other. "But you were given this, I wasn't given this," and, you know, it's a

total backbiting kind of thing. . . . The resentment on every level is gonna be
there. . . . It would be fantastic if *everybody* had *no* particular bias . . . and could
really do this. But you can't guarantee the professionalism of everybody that
handles that. I don't think [admission] should be based as heavily as it is on
grades. [But] you're gonna have to have some line in the sand that divides a—
that sets a standard, that people can compare themselves to. Otherwise, there's
no justification for somebody not coming back in . . . [with] nepotism . . . and
anything like that.

That left quotas; but while Steve endorsed race-normed cut scores, official
adoption of absolute quotas he rejected partly out of concern for minority applicants themselves. "If your target was not met, you [could] obviously have a
waiver. . . . There are waivers for income tax; there are waivers for medical exams; there are waivers for *everything*. . . . Even if it's just a [fake] cloak-and-
dagger minimum standard," official cut scores—that is, some minimum standard of achievement that even blacks and Latinos had to meet—preserved
"the dignity of the individual [applicant]."

Steve was forthright about his own personal stake in affirmative action. "If
I'm a particular . . . white male that got beat out of [admission because of affirmative action] . . . I'm not gonna say that I would not feel animosity." He
didn't feel that affirmative action could keep him from earning a law degree
or an MBA, but believed that racial quotas or targets might definitely damage his professional prospects if they kept him out of high-status programs.
"Because we're a capitalist country, and because that's how money is generated in America, I need to understand the business aspects of it/and . . .
[have] *other people understand* that I understand it"—a principal reason for
earning an MBA. *Which* program he completed, moreover, could have a big
impact on his future.

> I don't know if I'll get a better education [at the University of Chicago or North-
> western University's Kellogg School of Management], but I think [that's] the
> perception of those who'll be reviewing me, either for a job or for [subsequent]
> admission to law school. . . . I think, uh, [the] UIC [College of Business] is a
> great school, and the reputation is growing by leaps and bounds. . . . However, I
> think it might set limitations on me when I go up head to head against somebody
> who has the same type of credentials that I do, and the same type of . . . work
> experience . . . and is able to say, "Hey, this is what I have, and I'm from Kellogg
> . . . and you're *not*."

There were also larger social costs to consider. If schools ventured too far
from merit-based admissions—under a lottery system, for example—this would
result in

people not put into positions that they have an aptitude for or have an inherent skill to do. I am not gonna send somebody who can't add 2 + 2 into an engineering field or a physics field, and take somebody that's Sir Isaac Newton at 17 years of age and put them into something that was an advertising role, or as an artist. . . . What society is trying to do is get the *most* out of the resources that it uses. Putting people into a particular field that they have no aptitude for . . . could *undermine* society.

With the judicious use of racial targets and related policies, however, "I think that when you elevate that one black student, you're bringing up society." Blacks and Latinos, Steve felt, embodied a good deal of underutilized human capital.

There wouldn't be these programs if [white] people just thought, we're helping blacks out, and there's no benefit to society as a whole. . . . If you look back at the accomplishments and the things that blacks have done [in the military] from World War II on up . . . it shows that we cannot neglect such a valuable resource. . . . 20 years on down the line, society as a whole [is] benefiting [from affirmative action], because when you share power with different groups . . . you get more powerful as a society.

And in the long run, no one would suffer. As more blacks and Latinos found more places for themselves in the best paid, most influential strata of business and jurisprudence,

I don't necessarily think you have to take that away from somebody [else]. . . . [It] just makes the income bracket bigger. . . . You offer the opportunity for growth. . . . You don't have to take away my piece of the pie to get that.

THE BEST AND THE BRIGHTEST

None of the other twenty-nine men I spoke with put quite so positive a spin on affirmative action's larger impact as Steve Clayburgh did, or matched Joe Murtaugh's ebullience, or the self-sacrificing intensity of Pat Gaheogan's sense of vocation. But in general, there was good deal of common ground. However enticing the prospect of substantial modifications in admissions criteria, in the short run this might very well entail prohibitive monetary and political costs. Considerations of race in admissions decisions—or any kind of special consideration for the wants and needs of minority young people—must be balanced against the virtues of meritocratic allocation, which furthers the common good by rewarding exceptional capabilities and the effort to develop them.

Meritocracy: *Just desserts and collective advantage*

Pat Gaheogan was no more an advocate of meritocratic allocation than, say, Len Hellstrom, a card-carrying socialist and a staunch advocate of modified quotas and race norming, who was nonetheless very uncomfortable with the possibility of absolute quotas, unaccompanied by hard-and-fast, objective standards. "Who do *I* want cutting *me* open? I mean, I don't *want* a doctor who's been allowed to slip on through just because of some superfluous issue like race." Gatekeepers to positions of power and influence had an especial obligation to select for *individual* merits in order to best serve the *collective* good.

For the same reason, twenty-three-year-old humanities major Doug Peruggia drew the line at modified quotas. He had no real problem with absolute quotas "as far as driving buses . . . [but] as far as producing surgeons and airline pilots, you don't wanna do that." Endorsing outreach to high school and college students but rejecting race-conscious admissions altogether, twenty-two-year-old social science major Dan Lysenko explained that he favored an increase in black and Latino executives and attorneys, "but, well, how far am I willing to go? . . . I don't want to . . . hurt graduate schools. . . . I don't want to hurt the businesses that people go to after graduate programs."

Considerations of fairness as well as utility—getting "the most bang for the buck" out of our educational system—dictated that those resources be expended on the most promising prospects. How to *identify* the "best" prospects, however, was a good deal more problematic.

On one hand, common perspectives on educational equity were very much in tune with Lyndon Johnson's foot-race metaphor. Twenty-one-year-old, post-baccalaureate pre-med Sean Hanna, for example, stressed that equality of opportunity did *not* mean "that, you know, you have to give someone a crutch and force them through. . . . But the opportunity should be there. . . . Give somebody the tools to do the job and to do it well, and if they want to do it, then let them do it." In contrast to Sean, twenty-five-year-old business major Jack Uberhof disapproved of race-conscious admissions; but he too believed that, "Just for the benefit of society, people should—we should be able to take a person's talents and let them develop them . . . all the way up to where they can. . . . Saying, if you *want* to develop these talents, this is a route you can take, and there won't be any barriers based on anything except their abilities."

This helps to explain why "prime-the-pump" interventions with schoolchildren—what might be called a supply side approach to affirmative action—was the most widely endorsed of the several race-targeted options I'd presented. This option did not bear the same stigma of "reverse discrimination" partly because, strictly speaking, "It had "nothing to do with admissions," as Dan put it, "or, I mean, it doesn't *guarantee* admission." Even though such programs were expected to render blacks and Latinos stronger competitors against whites or Asians, those programs did nothing to interfere with colorblind competition at the point of admission.

But in any case, supply-side efforts to expand the pool of future candidates did not solve the problem of insufficient diversity here and now.

For Good Measure: *What is the fairest way for meritorious potential to be assessed?*

Among the men I interviewed, the most popular approach to diversity—endorsed by all but three of them—was to give more weight to a broader range of criteria. As for the most traditional criteria, no one wished to unseat undergraduate grades as one of the principal yardsticks of admissibility, but standardized tests earned mixed reviews.

There is an especially close relationship between the MCAT, medical school curricula, and the undergraduate coursework required of their applicants; so it was difficult not to see the link between test scores, grade point averages, and one's potential for completing an MD program. Sean Hanna, for example, toyed with the notion of an admissions lottery—"Depending on who enters the lottery, you might get a better cross-section . . . of different kinds of people"—but could not endorse it. "You know, if someone came to med school and said, 'Oh, I have all Cs in all my science courses,'" then as an admissions officer, he "might sort of look at them and say, 'Well, you get it, but you don't get it enough to be a doctor and have people put their trust in you.'"

Several pre-meds, however, also stressed the link between college performance and the kind of commitment professionalism demanded. One mark of a good physician, twenty-three-year-old Zack Pritchard told me, was "good character—like, when you're real tired, treatin' people nice, being concerned about other people," and this meant "pushin' through when you have to push through, doin' the hard work." Now majoring in one of the natural sciences, Zack still had mixed feelings about having dropped out of an applied arts program at another school, but he felt that the reason his fellow majors "survived and I didn't [was that] I wasn't willing to pay the price." If he were in charge of medical school admissions, what good grades would show him "is that the guy knows how to carry through on a commitment. You start a class, you end a class, you get a good grade, they're responsible, they're disciplined, that kind of thing."

I got a similar response from Len Hellstrom, who had serious reservations about going to medical school only because, at thirty-five years of age, he already had a wife and children and was just halfway through a BS program in a health profession. A self-described "pot-head" from age twelve through his early twenties, Len had dropped out of high school, earned a GED, then flunked out of college, not really "getting my act together" until he was almost thirty, when he made a fresh start at a community college because "UIC doesn't accept people with a 1.0 average."

> In the days when I couldn't possibly get it together to even enroll, those were days when my interpersonal skills were also poor, I was not as able to communicate, and I was not able to help myself out of a bad situation. . . . You couldn't count on me to get somewhere at a certain time. . . . Like, in those days, I might have been nice about [promising to do] something for someone, but I might not have been good at it, because I wouldn't have had the alacrity to go in and *do it* for them. . . . And those things tie together. . . . Your ability to get a good grade in class will indicate whether you're simply able to do something.

Comparing successful and unsuccessful people generally, twenty-three-year-old social science major Jeff McEwen had not observed any systematic differences in socioeconomic origins, or in natural gifts. "I think everybody—the majority of Americans, anyway, are pretty much almost all on the same intelligence level, I mean, there's only a little bit that separates everybody. So [the difference between success and failure must] come from somewhere else. I think it comes from desire." But desire per se was not enough. As Sean put it,

> Everyone would like to be a successful professional, earn an above average living, or whatever. But it's a question, I think, of following through. . . . You know, I have a friend who . . . used to say, I want to be a lawyer, I want to be a lawyer, blah, blah, blah, blah, blah. But he never *did* anything about it. . . . So I think it's more a question of wanting it and then going out and doing it and actually putting the effort into it.

But twenty-one-year-old Isaac Fedelovich had some doubts. A recent immigrant from Russia eager to scope out the professional landscape in his new country, he had already "talked to some [medical school] admissions officers, and they said that they had tons of people with *every* GPA accepted to medical schools, and they came out as the most wonderful doctors, some that are Nobel Prize winners." Moreover, the relationship between undergraduate GPA and professional accomplishments "was not just *random* ratio . . . people with lower GPA succeeded better than higher GPA. Not probably with GPA 1.0, but probably some average GPA." Prospective osteopath Tim Kovacs went even further. "The people that have the A average tend not to be the thinkers . . . [whereas] the people in the C range get the concepts . . . [they] don't have all the formulas memorized, but [they] know, like, what's going on."

There was considerably more skepticism regarding standardized entrance examinations. Some people just didn't test well; and several questioned the efficacy of the GMAT, LSAT, or MCAT as measures of potential. Thirty-four-year-old business major Charlie Kilgallen, who worked construction until "an argument with a steel beam" forced him to change direction, feared that the GMAT would be no more relevant than the pencil-and-paper test he had taken as an apprentice, which was actually produced by the same company. "[It] had nothing absolutely to do with whatever I ever did in ten years as an iron-worker." If it had been a relevant measure, "I would never have [lasted] a day." On the other hand, no one found it likely that these tests would be *especially* unfair to minorities, in the sense that blacks and Latinos would tend to earn lower scores than whites with the same degree of relevant knowledge, skills, or aptitudes. One reason Doug Peruggia could accept quotas coupled with race-neutral, but not race-normed, cut scores was that even if the tests *were* racially biased, "Why would you lower the standards [for blacks and Latinos]? Why don't you *change the test*, then? Take it from the root."

But in any case, giving more weight to alternate criteria was most often seen as the best antidote to any perceived inequities in traditional admissions policies. Twenty-three-year-old Rick Skilling, a science major likely headed toward an MBA, suggested that an admissions essay could not only reveal "how articulate you are" but also give a fuller picture of one's ambition. "If you come from Who'sville, and you've kind of made it this far, I mean, maybe you can still go a long way." Some alternate criteria would favor the men I was talking to: Doug, for example, played on one of UIC's varsity sports teams and felt that athletic experience "would be a good thing to have . . . because you get a lot of skills. Say you become a manager or a district manager of your firm; it's teamwork." Zack pointed out, "There's people who are geniuses, but, they're socially, like—some of my fellow [natural science] students are that way, don't have a lot of sense of what's going on around them, so I think you can do real well on a test and still be a bad doctor . . . [although] you can't do real *bad* on a test and still be a *wonderful* doctor."

Among physicians, communications skills and genuine compassion were generally thought to separate the merely competent from the best. Sam Turner, a twenty-five-year-old, born-again Christian who was considering a general practice in small-town America, believed that "a physician needs to have a servant attitude. . . . When you're taking on this job . . . you're a servant to your community." Len stressed that

> A good doctor is somebody who's very adept at . . . physiology, say, and chemistry . . . and even the physics of chemistry, and that's a very important criterion. But there's a lot of the human side of it, of just being concerned . . . doing the nurse things. . . . I think a lot of doctors, they don't look at the patient as a person. They become an automaton looking at a case. . . . A lot of doctors seem to be very nice, but a lot of it's bullshit, like, they're really pretending, and it's really obvious.

What was critical, then, to professional-managerial excellence was what some psychologists call "emotional intelligence," plus a strength of character that went beyond the sort of achievement-motivation that might be reflected in grade-point averages. From this perspective, the rationale for meritocratic allocation of opportunity seemed to demand considerable attention to what the numbers wouldn't tell you.

On the other hand, the relative lack of continuity between one's professional activities before and after graduate professional training might make it especially difficult to predict how a prospective lawyer or physician would actually perform on the job. "Something novel," Sean suggested,

> would be . . . sort of like a probationary period that you might have on a job. . . . Have your [stronger] applicants . . . come in and, say, for a week you're gonna follow this med student around and for a week you're gonna follow this resident around, and then have the resident or that med student come in and talk to [those responsible for admissions] or write up a little one-page report saying what they thought about this person. . . . How does this person react when you walk into the room, uh, while you were making the rounds, or whatever? . . . Does he ask intelligent questions? . . . Did this person seem empathic or, you know, were they just concerned about making money? Because I think you can learn a lot about a person, even in a short time like that.

At the same time, giving more weight to criteria difficult to quantify threatened the precision of rank-ordering that GPAs and test scores seemed to provide. A twenty-year-old business major, Greg Bogosian's fondness for marginal procedural consistency seemed to color his characterization of a law school lottery as "horrible" but "completely fair . . . that's almost *too* fair, it's pathetic." Twenty-one-year-old business student Chris Feraios challenged the whole notion of gauging applicants' relative potential once out of school: It was too difficult, and "I don't think that should be the school's concern, about who's gonna be the best business man" But he nonetheless upheld traditional criteria as simply "the fairest way to treat people. . . . With the GPA and the GMAT, you're getting a sure number that, you know . . . hard cash, where those other areas, you know, you can make your own decisions and—there's areas where you can, you know, pick and choose or whatever."

That kind of picking and choosing could be politically volatile and might not benefit blacks and Latinos at all. "Who's doing the interviewing?" Len asked. "That didn't change, did it? . . . I mean, there's too many guilty liberals and too many racist conservatives, you know?" The competition *among* minorities, moreover, might be politicized, leading to "a kind of small-group cronyism. . . . I mean, like, I'll get my buddies in." The same kind of thinking helped to explain the relative attractiveness of race-norming to some opponents of race-conscious admissions altogether, which was arguably less "wishy-washy" and more consistent in its application.

Perhaps the most interesting proposal came from twenty-one-year-old Marc Huston, a pre-med and part-time medical products designer who offered his own model of race-norming, of sorts, without quotas or targets. Out of each racial/ethnic group, each school would admit the top 10 percent, or 20 percent, or whatever percentage of medical school applicants was required to fill its entering class, to the degree that they did not fall below some absolute minimum standard. He saw this as a win-win situation, helping blacks and Latinos but not hurting whites very much: If whites deserving of a medical education were turned down by one medical school, they could still attend another somewhat less distinguished school that was forced to dip a little deeper into the applicant pool.

I reminded Marc, however, that there were still a finite number of places in medical schools generally, so that under his system, even the least selective schools might turn down the least qualified white applicants in favor of blacks or Latinos with lower grades or scores. On the other hand, those absolute minimum standards might mean that blacks and Latinos would still be underrepresented at those least selective schools, while Asians might earn fewer places at the top schools than they would otherwise. Gradually, this seemed to sink in, and by the end of the interview, Marc had renounced race-conscious admissions altogether. If he could not have it both ways, then the *degree* of "reverse discrimination" race-conscious admissions seemed to entail was too high a price to pay for diversity.

For advocates, though, the principle of marginal procedural equality was readily eclipsed by serious lapses in *cumulative* procedural equality. Special consideration for blacks or Latinos at the point of admission was seen as just compensation for systematically inferior opportunities to develop and display their true potential. But the devil was still in the details. Isaac had first encountered affirmative action in Russia, where the primary constraint on his own opportunities had not been that he was a Jew but that he was part of the better educated, more cosmopolitan, Russian-speaking minority of his region, whose university was determined to achieve more proportionate representation of the numerically dominant ethnic group. "You cannot distribute [professional positions] by force, by just . . . dragging people in who don't have qualifications . . . you cannot do that." To Isaac, race-norming made no sense unless the resulting differences in cut scores were, in fact, mathematically accurate corrections for the kinds of inequities responsible for systematic intergroup differences in performance. "It's probably hard to [calculate] . . . how much harder [the black] would have to work to be at the same level as the white guy. That's the problem." So his endorsement of affirmative action by U.S. medical schools fell shy of formal quotas or targets. "You can surely give 'em a break, but not—you know, moderate one."

All in all, though, the principal brake on advocates' deviation from marginal equality seemed to be their concern for the impact of the selection process on society at large, and their consequent desire to establish some floor of demonstrable, achieved merit below which applicants' abilities and motivation might fall dangerously short of what was required. As long as this floor was maintained, however, marginal equality was much less urgent than among opponents—and their concern for diversity somewhat greater.

Fair Shares: *Does diversity matter?*

Were there benefits to professional-managerial diversity—for blacks, for Latinos, for everyone? Was the relative lack of diversity in certain occupational strata a sign that equality of opportunity had gone awry?

Like Pat Gaheogan, Zack Pritchard was concerned enough about this to find race-norming less objectionable than other approaches to race-conscious admissions. "It appeals to my sense that . . . people are getting their share, you know. . . . It would be great if the best of every racial group were competitive and were equal." Several men echoed Joe Murtaugh's comments on the benefits of diversity to the common good. Phil Zeckman, a twenty-six-year-old social science major, saw advantages to

> bringing in a different thought process. Our laws are set on prior precedent, and those precedents are basically Anglo-Saxon. To give a different view is not necessarily wrong. Saying the *entire* current view is wrong . . . is false. But you know, bits and pieces of everything. I mean, I really don't think there's anything in the world—any view, any structure, any system that is entirely one hundred percent correct. And you can always learn something . . . a different culture, a different thought process, you know. . . . It's only positive.

Others cited positive consequences for minority communities in particular. Having grown up in a very self-consciously multiethnic society, Isaac Fedelovich took it for granted that "some patients feel more like going to some people of their kind." For Matt Vigoda, a twenty-year-old social science major who had recently interned with a downtown Chicago law firm, it was simply a question of equity.

> Maybe a [black or Latino] wouldn't be defended as well if his attorney can't empathize with his situation. . . . Also, if there were more black and Latino lawyers, there would eventually be more black and Latino judges, and [more] blacks and Latinos throughout the whole legal system, and that would really help us with judging, and with the rehabilitation kind of thing. . . . I think if they are going to be prosecuted by our legal system, they should have a hand in shaping it.

Len Hellstrom felt that greater diversity could go a long way toward breaking down negative stereotypes among practitioners. At a large university medical center where he worked,

> I see people come into the ER. An old white guy who's a member of the faculty at [the university] can be the biggest idiot that you ever met, but they hover around [him]. "Oh, yes, bring him right in." . . . That gets him anything and everything. . . . [Even] a black person of some high status doesn't get that. . . . I can't picture it. For all the [white physicians] that have good intentions, there's still this immersion problem. All of the junkies who have been shot, all of the people who live on the overpasses come in, terrible medical conditions, they're all black. . . . And you can tell from listening and speaking with some of the doctors, the ones that are aware of this problem . . . which is an interesting thing to watch, that some of them are actually *thinking* about that. They're thinking, "I go back to the suburbs and I'm surrounded by white people, all of them are someone like me. And here, you know, I have to be careful not to *get an attitude*, because here . . . here is what I see." . . . And it's interesting to see the ones that *aren't* making that effort , . . . that aren't concerned. . . . [With an increase in the percentage of minority physicians] white doctors . . . [would be] more acquainted with more black people who are of equal status to them, educationally and politically, and so would have a different attitude toward their [minority] patients.

The increasing visibility of black and Latino professionals might also have a positive impact on minorities' own perceptions of themselves. Even an affirmative action opponent like Jeff McEwen recognized, "Young blacks in a poorer neighborhood . . . need . . . people *from* the neighborhoods going into law school and achieving so that they can see, 'Hey, I can also achieve,' because, you know, Bill down the block achieved."

For most opponents of race-conscious affirmative action admissions, how-ever, there were few if any areas of endeavor wherein the desirability of di-versity was enough to challenge the ethic of free-market competition. "In terms of, like, *politics*," Dan Lysenko conceded,

> I wouldn't mind seeing a much better representation of, uh, the population. But in terms of a job, I think it's competition that should drive it, and whoever hap-pens to be the most competitive, I think should make it. . . . In business, it's the best people, the most competitive . . . and if the people with the best products happen to be, I don't know, some completely strange under-represented group in society that dominates the field, they have the best product, they run the best business, that's just the way it is.

Pre-med Tim Kovacs concurred, "It doesn't matter. . . . If 95 percent of [those with the top jobs] were black, as long as they're doing the jobs the way they're supposed to be doing it . . . I have no problem with that."

Regarding their views on affirmative action, however, the most critical issue for the men I interviewed was not the desirability of diversity for its own sake, but rather, *why* greater professional-managerial diversity had not happened by itself. The only thing that could trump the fundamental injustice of marginal inequality was a certainty that systematic inequalities of academic outcomes were a product of persistent and pervasive racism.

NOTE

1. Except where otherwise noted, all quotations are from author interviews.

VICIOUS CYCLES

Race, Class, Discrimination, Dysfunction,
and Other Explanations for Inequality

GIL JARREAUX: CONVERT

I was in Japan about a year ago . . . my father was working for [a large corporation] and we went to [the offices of a major U.S.-based multinational conglomerate] over in Japan, and [my father] said, "How come your . . . companies do so well here and, you know, a lot of American companies do?" And the guy . . . said, "It's simple. We don't have affirmative action. We don't *have* to place people in a position because they're a certain race. If they're qualified, they can do it." But then again, he also did say, "We do not allow blacks to get above a certain level of management," for whatever racist reason that was.

A year or so before our interview, Gil Jarreaux had undergone a conversion of sorts. Raised in Chicago by Western European Social Democrats, and a life-long participant in the social activism of a very progressive Protestant church, Gil spent two years as a human services major before his first economics course turned him into an acolyte of free-market capitalism. At twenty-one, he described himself as "a humanitarian and a capitalist at the same time—which is not exactly an easy balance—*but* I say, 'Let the best man win'; if they can do it, they can do it . . . survival of the fittest."

One can only speculate as to whether some longstanding tension between his parents' progressive politics and their employment by multinational corporations had finally born fruit. But in any case, Gil would now earn his degree in a business major, then pursue an MBA or its European equivalent. Having been born in a Common Market country, he might take advantage of his dual

citizenship to pursue graduate work in Germany or Switzerland; but he was
also thinking about Michigan State as his stepping-stone to a job as economic
analyst for some megacorp.

Would he follow through? I liked Gil; but in contrast to the urgent ambition
of several of the men I talked with, this young man was a classic underachiever.
His standardized test scores had always been high, and he was confident he
would do well on the GMAT. "I see all these people cramming for these . . .
admissions tests, and . . . I can't get into that sort of cramming, I could never
do that." But he didn't put much effort into his high school courses. "I wasn't
bored in high school, 'cause I didn't go," which had predictable consequences
for his grade-point average. This had actually led Gil to take advantage of affirmative action himself: For although he had always thought of himself as
white, and had identified himself as such on my questionnaire, one of his parents was part South Asian or Pacific Islander, and that had apparently helped
him get into UIC.

> It really *totally* depends on the situation. I've [identified myself] both [ways], and
> I've gotten different reactions, which is kind of funny. I remember . . . the first
> time I applied at UIC, I didn't get in because I had a really bad grade point av-
> erage. . . . And I applied as white, and then my sister said, "Why did you do that?
> Apply as Asian/Pacific Islander." And so with the same . . . high school grades I
> applied [that way] and I got in. . . . I usually do not use Asian/Pacific Islander un-
> less I *really* think it's gonna help me. . . . With my grade-point average and ACT
> scores in the past, I *needed* it. You know, I've boosted up my grade-point average
> to a 4.5.

A more serious student now, Gil was quite content with his job as a waiter,
even though job opportunities more pertinent to his career interests sometimes came his way. All in all, Gil was very much a work in progress, still pulled
in different directions, it seemed, with respect to his goals, his values, and
most certainly his views on race, inequality, and affirmative action. For he still
found the relative lack of professional-managerial diversity problematic. "I
don't think that it's just; I don't think it's a good idea for one race to have a
strong hold on all these positions. . . . You know, especially for a city, let's say,
like Chicago, which is so mixed, but . . . all upper-level management positions
in this area generally, you know, are held by whites. And I just don't think that
there's a fair representation at all."

Gil had no objection to reweighting admissions criteria to some degree. "I
think those GMAT scores just go right out the window when it comes to [suc-
cess in business.] . . . I know for a fact that most businesses nowadays, when
they're stuck between an A student and . . . a C student . . . they're gonna take
the one, you know—the C student may have incredible people skills and the

A student may be very smart, but street-dumb." But he was still "more comfortable" with quantitative measures. "I don't know why. . . . You know, it's something absolute, something you can rank against." Moreover, he could not condone any special treatment of minority undergraduates—"Subsidize anything, and the markets won't clear"—and the highest rating he gave any form of quota was a neither-here-nor-there 3 for the policy involving race-neutral minimums. Race-norming, he found "insulting to blacks. . . . It's like saying, well, because you're black, you can be stupider. . . . Welcome to our university, and we know you really can't cut it with whites, and so we're gonna, you know, give you a little extra edge here or there and bring you up to [our] standards."

Gil had observed minority students' academic handicaps firsthand. For example, "In some writing classes—you know, everybody's gotta take those comp courses—I've noticed that some black students just do not have the grasp of the basics—basic fundamentals. How to conjugate a verb." But whatever special academic difficulties these students might encounter, either in social science or business-oriented curricula, he did not take seriously the notion that college course content or teaching styles made things easier for whites than for blacks and Latinos with comparable abilities and preparation. "I don't think there's anything to that. Because they're teaching facts. You know, two and two is four to the white student and two plus two is four to the black student. . . . They're teaching facts, they're not teaching opinions. Well, hopefully not."

Success and failure generally, Gil attributed primarily to differences in motivation. "I can't think of any other reason for it. Because I'm thinking of examples in my head [in which] the one who makes it is just as smart as the one who doesn't make it: same background, but just have different motivation." Motivation might in turn be compromised by poverty, which Gil described as "a very inhibiting disease. . . after a while, it—you get used to not being able to get what you want." Among inner-city blacks and Latinos, moreover, economic deprivation was often association with a poverty of information or awareness of one's possibilities.

> A lot of times, blacks and Latinos feel that they don't even stand a chance, so . . .
> you know, they won't even try. . . . I have a lot of friends in the inner city, and a
> lot of these black kids that I know are very clueless as to what's out there. . . . For
> some reason or other, they just don't know. [At the church that my family belongs
> to] we did a lot of work with inner-city kids, and they are just not aware that there's
> a lot more to life than, you know, going and working at the gas station or whatever.
> . . . *maybe* [there is] less of a desire to succeed, only because they think they can't.

But he did not think it fair to attribute either sort of impoverishment to racism. "Maybe in the '50s, [racism] would have been a good excuse, but, honestly, I honestly do not believe that now. I do, however, think that poverty is a cycle, and I think that if you're in that cycle, it's hard to get out of it. *But* I don't think that they're in that situation because of discrimination. . . . I really don't think it's that bad, that it keeps them there."

Contemporary animosity toward blacks, at least, Gil blamed largely on affirmative action itself.

> My best friend is—he's always been, you know, wary of black people. Now he just outright hates them. . . . I really don't know that many white students who *aren't* offended by [affirmative action admissions and financial aid]. . . . Every time the subject comes up, when I'm talking to another white student, they are offended. . . . I still think that some amount of support's necessary for black students. But not to the point where it discriminates against someone else.

To a considerable degree, moreover, racism seemed to be a self-fulfilling prophecy.

> Most of my friends are right here at UIC . . . [and] a lot of my friends lately have gotten very sick and tired of black people because of, like . . . the Rodney King thing [wherein white police officers videotaped beating a black suspect were acquitted by a California jury, which led to riots in African American neighborhoods of L.A.]. They are very sick and tired of being accused of racism, and they have a very negative attitude towards black people.
>
> I know, I can say for myself, I'm very sick and tired of being called a racist . . . of, you know, being blamed for a lot of people's problems because I'm white. I think [blacks] maybe encountered [racism on the UIC campus] in the last two years . . . [because] they bring it out. . . . They make it a problem when they make it sound like they're being abused and then they go on the news and they say, "Oh, here we are a UIC being, uh, discriminated against."
>
> Last year, for example . . . a friend of mine lived on campus, and she was accused of being racist because her roommate was black and she didn't always get the phone messages so that meant [the white roommate] was a racist. . . . And I hung around with [the white roommate]. . . . And so I was accused of being a racist, some people started yelling, "Racist!" and they threw eggs at us. . . . I felt more like *I* was the one who was discriminated against. But it's, you know, I would say I think [overt racism] is more of a backlash.

If black and Latino graduate business school applicants' inferior credentials, on the average, could not be traced back to racism, then how did Gil explain it? He responded candidly to the notion that inequality of outcomes between different racial groups might be due to heredity.

> [It's] a difficult question . . . because, to categorize any group in that sense—to say, well, blacks are low *because*—can sound like racism even if it's not. And it's

just—it's kind of tricky, because I wanna—I seen studies done, I—the thing is, I really don't know what to believe. I have good reason to believe—there's a number of studies that I've seen done, that say blacks just are not *capable* of learning as much as whites, and I don't know whether to believe that or not, because everybody says that's not true, but I haven't heard any other good reason for it. I think you can say social conditions, but I don't believe in that kind of thing.

At the same time, he clearly understood the potential impact of cultural differences. Like all of the other men interviewed, he had no problem with the *over*-representation of some ethnic groups—like Jewish or Chinese Americans—in some graduate programs and career paths. As to why that was, Gil felt that Jews "are just smart enough, and they know the value of education. I can't remember exactly where—I just read this book about the Jewish, uh, tendency to succeed. And it's just *really* all it is. Education is a very important thing." Having grown in a neighborhood with a large Jewish population, Gil observed that

Jewish culture is . . . a very competitive culture, and . . . I think that the Jewish people tend to know the value of hard work. And they know what to do with their money—they know how to invest it. And unfortunately, because they're good at this, a lot of Jewish people are, you know, they get the reputation of being stingy and cheap. But that's not the case at all.

Blacks, by contrast, "deal with things a different way than white people do. That's not a racial statement, that's just a fact, that's something they just do. . . . Certain cultures just do not, as a majority, tend to go to college, and they do not, you know, they do not tend to get on track."

MEL GIBRAN: PEOPLE TURN THEIR BACKS

People I know that are unsuccessful are generally lazy people [who] don't want to get any more out of life than to eat, sleep, and, you know, . . . just have simple pleasures. . . . I'd have to say, part of it, it's somewhat inherent. But I think a lot of your interpersonal characteristics are the result of your environment. And, you know, a lot of those people who are lazy probably have—deep down inside, they have a drive within them to *be* successful, but because of the way they were brought up, or the environment they lived in, whatever, *they became* satisfied.

Mel Gibran was "brought up in a family where education was *the* most important thing. No matter what, you know, I was gonna go to college and all that stuff. My brother isn't crazy about going to college, and my dad said, 'Well, you can leave the house. . . . You can move out, or go to college.'" One of the legion of Middle Eastern immigrants driving taxicabs in Chicago, Mel's dad had done well at it, earning enough money to buy his own medallion, and he continually impressed Mel with his intelligence and breadth of knowledge—although occasional outbursts on the topic of college grades had encouraged Mel to start paying his own tuition. "People that I know that are successful . . . generally were brought up in an environment where they were urged to do well . . . or they had somebody to look to do well . . . combined with their own personal drive."

Mel had graduated in the top 10 percent of his class from one of Chicago's most selective, top-quality public high schools; at UIC, he was an engineering major and "Vice President for Personnel" (a.k.a. rushing chairman) of a campus fraternity. Like most of the MBA aspirants interviewed, he expected to work full-time for a few years—perhaps as a floor trader at the Chicago Board of Trade—before going back to school. A big fan of Milton Friedman, the University of Chicago's guru of free-market capitalism, Mel was also a strong supporter of affirmative action.

Reweighting admissions criteria appealed to him because,

When you read a person's essay, you interview somebody, you kind of get an idea of what that person's like and what contributions they can make—not only to the school . . . but to society at large. You know, accepting somebody to graduate school, you want to send them out into the world so they can do something better. This may sound a little corny [and] I don't know if people really look at that, but . . . you wanna send out the best.

But Mel also approved of race-conscious admissions and flexible cut scores for minority applicants, mostly because he *dis*approved of welfare. Individuals should be "free to make their own choices and decisions"; moreover, "They've proven [social programs] don't work anyway. They screw up. You can put more money into them, but there's all kinds of waste . . . and the people that are supposed to be the recipients . . . it never really reaches them, or not to an adequate extent."

Even something as admirable as increasing opportunities for blacks to reside outside black ghettos had its downside.

One time, a black man was talking [on a TV program]. . . . He was a professional black male and everything [with] a well established position somewhere . . . talking about . . . when he was brought up, back in the 1920s or '30s . . . when, "We [blacks] all lived together." You know, "I could come home [with] my report card, [and if] I had a bad grade, [then] on the way home, the lawyer who lived a cou-

ple blocks away from me would see me and ask me what my grade was and . . .
give me a whack across the behind."

He . . . had role models from different people. . . . I mean, it was just [a] very
[economically] diverse environment. . . . You know, some people were considered undesirables, but you had [people] that you could look to . . . as role models. Not necessarily now; when you think of a role model you think of somebody
in the public eye—[Chicago Bulls basketball legend] Michael Jordan or something like that.

Not that Mel had any problem with middle-class blacks or Latinos taking
advantage of greater choices of where to live. But he felt very strongly that
those left behind deserved more help finding their own path to a better life.

You should get rid of [welfare programs] but provide people who are less fortunate with the opportunities to better themselves. . . . [Black and Latino] students
from underprivileged backgrounds—not in every case, but in many cases [that's
where] they [come from]—don't have the same opportunities, so they might not
be on a par academically [with whites]. . . . But they probably have the same if
not better capabilities. . . .

I'm not trying to say you should *hand* anything to people. I don't believe in
that; you gotta work hard, you know, and that's where I have a dilemma in a way
with affirmative action . . . because . . . I don't believe you should *give* anybody
anything. . . . I don't believe anybody should be [told], you know, "You're special,
here.". . . [Appropriate] compensation lies in programs like affirmative action . . .
which may eventually *lead* to those betters jobs.

The notion of "compensation" was critical: What kept Mel from rejecting
the possibility of even absolute quotas was what he saw as an obvious link between being "underprivileged" and racial discrimination.

The whole reason for affirmative action anyway is really to compensate for
what—what hasn't been done in the past. . . . You're trying to compensate for
what you wouldn't give people to start with. I mean, you won't, like, help them
achieve their education earlier on or help build up the neighborhood or, you
know, all that stuff. . . . so, I mean, it is a necessary thing. . . . If, you know, . . .
maybe twenty years down the road . . . the station of blacks and Hispanics in
this country is better . . . in terms of getting equal in the economy and everything like that . . . then I'd say affirmative action . . . wouldn't be as necessary.
But . . . [right now,] I'd say it's very necessary, just considering, you know, stuff
that's going on.

Like several of the men I interviewed, Mel lived at home in a part of
Chicago that was "really prejudiced. I have [black and Latino] friends that

might come over . . . and, you know, I can see some of that prejudice—
I mean, I can understand some of [it] because, now the neighborhood's changing: There's, you know, some crime there every so often—not major things,
but nevertheless. . . ." But Mel also had friends in a west suburban community

> which is predominantly an Italian neighborhood. . . . And to be honest with you,
> I mean, it kind of shocks me, they aren't really prejudiced so much [as] they [just]
> haven't come in contact with black people—or minority people, for that matter.
> Like, nobody in the high school was black . . . not one, probably never. . . . They're
> so limited . . . they're so isolated from other people.

On the other hand, Mel was no stranger to the kinds of negative feelings affirmative action could generate among whites. While in high school, Mel had
applied for admission to two U.S. service academies:

> Actually, I applied two years in a row; the second year, I just kind of got . . . sick
> and tired of all the b.s. that was involved. Some of [those accepted the first time
> around] might have been more qualified than me. . . . You know, so be it. But . . .
> I had a [Hispanic] friend that coming out of high school didn't—and I don't mean
> this in a bad way, but really didn't match up with me in terms of academics, ath-
> letics, all that stuff. But he got in. And that's not taking anything away from him,
> but . . . you know. . . . You are taking away an opportunity from somebody else.

Senior year, two of Mel's best friends in high school were an African American and the son of a Jewish college professor.

> [The African American was my] lab partner in chemistry . . . and I was on the
> track team with him and, you know, he's a real good student. He was a National
> Merit [Scholarship] semifinalist, you know, excellent student. To be honest . . .
> I had better grades than him. But what impressed me about him was just that—
> I mean, in chemistry and things like that, the guy wanted to know every—I mean,
> he was very inquisitive and he wanted to know more about a lot of different
> things. I mean, he might have been weaker in other areas . . . but he was still a
> brilliant student. . . .
>   [After] I applied for [the] University of Illinois [flag-ship campus in] Cham-
> paign-Urbana, I had to wait I don't know how long, several weeks after my ap-
> plication was finalized, to find out whether or not I was accepted. [But right af-
> ter my black friend took] his ACTs, Champaign sent *him* a letter [that] said,
> "Congratulations. You're accepted. Send in the application.". . . There were three
> of us in this class that were kind of, you know, hung out. This [third] guy . . . is
> sittin' there raggin'—you know, he . . . was real candid. . . . He's, like, "What the
> hell?". . . And we were laughin' about it. . . . But, I mean, see, a lot of people . . .
> get upset by that.

At UIC, Mel saw nothing in the faculty's approach to teaching that posed any greater challenge to blacks or Latinos than to whites. For example, "Some professors might be very demanding, but at the same time very explicit in their requirements. Whereas others, they've been good professors, but, you know, just difficult to deal with, they're hard to talk to, their tests are impossible. . . . You have to kind of adapt yourself to their methods so you can end up gettin' the better grade."

Students' best efforts, however, might not be enough to compensate for persistent racism on the part of the Chicago Public Schools. Even well-intended reforms sometimes backfired. For example, the CPS had recently decided to democratize access to traditionally elite, selective public high schools like the one Mel had attended. Mel seemed much less concerned with the reverse discrimination this might entail with respect to whites than with its adverse effects on those bright, well-motivated blacks and Latinos likely to benefit the most from a more rigorous, more competitive academic environment, and whose parents could not afford private alternatives.

> [My high school] used to . . . select students on the basis of their academics and all the other factors that they use. . . . But now, with the quote-unquote reform movement, they're basically eliminating [that]. . . . At least [Lane Technical, Lindblom, Whitney Young, and other traditionally selective high schools] were the schools that [could make you] proud of the public school system. . . . Now what you're looking at is . . . eliminating that and bringing all the schools down at once. . . .
>
> [In the past] a good student . . . could go to one of these schools . . . [and] that good student is gonna succeed. And in general, I believe the good student will succeed anywhere. But, I mean, now, you've gotta compete with all kinds of, you know . . . outside influences and negative aspects. . . . You should just leave the system the way it was, and allow these better schools to stay better.

But in general, the public schools were handicapped by inadequate funding.

> Actually, a lot of the poorer schools are the schools that have more funding, but . . . [what] they have to use it for, unfortunately, is . . . like, police and all that stuff. I went to a Chicago public school and . . . my brother does now. And the funding isn't there. . . . There's all this constantly cutting back. They acknowledge that there is a problem but . . . you know, everything you hear on the news on TV and from politicians is just a bunch of rhetoric. . . . They talk about getting money. . . . But they don't have all of the things that a lot of schools in the suburbs and private institutions have. . . .
>
> The Chicago public schools are basically—I mean, the large majority are minority students. And I honestly think people turn their back to that crisis,

because, you know, it's just the minorities. . . . You know, screw them . . . , I mean, politicians would talk and everything like that, but anybody could talk a good game anyways, but it was just a bunch of b.s., the whole thing, and I honestly think they turn their back. . . .

I think they're representing the white public's view. In my neighborhood, nobody sends their kids to the public schools. . . . The large majority . . . all go to . . . St. Ferdinand, which my parents, after sending my brother to the [public] grammar school . . . for one year, enrolled him in . . . simply because the public school was horrible. . . . There're a lot of non-Catholics . . . that send their children to the Catholic school . . . because it's a better school, period. But in a way, you see, that's a cop out.

DAVE ZALUBA: PLAYING THE PERCENTAGES

> [At my high school] peer pressure was more or less [in the direction of] doing better in school, because the stars of the school—the stars of your friends—were the people who were doing good. . . . Even the jocks still had the pressure of—Like, if you were a smart jock, you were probably *the* person, you know . . . the most popular. . . . [Whereas blacks' peers are] encouraging them very strongly *not* to do well. . . . The peer pressure is not to get A's in school; it's to be tough, to make it through the next day, it's to get some money, you know, it's to buy a nice set of shoes . . . or to buy that leather, I don't know, Bulls jacket or something.

Dave Zabula's own family never had much money to spare, so it had probably made good sense for him to start off his college studies with a two-year electronics degree from one of Chicago's community colleges. At twenty-six, he was working his way through UIC with one part-time job as a computer technician, and another as a research assistant for one of his science professors. He had his heart set on medical school—saving lives "would be such a fabulous thing"—and was especially interested in cutting-edge developments in neurology and immunology.

Dave's interest in research fed his enthusiasm for cultural diversity. "Being from a different culture, you have a different flavor on life, you know different things, and by sharing those differences, you can make yourself stronger." With respect to medicine in particular,

> Other cultures have so much to offer, and by discriminating against them, you lose what they give you. The American Indians had tons and tons of medicines that . . . we never learned about. And now, we're, like, "what if their thing is true?" . . . And we're going into all kinds of countries now [where] folk doctors

. . . [will] say, "Oh, yeah, this helps, look at this.". . . It's, like, aspirin, your [American] Indians used to chew on the bark of a tree, and that would help toothaches. . . . It's the Indians who knew it, not us. . . . The whole world could be so much more efficient.

Regarding his own talents, Dave was well aware that his strengths in math and science far exceeded his linguistic abilities, and he feared that he might not do well enough on the readings-based sections of the MCAT—a test he viewed as a "totally useless screening process, because . . . as far as I understand, there would be no correlation between how well you do on these entrance exams to how well you do in med school." Like several others, however, he had a good deal of faith in college grades, as a measure of learning, of "just deserts," and the probability of superior performance in the future. That was his problem with a hypothetical admissions lottery: Failing to take into account the likelihood that prospective medical students would know about the lottery, it upset him that applicants

who have maybe worked hard their entire life to get into medical school . . . just by the luck of the draw may not get in . . . and some guy who, you know, just drank all the way through college . . . and . . . squeezed on by, he gets in. . . . I think if you look at the majority and the average, people who work hard during medical school and during high school and college will work hard when they're *out* of that, it's their work ethic, their work habits.

Regarding affirmative action, he had a problem with race-norming, which seemed to violate what he took for granted as the utilitarian rationale for cut scores in the first place. "If there's a minimum standard to get through medical school for a human being, then it's the minimum standard. If you have two sets of standards, and one is the [actual] minimum, and then the other one is set *higher* for white people, because they've had better opportunities, then what are you trying to get at?" He also felt that a double standard would have a negative impact on those it was designed to help.

By *getting* these quotas, you're gonna strive to achieve a *lower* status. . . . A white male says, "Well, I have to have a GPA of 4.5 [to get into medical school]"; he's gonna work to have that. Whereas a *black* male says, "Well, I have to have a GPA of 4.2." So *he's* gonna work [just hard enough] to get that GPA of 4.2. . . . In a way that's *hurting* them because . . . it *keeps* them [unequal]. It keeps the status quo. . . . The goal is to achieve a common ground. . . . I think it's bad for a social group to strive to achieve less than anybody else.

Like Gil Jarreaux, Dave did not buy the argument that black and Latino undergraduates might be further disadvantaged by any sort of cultural bias in their college studies.

> Basically, learning knowledge is learning knowledge, reading a book is reading a book, memorizing something is memorizing something. . . . If you can say that the way [whites] teach is biased towards the white people, and makes it harder for the black people, you're saying that these people's *minds* must be different. . . . I don't think there's that much difference in the way people *process* things, you know. . . . I think there's . . . maybe different ways of *presenting* things, and if there *are*. . . . Let's say, Latin American culture, they tend to represent this one thing a certain way. And maybe *because* they present it this way, 80 percent of the students will grasp, uh, 90 percent of the information. Whereas the other way, 50 percent of the students will grasp . . . 90 percent of the information. So maybe you could adapt the Latin American way of teaching that [to everyone].

But as long as there was a single cut score, Dave endorsed affirmative action admissions in the form of modified quotas. For on the average, Chicago's blacks and Latinos had *not* had a fair shot—not because of poorly run, underfunded schools, but mostly because of the behavior and worldviews propagated in the communities they'd grown up in, full of welfare mothers, substance abuse, and gang violence. Dave believed that kids growing up in Chicago's ghettos and barrios wanted to succeed as much as anyone else, but they were much more likely than whites to be diverted from mainstream avenues of achievement.

> They're out there trying to survive, you know? They're not out there trying to get a decent job like me, they're out there trying to survive. Make it into the next day. So they're not shot, so they're not mugged, take care of their mom or their brother, you know? . . . The reason why the blacks go out and sell the drugs is not because they don't want to succeed, but because they *want* to succeed. They *want* to make the money. They want to get through and . . . it's just the way they're pushed into doing [it] , you know. . . . A gang neighborhood could *keep* people from going to school. If the smart people go to school, they'll kill him because he's done well.

So the correlation between interest, effort, and achievement might not hold true.

> [Even] if a black is as motivated as a fairly *un*motivated white, where a white would get through college with maybe Cs and go into the work world . . . a black who's just as motivated as that . . . I don't think he's going anywhere . . . because . . . not only does he have to *want* to get into college, he's gonna have to want it so hard that he's not gonna go off with his friends.

For this reason, Dave saw real advantages to inner-city blacks or Latinos living on campus (although my memories of dorm life suggest he may have been too optimistic). "I think once they're removed from that [environment]—say, they're removed to a dorm here, and sent to this lifestyle, where now you have *everybody* studying—the peer pressure now is [to] study, and it'd make it a lot easier." But while he felt this would be "more equalizing . . . like, if he makes just as much effort [as I do] to get an A, we should both get A's," one of his arguments for affirmative action was that, "The obstacles in the past . . . they hurt them . . . *now*, you know what I'm saying? . . . Even if they are totally removed from their high school . . . they come to college less well-prepared."

Parents could sometimes fill the gap: Dave had "one friend who's black and he grew up in a black neighborhood. It wasn't the worst neighborhood, it wasn't the best. But he came out good because, I feel, he had a mother that would love him, a father that would love him, that worked hard, and they kept him off the streets. You know what I mean? They tried. They worked at it. And he came out pretty good." But, on the whole, Dave saw black families as part of the problem.

> There's really not a very strong family commitment in a lot of black relationships . . . like, a mother doesn't believe she has to be married. . . . The mother tries to raise the child by herself, the father really doesn't have a whole lot of room for the child, there's not a strong family group, and the mother, naturally, she needs money, she goes to welfare. . . . It's usually the mother saying, "I don't want you to get involved with gangs, you know, you should go to school," and stuff like that. But they don't have a father . . . they don't have *both* of them harping on it.

The pressures of inner-city life, moreover, might take their toll on one's whole approach to parenting—especially if the parent herself had grown up in the same environment.

> It's not just blacks. . . . I know a white lady who drank all the time, treated her kids like shit, like they were her possessions instead of her children. If she wanted something, it would be, so-and-so, get this, so-and-so, get that. She wound up eventually deciding she didn't want them anymore, so she gave them up [to] her husband. . . . But I think it tends to happen more in the black neighborhoods because of the way *they* were brought up, and that's hard on the kids, you know. So now they have, like, *everything* against them.

For the most part, Dave blamed all of this on poverty. Regarding criminal activity in and around black neighborhoods, for example, "I don't look at it, 'Because they're black, they're doing this.' . . . It's that they're in a depressed area. . . . If you had a bunch of upper-class blacks and there was a white slum, then the whites would be the same way. You know, it has nothing to do with the color, it's just a fact of their economic status."

My rejoinder, at this point in the interviews, was the common argument among many opponents of affirmative action that many other ethnic groups seemed to have overcome poverty, geographic dislocation, and often serious discrimination a good deal more readily than the present-day black and Latino underclass. How come? Dave pointed once again to communal solidarity and familial concern. He did have some qualms about child-rearing among East Asian immigrants to this country, who "tend to push their children *very* hard in school. And they also have a strong sense of *controlling* their child, as far as, well, they *have* to do so much home work. . . . And then you end up in a debate [over] whether you *should* push a child so hard in school, and not injure their life. . . . I would never want to put my kid though that much torment." But he had no quarrel with the consequences overall.

Dave was also impressed by certain patterns of Asian self-help he'd heard about. "Oh, it's elaborate, the Asian people will get, say, a group of twenty families together, and they all throw in money to this pot," from which each family in turn could draw money to start a business. "And this way, not only does the family support each other, but a whole group of people support each other and get each other through difficult times." Dave had good things to say, as well, about his own ethnic group. "There's this *strong* [Eastern European] neighborhood in Chicago. And when you come here, you go into [that] neighborhood. [It's] *still* there . . . sticking together, because these people stick together. . . . But . . . not [the blacks]. I don't know why not."

Were there perhaps inherent differences between the races that might help to account for contrasts in social mores or academic achievement? Drawing on substantial training in the relevant disciplines, Dave admitted that natural selection among relatively isolated populations exposed to different conditions might very well have produced *minimal* differences, "[not] so much [in] the size of the brain being different, but maybe the way the brain is developed or hooked up." And then he stood one of the classic arguments for white superiority on its head: "If you say blacks are better with their hands, that might make them better surgeons, or make it *easier* for them to be better surgeons—just like women in general are better with their hands. . . . But I think that it is so *subtle* [a difference] that to say they have an advantage is barely true."

Dave was more sympathetic, however, to the notion that long-standing cultural differences, predating extensive contact with whites, might have something to do with present-day difficulties. For one thing, it could help to explain some differences he had observed among Chicago's Latino communities. If Puerto Ricans "do not have strong . . . family togetherness, it might be the result of their culture *before* they came over here. . . . Where maybe Mexicans *did* have strong family togetherness, and *definitely* Asians [did]." Regarding blacks, "I don't know if it varied from tribe to tribe, [but] I have seen documentaries on tribes in Africa and . . . I do not think they actually marry there. . . . I saw *one* not too long ago, and it seems to me that they did not have a lifetime mate."

Regarding present-day race relations, Dave agreed with Gil that blacks often exaggerated what they were up against. For example, "I don't think the KKK is a very strong influence. When they rally, they don't have a lot of people standing around and going, 'Yeah, yeah, yeah!' There are [actually] a lot of [white] people standing around and throwing bottles and stuff [at them]." And blacks' efforts to counteract racism were often too extreme.

> Everybody talks about, oh, yeah, this person is discriminated against. But . . . I won't say all, I would say 95 percent of [the] resentment that I have, or discrimination that I have seen, is more [in response to] the black attitude toward the white. . . . [When sports handicapper] Jimmy the Greek . . . [said] something like, they're better at sports because . . . they're more flexible because they have that extra tendon . . . he was fired from his job and everything, and criticized *immensely*. He didn't say anything about how bad blacks are, that we should go out and kill blacks. And here [rap star Sister Solja] goes out and says how [blacks] should kill whites. . . . She's saying, "Oh, I didn't mean to," like, but still she said it. . . . And she is *defended* for it. . . . A lot of [white] people are . . . saying, "Enough! Enough!"

On the other hand, Dave felt that there was more than enough good old-fashioned racism out there to explain blacks' anxiety on a white-majority campus.

> Just one act of discrimination could very much affect everybody. . . . If I walked through a campus that was mostly black . . . actually, even if we were in the majority and [some blacks had] perpetrated racist acts against some whites . . . just walking around through a group of blacks . . . you would feel [hostility], because it was the blacks that did racial discrimination against you. . . . Even if . . . there were . . . [just] 10 percent that might be problems, [any time] you walk in front of [blacks] . . . you know that some of those people have so much hateful thoughts . . . and that makes you uncomfortable, that makes you not want to be there . . . it's not a good thing.

And he seemed to grasp the power of stereotyping to shape even his own attitudes. Explaining the depth and persistence of poverty in much of the black community, for example, he ventured,

> It's part of their own—it's, like, they're a community where they don't actively go out and seek jobs. Well, they can get welfare. . . . Mothers . . . have another child

to get more welfare money. Not that that happens all of the time, but as a bad image of what's goin' on. . . . You hear a lot about them going on welfare and getting
a job and collecting unemployment. . . . That might not be what's goin' on at all.
But . . . whether it's true or not . . . you hear about it happening. . . . Whether
that's true or not, I don't know.

On the other hand, Dave's own experience suggested that at least some negative stereotypes had solid foundations. For example, he described an experience I had had numerous times myself, riding the Chicago Transit Authority's
buses and rapid-transit lines.

I can get onto a bus, and the bus will be quiet, and [then] the bus will pass a
school [that's] letting out and a bunch of black students walk on. And from there
on, all you hear is screaming, cussing, very much disrespect of anybody around
them. . . . And so what kind of attitude—When you look at the—You could say,
"Okay, this is just *them*." But, still, this is what you see.

But the real problem was not that black youth might be uncouth, but that
blacks posed real dangers to whites, which went a long way toward explaining
white flight from "changing" neighborhoods.

I had some neighbors that *moved* from [what had become] a black neighborhood.
. . . Their daughter was riding a bike, and some black guy threw the daughter off.
. . . Blacks had moved in, and then [there was] more crime and stuff like that. And
then when their child's bike was taken while she was riding it . . . that's when they
moved. So, in a way, you can't expect me not to have some feelings. . . .
    Although we're not far from the black dividing line, the blacks don't come into
my [northwest side] neighborhood, and . . . walking into their neighborhood, I'd
be very uncomfortable [about] being jumped. . . . There [is] a lot of distrust on
the part of blacks, that we don't like 'em. . . . You know, the blacks complain that,
"As soon as we move into [a] neighborhood, the whites move out." Well, you can't
expect me . . . to live in a neighborhood where I have to be afraid when I walk
out that door. . . .
    Right now, I can come home, or walk out of my house one o'clock in the morn-
ing, feeling fine. . . . [If my neighborhood begins to change] I could say, "Well, I
don't want to be discriminatory, I'm not gonna move." But then again, that's kind
of like what happened to that neighbor, and it affected their child. I don't want to
walk out of my house, ten o'clock at night, and have to worry. I don't want my
mom saying, well, it's dark out, she can't leave the house.

Explaining whites' more general fear of blacks, Dave once again talked
probabilities. "If the percentage of times that I see a black person [committing
a crime] is 75 percent of the time, I see a white person doing this 25 percent
of the time, naturally I'm going to feel more leery. . . . So I would think that's

more the discrimination [that blacks encounter] as opposed to just hating blacks in general." All in all, what Dave seemed to be telling me, is that what might *look* like white racism was often simply a reasonable effort to survive the urban jungle.

I'm not saying that all—'cause I have some—a lot of friends, I should say, that are black. And they're just like me, or I'm just like them. . . . But if you see some-body, well, you [respond on the basis of] what you relate to them the most, you see what I'm saying? There's probably some real nice, tame lions out there that you could walk up and pet. But the majority *aren't* going to be tame, and they're gonna pounce on you. And so, knowing that, if you're gonna approach a lion . . . you're gonna go with what you see the most.

RATTLING THE CHAINS OF CAUSALITY

Were some minority groups *inherently* dangerous? Or in some other way less genetically suited to legitimate avenues of achievement? Chris Feraios, for one, felt that the rioting and looting in L.A. that Gil Jarreaux alluded to was good evidence that blacks were by nature violent. Sam Turner thought that blacks' "quickness in athletics" might possibly be related to group differences in genetic endowment. Tim Kovacs agreed that, "Physically, I mean, blacks ex-cel in sports," and that this had "something to do with muscle placement in their leg or whatever. . . . As far as . . . mental capacity, I can't say. I would say, no, just in general. But—uh, yeah, I would say probably not." He did suggest, however, that Asians' tendency to be "more science oriented" might be related to some "innate capability they have;" but then again, it might just be "a soci-etal thing . . . I'm not sure."

But for the most part, everyone agreed with Mel Gibran that most of the blame for inequality of academic outcomes between whites and blacks or Latinos lay largely with the public schools—or they agreed with Dave Zaluba that the problem was what social scientists, politicians, and journalists have come to call the "culture of poverty"—or a little of both. There was much less agreement, however, on the severity and impact of racism past or present, and to what extent bad schools and the culture of poverty could be traced to prej-udice and discrimination on the part of whites.

Still Racist, After All These Years: *First-hand experience with inter-ethnic hostility*

None of the men I interviewed claimed that this country had put racism be-hind it. Jack Uberhof's experience was similar to Dave's.

Whenever I feel like arguing [with my parents], I'll bring [race or affirmative action] up. . . . They're really good people, but as far as this goes, I think it all goes back to, when they first moved to [a suburb just west of Chicago] back in '72, my mother was assaulted by about four or five black gentlemen. . . . They had gotten out of [their] car and grabbed her and tried to throw her into the car, and I think that's when it really started. Then, you know, she just generalized from then on.

Other interviews as well touched on white anxieties concerning "changing neighborhoods." Joe Murtaugh had grown up in a largely Irish-Catholic enclave (immortalized in the novel and stage musical *Do Black Patent Leather Shoes Really Reflect Up?*[1]) where "They're trying to keep it white. . . . Not that we're busy burning crosses on somebody's front lawn or . . . a black guy [who] gets on this side of Western Avenue's gonna be beat up, but, uh. . . . It's just extremely realized, if there's anybody [black] at a drugstore on my corner . . . it's 1945. . . . They aren't wanted in that mile-and-a-half square." Twenty-one-year-old pre-law business major Greg Bogosian could

still remember, it was three years ago, when a black family moved in on my block. It was like—like the neighborhood held its breath. It was *unbelievable*. I mean, I was waiting for the crosses on the lawn to go up. And, I mean, I didn't care. . . . Just don't mess with the neighborhood. Whether you're white or black. . . . And, you know, they've been the perfect family: No problems, you never see beater cars out there. No late night, you know, drinking or drug parties. . . . None of that happened.

Along with a public housing project, UIC itself had been eminent-domained out of the heart of Chicago's Little Italy, and Marc Huston recalled seeing "a couple of black kids [walking down] Taylor Street [just south of campus] . . . and one of the Italian older men kicked 'em off the street and told 'em to walk on the other side. . . . The people down here— well, these people have lived here all their lives, and they don't like to see blacks in their neighborhood."

Back on the northwest side, "You know where the boundaries are at," Chris Feraios told me. The very presence of a black visitor to Sean Hanna's home had provoked hostility, including

death threats to myself and my family. . . . I mean it wasn't that my black friend came over and [later] someone called [and said], "I'm gonna kill you." It was more like an ongoing conflict. . . . We had people break into the house . . . racial epithets. . . . I don't know if you've heard of the cross-burnings a couple summers ago. These were the same people.

Was there racism on the UIC campus? As Dan Lysenko put it, "If you're gonna be here for four years, you're a member of a minority, yeah, I think at some point, something's going to happen. Maybe a major incident, maybe a minor incident, but I don't see how . . . it *couldn't* happen." On the other hand, there was general agreement that the campus was a safe haven of sorts. "It's going to happen," Jack explained, "[but] the predomination of the university student is more of a broad-minded person than of a narrow-minded, so I think that within the university, the people attending and the faculty . . . at any university, I think [blacks and Latinos would] be less likely to become victims of racial prejudice than outside."

And several men seemed to agree with Gil Jarreaux that racism was "really blown out of proportion," as Jack put it, "and how often and how many times it has happened." In UIC's principal student newspaper, Marc observed,

> They always have black people crabbin' about being racially, you know . . . [but] I think it's just their perception, because [everybody] who works here, just about, at this university is black . . . civil servants, I should say, working for this university . . . [so there aren't] too many white people to be discriminating against blacks here. [It's] just . . . that . . . if something happens to one person . . . all of 'em band together and it's a whole racial incident.

Here's that newspaper's description of one incident referred to several times in my interviews.

> Greek Week . . . erupted into controversy on Wednesday . . . when Caucasian members of Sigma Alpha Mu fraternity painted their faces black and portrayed Ray Charles and other African-American artists during a lip sync contest. . . . Another performance, by sorority Gamma Gamma Gamma of "The Lion Sleeps Tonight," portrayed a sleeping lion with three dancing monkeys singing back-up to a bird, while a gorilla did harmony. . . . [It] won a second place award, but some [African American] students found it offensive.[2]

And Pat Gaheogan's take on the same incident:

> This school's highly tense about racial things. I mean, it's almost to a point where it's comical. Because I remember reading, last semester, they had their "Greek Week," or whatever they had. . . . They had a show where they were singing, "In the Jungle," or something?[3] And they had a gorilla come out in a gorilla costume, and people took it racially. . . . I don't believe for a second that was the intent. That would just be silly. Granted, when they did black-face, I think that was in very poor taste. . . . But the racial tensions are at an edge. It's like a rubber band that's getting ready to snap, it almost is.

Like Gil, Joe felt that he had been victimized by blacks' tendency to see racism when it wasn't there.

> Blew my mind. . . . It was convenient. . . . A [black] girl . . . was trying to pull a game. . . . She was very difficult. It turns out she had major head problems. . . . She was [involved] in a [project] I was [in charge of]. And I wound up dropping her, and she was completely psycho.
>
> She later attacked one of the [other students] with a weapon, and cut up her face. . . . She accused me of being a racist.

With several others, Joe seemed to agree with Dave that interracial hostility in the present day was to considerable degree something that blacks brought on themselves through "reverse racism." At a school Joe had previously attended, "I did a lot of stuff with . . . a black fraternity, and I almost joined them. . . . I'd say the biggest reason why I left [that school] was, I was in the wrong place at the wrong time, and I ended up spending a couple of days in the hospital. Somebody beat the hell out of me for being a white guy." Joe had also worked with and managed both blacks and Latinos. "I don't want you working for me wearing a [Malcolm X] tag on your cap. . . . Malcolm X was a stone racist. Anybody that's read any of his stuff goes, Whoa! Black supremacy; look out! That doesn't make me a racist for questioning those [people]." A state-licensed teacher, Sam Turner recalled a job interview at one inner-city school.

> They looked at me, and they gave me about five minutes, and said, "Thank you, we'll call you when we're ready." . . . The guy was, like, in shock that I was even applying. . . . It was a primarily black school, and I would have felt better about it if I had been able to express some of my opinions and so on, my ideas and things like that. But it was just such a cold turkey type of thing where they just said, "See ya." And it was very obvious.

As both Gil and Mel Gibran noted, moreover, affirmative action could be part of the problem it was trying to solve. To Chris, "The whole reason why there's campus violence and everything [is that] the whites just feel that there hasn't been any, you know, fairness in the way [blacks and Latinos] have gotten here and the way other people have gotten here." Pat seemed a little embarrassed to admit that he would "feel a little bit of animosity" if affirmative action kept him out of law school. "'Hey, I scored better than you, *but you're in and I'm not.*' That may give me a complex, I guess, but that's just the way I feel."

But whatever its source, however intense or widespread, free-floating, interpersonal prejudice or discrimination was not really what kept blacks and Latinos down.

An Unlevel Playing Field: *Institutional racism and inequality*

None of the men I talked to saw much of a link between inequality of outcomes and direct, *mano a mano* experience with racist whites. But most of them made the same connection Mel did between inequality and institutional racism in schools or the workplace, or like Dave, linked *long-term* structural racism—in American politics, our job market, our housing patterns, you name it—to communal obstacles to mainstream achievement.

There were differences of opinion, however, as to whether this kind of racism had survived the civil rights movement. "I'm sure they don't have the same amount of [executive] jobs that they probably should," Chris Feraios told me, "but . . . it's just [since] the sixties and all, you know, the civil rights thing, and I think it's just taking time for, you know, to climb the ladder." But Steve Clayburgh, who had spent most of his early years on relatively color-blind overseas military bases, saw something quite different when he moved stateside after his parents' divorce.

> I worked as a bagger at a grocery store [in the South] when I was in high school, and I was stocking one of the shelves and a guy who was black came up to me and asked me, "Hey, man, do you know where I can get a job application, or if they're hiring right now?" I said, "I don't know if they're hiring, but if you go back up to the management office, the boss ought to be able to give you one." . . . [A few minutes later] . . . I went up there . . . [and asked] "Was there a gentleman that came up here to get a job application?" And the manager sat there and scratched his head and looked up like he didn't understand me and said, "No—No, I can't—Oh, there was this colored boy that did." And I'm, like, "Well, ain't he a gentleman?" And then he realized what I was getting at, and corrected himself by saying, "Oh! Oh! But I gave him an application." Like that was his saving grace. But the attitude that I saw in there meant that even if he turned in the application, they were going to throw it away.

Greg Bogosian was not the liberal that Steve was and opposed any form of race-targeted affirmative action, but he saw himself as one of the *least* racist people he knew. Where he worked, at a north suburban branch of a national chain of discount stores,

> What I do is, I'm the security manager there, and I investigate, you know, all sorts of theft and shortages and all that other garbage they have around the store. And the first response I hear from a lot of people, when a black cashier comes up with a register shortage, is, "Oh, it figures." You know, like, I just want to crack 'em upside the head one. It *doesn't* figure, you know, it happens to everybody. . . .
>
> You know, they claim where it's all equal and stuff, as far as the work stands, and it really is, you know; they apply the same standards for hiring [minorities] as

they do for everybody else. It's just—it's just real interesting how, when we started with twenty black employees, we're down to two. And it just seems the way [the people in charge]—I mean, I suppose it's also our location, we're up in [a suburb just outside the city limits], so that's sort of out of the way for them. But it just seems, you know, sometimes you want to say, "Something's a little fishy."

Joe Murtaugh had seen similar responses to black customers. "A white guy walking up in a business suit trying to return a dress shirt? Yes, sir. Yes sir. I think a black woman walking in with the same problem wouldn't. 'Let's check this again for shoplifting.'" Something more blatant confronted Jack Uberhof, who worked at a Chicago placement agency for degreed professional and technical employees.

We get orders from big companies . . . and I've heard that a lot of times, it's not . . . written anywhere. . . . But [a major consumer-products conglomerate] called in an order, and they were saying it's corporate policy that as far as that one department is concerned, he made it clear that he didn't want any blacks. . . . I realized that you have to keep this relationship going with this huge client that was . . . giving them a lot of business. I just, I wouldn't have took [that kind of order] myself. Of course, I don't know how much trouble I would have got in.

Several men, moreover, shared Mel Gibran's concern with the poor quality of preparation blacks and Latinos were likely to have received in the elementary and secondary schools they'd attended. "The high school curriculum may not have been meant for them to go to college," Pat Gaheogan speculated; rather, "they're trying to teach [them] to work with their hands." "They don't get the attention or they don't have as good teachers in the primary grades," Tim Kovacs observed. "If you don't learn step A, you're just memorizing step B instead of really understanding what step B is, to get to step C." Although he hadn't been in this country very long, Isaac Fedelovich already recognized that, "When [blacks and Latinos/] go to worse schools, they're not *required* to do as good as white students would be required to do. . . . By the time they enter college, they don't have the same [academic] background. So even if they take the same classes in college, and they're treated equally in college, they don't have the basics, and that might hurt, you know?" Doug Peruggia emphasized disparate levels of funding:

The kid from [upper-middle-class, suburban] Winnetka [is competing] against the guy from the inner city. The school teacher [in Winnetka's] making $65,000 a year, the school teachers here are making $21,000. You know . . . at second grade, [children in Winnetka are] on IBM computers, and these people are still plugging through.

As discussed further in the next chapter, views on inner-city schools had a lot to do with my subjects' enthusiasm for graduate professional school outreach to schoolchildren. But were blacks and Latinos *further* disadvantaged by the educational policies and practices of the colleges they attended? Minority advocates and scholars have often argued that even if majority-white colleges and universities are relatively free from traditional forms of prejudice or discrimination, they might still be guilty of institutional racism by virtue of their failure to make adequate adjustments to the needs and perspectives of students of color. Did blacks and Latinos seem to have that problem at UIC?

Matt Vigoda thought that, to some extent, they did. Different ethnic groups were bound to bring different perspectives to bear on their studies, "especially in the liberal arts, where you deal with a lot of humanities and things like that. And race kind of colors any subject there. And I think maybe a lot of times, like, professors are insensitive to that." Twenty-one-year-old humanities major Hal Voorhees was not always sure himself "where [professors are] coming from sometimes . . . or they have this annoying habit of getting off on tangents or whatever . . . and my grades have suffered because of that. . . . If within one race, that sort of thing can go on, it would seem very plausible that it could happen *among* races as well. Perhaps even more dramatic." But most of the others felt that any special problems minorities encountered in UIC courses were simply a matter of inadequate preparation in high school and had very little to do with culture-specific teaching styles or slants on content. As Jack put it, "I don't know how differently you can teach accounting."

Doug argued that cultural differences might actually work to blacks' and Latinos' advantage. "Western civ . . . based on white culture . . . is what [everyone was] taught in grade school and high school. But [blacks and Latinos] also have the knowledge of their own culture[s]. Actually, they know a little bit more than we do, 'cause they have that interest enough to do it themselves." Pat was more succinct: "They have just as much chance to fall asleep as I do."

In contrast with its public schools, America's military forces have earned fairly high points over the past few decades for having overcome a long history of institutional racism, and this was born out by the veterans I interviewed. But while Steve had observed a good deal of affirmative action, twenty-five-year-old business student Bill Sajak had had a different experience.

> Being in [that branch of the service] had a lot of influence on my [opposition to] affirmative action, because I saw that there were plenty of minorities who were treated exactly the same as I was. 'Cause in the military, everybody's equal; there actually is no affirmative action in the military, at least that I saw. None of the minorities received special treatment and none of the whites received special

treatment, so it was really up to the individual to pursue his own interest and motivation. . . .

I think it made me less in favor . . . of affirmative action, because I saw that everybody could be given an equal amount of opportunity, but there's still so many people that won't take advantage of it. I also saw a lot of racism in the military. But a lot of [minorities] complained that they weren't being given a fair shake in relation to the majority. That wasn't the case at all. It's just that there's some people that don't take advantage of opportunities that other people take advantage of. . . . I don't know what the reason would be. They feel that they've been left out, but I feel it's their own fault.

On the whole, advocates of affirmative action seemed more likely than opponents to link inequality of outcomes at least in part to interpersonal and/or institutional racism. Nonetheless, the great majority of the men I talked to agreed that blacks, especially, did not take full advantage of the opportunities open to them, mostly because of the sorts of negative influences on inner-city youth that Dave Zaluba had talked about. Present-day racism might still be part of the equation; Zack Pritchard, for example, felt that "The kind of prejudice that they have to experience would wear you down, and give you less strength to say no to the other things," like street gangs. Even those most sensitive to contemporary hostilities, however, tended to give more weight to the sustained impact of a long history of racism on minority communities and their youth.

The Culture of Poverty: *Communal constraints on academic motivation and achievement*

I'm from Joliet, and they have a terrible gang problem. I've known many [African American gang members] . . . and they were great kids . . . did okay in school, but they weren't interested in going to college. . . . Their parents hadn't gone, their brothers didn't go, and they just weren't gonna do that. . . .

I was really close to some of them when we were, like, fourteen. By the time I saw them again, when we were seventeen . . . where they lived [had] just caught up to them, and they were into drugs and guns. One particular [black high school] friend that I had, he *did* go away to college, he went to Robert Morris College here [in Chicago], and he made good. . . . But then he got shot [on a visit home] and now he's blind. And so you can't get away from it.

—Matt Vigoda

A city of about 100,000 about forty-five miles west-southwest of Chicago, Matt's home town is "particularly well known," its Chamber of Commerce website tells us, "for its unique expression of identity through public art."[4] Chances are, it is better known for Joliet State Prison, immortalized in *The Blues Brothers* movies and long the home of some of Chicago's worst and baddest. The website makes much of the city's comeback from the same economic doldrums that decimated hundreds of Joliets across America's rust belt in the 1970s and 1980s. But its new corporate offices, its theme parks and riverboat casinos, and its impressive growth as an "exurban" bedroom community for Windy City commuters had as yet done little for a substantial minority underclass very much like Chicago's. And it was the lifestyles and worldviews of this underclass that the men interviewed were most likely to point to as the most immediate source of minority underachievement.

Like Dave Zaluba, they rounded up the usual suspects: chronic unemployment and welfare dependency; inadequate housing in rundown neighborhoods; dysfunctional families created by teenaged mothers and absentee fathers; widespread abuse of alcohol and illegal drugs; gang violence, often related to the sale of those drugs; and not nearly enough successful, law-abiding adults for young people to emulate. Twenty-one-year-old pre-med Mike Benedetto could imagine what it was like

> to grow up in a set of [public housing] projects where . . . [so few people] are striving for anything . . . the overwhelming majority are just on welfare. . . . You don't see role models . . . you don't have people pushing you. . . . You might want the out, but you have no way of knowing how to.

But of course, there were more than enough successful adults with a powerful influence on young people's behavior and attitudes. Len Hellstrom made the point, "Who has the money in the poorest black neighborhoods? Drug dealers. That's a fact." Peer pressure and peer norms were at least as powerful. Doug Peruggia was matter-of-fact: "The majority of blacks live in the ghetto; the majority of those fourteen-year-olds join gangs; that's what the majority's going to do, you know?" Young men "that are constantly worried about their own personal safety will join a gang just [so] . . . if somebody messes with them, they'd have somebody watching their back."

As far as schoolwork was concerned, Joe Murtaugh had observed, "If a black guy's doing good—and I've seen this happen, too—other black guys will say he's Uncle Tom-ing . . . instead of saying, 'Hey, nice job,' you know? . . . If I'm . . . afraid to walk home with school books in my hand without gettin' the hell beat out of me, I won't bring those school books home."

Like Dave, Mike stressed that parents could serve as a critical buffer against those kinds of influences. "When I grew up, my parents were always pushing me. If your parents aren't sitting there to help you with your homework, if your

parents can't even *do* the level of homework you're doing, how are you supposed to get ahead?" Greg Bogosian agreed,

> If you're brought up to want to succeed, you'll succeed. . . . Having one parent or
> two parents, it's how your parents . . . bring you up that makes a big difference.
> . . . It has a lot to do with discipline. . . . Right now . . . black and Latino children
> may be less supervised or less—It['s] . . . not that [their parents] *care* less, but
> they've almost given up on everything. . . . [But] the ones that haven't given up,
> you can see . . . that the results are considerably better for their children. And
> their children get better grades . . . they stay out of trouble, they don't get killed
> by age fifteen.

By contrast, ineffectual parenting might help to explain just why inner-city
schools often failed to provide a quality education. "A bad family background,"
Sam Turner argued, "can eventually work its way so that teachers feel ineffec-
tive and essentially the schools kind of break down." What was often lacking
was "some sense of stability" within the home.

> If your stability is shaken, then you don't have *time* to worry about things like ac-
> ademic achievement. . . . Lately what we're seeing is a breakdown of the family,
> and that's had devastating effects . . . especially on the black community. . . . It's
> not that [the children] work any less hard, they just have—there's limited hours
> in the day, and if half of your day when you get home is dedicated to raising . . .
> your little brother, or . . . changing diapers as a nine year old. . . . I mean, you may
> not get your homework done that night, and then it may eventually unfold that
> you don't get to where you wanna go.

On the other hand, even parents with the solidest of characters, working full
time and then some in draining, low-wage jobs, might not have enough time
or energy left over to offer the supervision or encouragement their children
needed. Or the kids might "receive less *useful* encouragement," as Matt put it,
from parents with little education or limited experience in the work world
themselves. Their children "may be encouraged to do *better*, but the person
encouraging them may not know how that is done."

Single-parent families were of special concern. Like Mel Gibran, several of
the men I talked to provided vivid glimpses of their relationships with their fathers. Pat Gaheogan, for example, stressed that what kids needed was not "just
a presence" but

> a father . . . who you see coming home every day, working hard. Someone who
> says, "Wow, you did a really good job with that," every once in a while. Not some-
> body who coddles you, [but] who tells you the truth. Who says, "Hey, you have to
> start doing better. You gotta straighten up your act." And maybe every once in a

while will slap you around, if that's what *you* need. Someone to help you, I guess.
. . . I looked up to my father, and I still do. He was a very important part of my
life, and I take a lot of what I am from him. And I could not see growing up without the figurehead.

Fighting the Undertow: *Racism, resilience, and the unintentional consequences of collective intervention*

Don't get me wrong: No one I interviewed had abandoned his all-American
faith in the power of the individual to overcome adversity. Perhaps Hal
Voorhees put it best: "I'm a strong believer in free will. And while I think that
there are many environmental influences, I don't think that there are really
environmental causes, as far as that goes. [But] I think it's more *difficult* to
make [good] choices, if not given the correct influences." The culture of
poverty was seen to feed on itself largely through its *psychological* impact on
minority youth: muting effort, sapping self-esteem, blocking those in its grip
from escape routes much more visible from the outside.

Growing up in the inner city, it was easy to internalize values antithetical to
long-term academic and professional achievement. "Maybe the problem with
the blacks," Joe Murtaugh suggested, "is that they're seeing, you know, my dad
didn't work, why should I work? And my mother didn't work, why should I
work? You know, if they're pickin' up a free meal ticket."

Moreover, minority youth might not put much store in delayed gratification.
Sean Hanna recalled running into a black friend from high school, "and
[when] I told him what I was doing, bio major . . . he just kind of scoffed and
he said, 'Well, what's the point? . . . What are you going to do with that? . . .
You know, I've been working for years and I'm makin' seven bucks an hour and
I got a new car.'" As Rick Skilling saw it, blacks and Latinos "might not want
to work as hard [at academics], not because they have less desire to succeed"
but because they

don't get it kind of kicked into 'em that school is gonna pay off some day. . . .
'Look at my parents' or 'Look at my family,' stuff like that. . . . White gangs, black
gangs, Latino gangs, what have you, [have] a mentality of getting whatever you
want right then. . . . And to work for somethin' now that's gonna pay off twenty
years from now—the desire for *that* isn't as great, maybe.

It did not help matters that so many of the most visible blacks in the United
States were pro athletes.

To dribble a basketball, you don't need a whole lot of books. . . . Is there any
payoff for me sittin' home like a dork studyin' algebra while everyone else is out

playing basketball, or football, or whatever? I don't want to be stereotypical, but it's just, like, [in] America as a whole, there's a lot of people watch a lot of [sports on] TV, and a lot of . . . players have a lot of money. It sure seems like an easy way out.

As Gil Jarreaux noted, however, an even bigger problem might be a general sense that real success was simply out of reach. "At a very early and crucial time," Matt Vigoda argued, negative environmental influences "can take away your belief in yourself, so that no matter how talented you are, and hardworking . . . you become blinded to your possibilities." From the perspective of an inner-city youth, moreover, lack of effort might even look like a rational or psychologically healthy choice. As Doug Peruggia put it, "I'm placed in an inferior position. So I can try as hard as I can, but it may not make a difference. Or else I can just go with the flow, and just accept the position I'm in, and not bust my ass. I may bust my ass and be here in twenty years, the same place."

Tim Kovacs as well described a kind of culturally constructed stoicism: "I don't want to achieve anything, 'cause I'm not going to, therefore I won't desire it." Bill Sajak pointed to the *expectation* of discrimination, of a double standard in whites' favor. "[If] they['re] constantly comparing themselves with whites who are the same age as them, living a higher lifestyle, it would make them feel that it doesn't matter how hard they work. . . . 'Why work hard if . . . it'd be so much harder for us to gain something compared to our white peers, who don't have to work as hard?'" In Greg Bogosian's view,

[Blacks have] just given up. . . . If you've ever seen the [mostly African American] *In Living Color* [TV] show, where [some characters disparage] "the Man," and the Man is always the *white* man. You know, it's a spoof against white-dominated society. But, at least in their spoof, the black person hasn't given up and he's always fighting against the Man. . . . You know, he's *trying* to succeed.

The very rhetoric of minority rights activism might be partly to blame. Tim, for example, recalled "interviews where [blacks] are saying, you know, there is no justice, or, we can't do this, we can't do that. . . . even by their own *race* they're told that." In Joe's experience, blacks often seemed all too ready to take a back seat to whites.

I've worked a lot of jobs where I was the [only] white guy. It doesn't bother me bein' the white guy. I think what hurts blacks the most is their reverse discrimination within their own race. . . . [When] I worked . . . [for] Wendy's hamburgers . . . I was the white guy, so they told me to work on the register. I was the only white guy in the joint. There'd be a [35-year-old] manager standin' next to me at the time, there'd be a problem with something, the black customer would wanna talk to the manager, "Get me him"—*me*. . . .

The blacks . . . wanna talk to the white guy to solve their problem. And it happened *all* the time. These black managers, I mean, I'd yell at 'em, "Go in the back, do your paper-work, I don't need you up here." . . . And they loved it. They didn't have to deal with *any* problem when I was there. And everybody was willing to take orders from me, which was so confusing. People who worked thirty-four hours [a week] were willing to take orders from me. And it's happened several times.

I was reminded of anecdotes I'd heard from health care professionals, echoed in an episode of the television series *ER*, concerning minority patients who shunned physicians of their own race in favor of whites, from whom they expected superior skills and better care. Media depictions of lifestyles or behaviors characteristic of any culture of poverty did not do much for racial pride. "The newspapers love to tell garbage about everybody," Pat Gaheogan observed. "You see in your movies, who's the drug dealer?" Jack Uberhof, enrolled in UIC's Honors College, recalled a class discussion in an honors seminar he had taken on the development of moral reasoning.

There was a black gentleman in the class . . . [who] brought up a good point, in that because of what's on the news, whenever you see a gas station's been robbed or all the attacks [on other retail outlets]. . . . Primarily they're economically based, you know, because of the drugs and whatever's involved. Unfortunately, the vast majority of [the perpetrators] are black. . . . [The newscasters] always mention it—you know, "it was a 35-year-old black male.". . . [So blacks] develop sort of this inner hatred. . . . Someone . . . in grade school can't make that real distinction between, is it an economic thing, or is it a black thing?

No one I talked to really questioned the notion that the culture of poverty had contributed substantially to differences in academic outcomes between blacks, Latinos, and whites, by virtue of its powerful influence on their worldviews, their attitudes, and their choices. And while several also pointed the finger at underfunded inner-city schools, they were not unaware that gang violence, teen pregnancies, and peer pressure not to "act white" by doing too well complicated the difficulties of providing inner-city kids with a quality education.

But every high school, every neighborhood had its success stories; defeatism and underachievement were hardly a forgone conclusion, even for second-generation welfare families, or those burdened with alcoholism or drug addiction. Even if racism had something to do with putting blacks or Latinos in the underclass in the first place, plenty of other ethnic groups had overcome substantial prejudice and discrimination to achieve levels of success comparable to—or in some cases, greater than—White Anglo Saxon Protestants. Why hadn't blacks and Latinos taken better advantage of that?

Like Dave, Zack Pritchard pointed not to genetics but to cultural inheritance as a contributing factor. "Different cultures place different emphasis on career. Even if there was, you know, no economic differences or anything between blacks and whites, who's to say that as many black people as white people would want to be doctors?" Like several others, Bill traced unequal outcomes to the simple failure of blacks to work as hard as whites. But why *didn't* they, I asked him? He explained,

> I just think it's as a result of those who were never taught to work hard, and it's just been passed down the line. . . . I guess you could say that it is a cultural difference, because if you look at the countries that these minorities' ancestors are from, the lifestyles that their ancestors had . . . it's not at the same level as the white majority of people in this country. . . . That's where it originally comes from, and that's why they haven't been taught to work hard.

Assumed links between parenting styles and academic or professional success were evident in responses to another question: Why were Jewish and Chinese Americans, who had been victims of serious prejudice and discrimination themselves, nonetheless routinely *over*-represented, these days, in the best graduate professional schools? "The fact of honor to your family," Steve Clayburgh argued, "is more intrinsic to them than it is in—You know, if I as a white male fail, my dad'll be pissed off, but I'm not gonna take my life because my whole entire family is shamed forever and ever." Asians and Jews may "try harder," Pat ventured, because "They . . . have been told that their education is their key, that's what they have to do to get their end-all-be-all; that may have been drilled into them as small children, and they just ran with it." Rick had talked about his own love of learning for its sake and felt that the same thing helped to explain ethnic differences.

> Asians are, from what I know are . . . just kind of united, and the parents teach the kids, and the kids teach their kids, and so on and so on. . . . I think for certain nationalities, knowledge is power, just to get smart, and for others, knowledge is money, to go get money. And I think there's a different motivation. You can only stay motivated for money for so long, whereas goin' to learn because you'd like to learn, you learn a lot more and become a lot smarter. I think that's the way the Asians and the Jews and a lot of people look at it: That they're educating like in the biblical sense, you know, to teach their children so they can teach their children—not to only go out and get a job. . . . It's kinda like, you know . . . the thing in the 1700s in Italy. . . . Yeah, the Renaissance. . . . to get smart just to get smart; to become educated.

Greg recalled that, "Every year, our number one student in high school was always an Oriental," and traced their success and that of Jews to their upbringing: "'Read your books,' you know, 'Succeed, succeed!'" He spoke well about his own ethnic group in this regard, noting

a real interesting cultural difference to grow up in an Armenian family versus . . . a typical [white American family]. . . . There [were] major differences [from] what some of my friends were brought up with. . . . My parents weren't strict to the point of where they were prohibitive. But it was almost a matter of, "You want something? That's fine. Prove to me that you've earned [it]." . . . All of my privileges were *earned* privileges. When I wanted to start driving a car when I turned sixteen, God knows, I had to earn that one.

Charlie Kilgallen, too, spoke well of his own "strict, ethnic parents" in this regard: Between them and the Christian Brothers running the Roman Catholic high school they sent him to, he was "forced to study, whether I wanted to or not." Joe said little about the Catholic schools he'd attended but had an interesting take on the differences in academic achievement between Asian Americans and Latinos.

I think with maybe Orientals, they see more of that drive on education because schools *were* [*there*] in the Orient, and [then the Asians] came over here. There ain't a lot of schools down in Mexico, you know, and assorted countries. So I think the nature of schools is kind of lost for Latinos a little bit.
   Some of it might be the fact that, uh, Latino family businesses. You know. Family business comes before school. Family business is feedin' us, not that school. . . . I think they're encouraged to put the energy into the business because the business is taking care of the whole family, you know, all the generations. And maybe they just aren't used to an investing type of thing, investing in the future. . . . [Or] maybe they see their investment as the business. I get the kid in the business young, you know, I can retire a little bit earlier, everything'll be wonderful . . . and we can open up a separate [store] for him, and we can build a family dynasty that way.

When intracommunal supports were insufficient, however, did it make sense for government to fill the gap? As to "why the black problem exists . . . why those people aren't being motivated to work at something," Joe pointed to cultural patterns of a much more recent origin. "The best I can say is, it's the fault of our government. . . . [Blacks] were given too many crutches to lean on." Joe also pointed to federal housing projects: Designed to provide affordable housing to the urban poor, their tightly packed concentrations of economically marginal, single-parent families had been ideal breeding grounds for gangs and other ills. "They show these studies, you stack people up and make them live like rats. Do it to rats, rats start eating themselves. I mean, there's a destructive nature from this environment that we placed them in."

There were also concerns about flawed welfare policies: One reason that so many minority youth grew up in single-parent families was, as Sam Turner put it, "because it is more economically sound to grow up in a broken home than it is to be married." In Mike Benedetto's view, unemployment compensation encouraged sloth.

> The [blacks] I've worked with . . . weren't successful because they were just plain lazy . . . of the worst sort. They essentially said, "Well, I'll come here, I'll work for a couple months." They . . . know the rules—you know, you can't get fired until you've been written up three times—so they're willing to milk it for what it's worth, and then, it's, like, "Okay, great, I worked here long enough, now I'll get unemployment."

Hal took a broader view:

> I think it may be controversial, but I don't think that either a Latino culture or black culture is one which does not place an emphasis on working hard like the white culture. I mean, I don't think that at all. . . . Whites are not by *nature* industrious, no more than a black or an Hispanic. . . . Before the '50s and '60s, the black family was incredibly strong. I mean, a black birth out of wedlock was comparable if not [more stigmatizing than among] whites. . . . [It's] entitlement programs from a bureaucratic government [that] start fostering an attitude that, "I deserve this," or, you know, "I need this to live," and "I *cannot* work on my own," or, "I *should* not work on my own," . . . [rather than] all blacks believe this, all Hispanics believe this, because it's a common heritage or something. . . . As people become dependent on welfare . . . it's a kind of a learned helplessness sort of thing. . . . I think that whites on welfare might have the same problem.

Affirmative action itself could exacerbate inequality. As Sam put it, "Everybody knows that [certain minorities] had special treatment. . . . If somebody wants to get the best physician . . . well, naturally, you're gonna *still* be looking for the others that weren't [held to a lower] standard." Sam had observed at another college he'd attended that race-targeted support services might actually impede minority achievement. "Pretty soon, what happens was that these people were going to these special classes . . . to basically have their homework done, and they don't see that that's a rip-off for them, they're not getting what they should out of . . . college."

In the business world, Dan Lysenko had observed that people may "kind of not try their best if they know they're gonna make it anyway." He recalled a Latino coworker who had been trying for a promotion. "Once he found out that . . . they needed some Latinos for this *specific* position, and that no matter what, he would get it, he *definitely* didn't work as hard, didn't do his best. . . . I don't think he's gonna be able to advance in the future as far as he'd [otherwise] be able to."

For similar reasons, Rick's endorsement of modified quotas did not go as far as race-norming, which he felt would spare blacks and Latinos unvarnished comparisons with those of other ethnic backgrounds and thus "wouldn't foster much competition. . . . Through competition, I think, you can be at your best level. . . . I think then you're *looking* for people that are lower, rather than [black and Latino] people themselves are looking at [the schools] and thinking, I have to achieve that certain amount. It's kind of like a goal, I think; there's a minimum standard, and you have to go reach it."

Len Hellstrom could handle race-norming—as long as it didn't go too far, to the point where it came close to an absolute quota. One reason was that, "If they let anybody in, but then were perfectly willing to blow them out if they couldn't handle the first semester, couldn't handle the turf, then . . . a lot of materials, resources, and time would be wasted." But like Joe, Len thought it much more likely that, "There would be a tendency to let [blacks and Latinos] go through. . . . It would just be known that, well, blacks don't have to work as hard, don't have to be as good at it."

That frame of mind, Greg pointed out, could be devastating in the field of law, where *no one* was cut much slack. If as students,

> they have this cushion, they're going to get used to saying, "Okay, I don't *have* to be as good as you, because I'm black, 'cause I'm Latino." When they get to the real world, there's lots that aren't going to care if you're white, black, green, or purple. . . . You can't do the job, you don't get the job. . . . They're going to end up paying for being lazy. You know, I would say it would be better to pay their dues now, and learn where they can fit into the job market.

Like Mel Gibran, Joe had seen similar negative consequences of some misguided forms of affirmative action at the high school level. "I've worked with—Jesus, over fifteen people who could not read, who went through school systems. Amazing. And why? Because they have quotas. 'Well, I can't flunk the black kid.'" Len attributed part of the "slippage" in expectations in many minority-majority schools to "an effort to see more black [and Latino] kids graduate from high school." Bureaucratic pressures could have the same effect at community colleges. "A friend of mine who took a job as a teacher at [an inner-city] community college . . . was *told* that he wouldn't fail any black students. Apparently they've changed that. But when they were starting . . . they wanted to have a [high] success rate, regardless of the damage it did."

But the greatest damage might be to blacks' or Latinos' self-esteem and their sense of their own potential, perhaps already battered by the culture of poverty. "The direct message [of race-norming] to blacks is, 'You don't quite measure up . . . so we're gonna lower our standard for you.'" Tim came down hard on race-norming because it was not only reverse discrimination but "just perpetuating the whole system" of racial discrimination. "I mean, you're saying, 'Okay, we got a certain standard for whites because they can reach it, and we got a certain standard for blacks because they can't.' . . . You're almost coming out and saying, 'We realize that blacks can't compete with us.'" This was a judgment minorities could easily internalize, Hal argued. "Well, because I come from this racial group, *I* can't do it [myself] , so these [white] people . . . [are] being charitable to me . . . helping me to do something that I couldn't [do] otherwise." If the principal justification for affirmative action was the link between racism and group differences, and if much of that linkage involved *psychological* barriers to motivation, self-confidence, and achievement, then the wrong sort of affirmative action could easily turn into a treatment worse than the disease.

This might have an especial impact on exceptionally capable blacks and Latinos who *could* have made it on their own, but might nevertheless bear the stigma of a double standard, both in terms of how the world saw them and in terms of their own sense of accomplishment. Tim recalled a Mexican American high school friend who had received a National Science Foundation scholarship.

> He was [ranked] number one out of everybody. . . . [But] instead of giving him the number one overall, they gave him the Mexican NSF, so I guess they set aside, you know, so many for minorities. And that's kind of a slap in the face, that they have to give you the Mexican one 'cause you're Mexican, you can't compete against anybody else, you have to compete against other people of your ethnic [group]. And when people see that . . . that takes away from a lot of people.

Sam agreed,

> A black student that is a super-achiever—which there are a number of—how is that fair to him, to say once again that he was set apart, in some way? There was already a place for him [without affirmative action]. . . . [It] totally takes away from the great doctor that he could be . . . [because it] devalues the hard effort and work he's put in. . . . It looks like an advantage. . . . But it's really not.

On the other hand, affirmative action might also do considerable damage to self-esteem and achievement when it placed blacks or Latinos in situations that were simply beyond their capabilities. Dan anticipated,

If I was up for an interview at a job, and they hired me [just] because they didn't have enough . . . [whites] but I didn't meet the minimum standards, I don't think that's fair to me. I'm not going to fit in there. . . . [Affirmative action can put people] in a situation where they're not going to be able to compete with people, they're not going to be able to rise with the rest of the people, 'cause everyone [else] is gonna be a step ahead.

Something like that had happened in the faith-based, nonprofit organization Hal worked for.

I just read a letter today from . . . our ministry down in Atlanta . . . talking about an inner-city . . . lower class . . . black [woman] who they had promoted to manager. . . . [But] they found out later that . . . that's not where her talents lay, that's not where she flourished. They were most happy about [helping to] empower someone and move someone up the economic ladder. But she foundered and eventually had to be taken out of the position. And that's—I mean, I really don't want to emphasize self-esteem, but that *was* a blow to her self-esteem. . . . She was really the person who benefited *least* from it.

Or maybe no less than blacks in general. "To reward somebody [just] because they're black," Steve observed, might in the end seem to vindicate the worst kind of prejudice—"because people who have been putting blacks down . . . would only have something to point to and say, 'See? We did something, and it didn't work; that just proves our theory that they're a lesser race.'"

An Elusive Consensus

These difficulties notwithstanding, there was no question that the policies most damaging to blacks, at least, had been several centuries of state-condoned slavery and another century of discriminatory legislation, regulations, and judicial decisions. Among the men I interviewed, no one thought racism *alone* could account for the gaps in academic achievement between whites and blacks or Latinos, and opponents of affirmative action were less likely than advocates to recognize our public schools as a venue for systematic inequality of opportunity. Almost all the men, however, seemed to recognize that the legacy of slavery and Jim Crow was sufficiently distinctive to warrant some special efforts to help young blacks mired in the culture of poverty climb out of it.

But should that something extra extend to blacks *outside* the ghetto? To Latinos? To college students or college graduates? All things considered, it was not really a question of *whether or not* to reach out to those in need, but rather a more complex set of questions regarding just *whose* needs deserved special attention, and just how far and how often the outstretched hand needed to extend.

NOTES

1. John R. Powers, *Do Black Patent Leather Shoes Really Reflect Up?* New York: Samuel French, 1982. "I went to that school," "Joe" assured me, "I had that nun."

2. José Vargas. "Fraternity Skit Revives Racial Tensions." *Chicago Flame* 4:30 (April 14, 1992), 1, 9.

3. The fraternity most likely lip-synced the very successful rendition of the song by the doo-wop group The Tokens, released by RCA Victor in 1972. It was based on "Wimoweh," a South African Zulu folk song, first popularized in the United States by the folk group the Weavers in the 1950s.

4. www.jolietchamber.com/aboutjoliet/artsandculture.htm, December, 2004

3

ENOUGH IS ENOUGH

Targeting Affirmative Action on the
Basis of Age, Ethnicity, Educational Level,
and Socioeconomic Background

DREW KAZINSKI: GETTING BETTER ALL THE TIME

It was quite a learning experience. . . . Three white students wore their
grandfathers' Ku Klux Klan outfits to the high school . . . and . . . they got
into a fight with one black student, and the Ku Klux Klan got hold of this,
and they came down for a major demonstration. Uh, most of the [KKK]
members in the Midwest were there, including the Grand Wizard, who
lives in Indiana. . . . It was quite an experience for the whole university.
. . .They just marched through the main street, and they lit their torches
and, you know, did their big ceremonies, had their speeches. . . . And, I
mean, they're not just racist against blacks; they're racist against many different ethnic groups. And I think often—up until that point, I thought
that [race relations were] *much* better than it was; it was a real eye-opener
for me. . . . So, yeah, I still [see racism] occasionally. . . . Just with the
whole Rodney King thing, I didn't realize that there was so much racial
tension in California.

The minute I got off the elevator, I knew I was underdressed. At his invita-
tion, my interview with Drew Kazinski was conducted in one of the richly ap-
pointed office suites of the marble-clad lakefront office tower where the
twenty-two-year-old was employed. An internship with one of the companies
housed there had led to a full-time professional position, which Drew juggled
with full-time study at UIC's College of Business. After completing his BS a
couple of semesters later, Drew expected to remain with the firm, which he

hoped would pay his tuition to law school. But he also expected to earn an MBA or an MS in economics, to further strengthen his technical skills, his managerial expertise, and hence his marketability. Eventually, he hoped to make partner of a consulting firm, or serve as CEO or CFO with a large corporation. An uncle was involved in politics, and Drew could see himself as a U.S. senator someday.

Drew had never been fond of affirmative action. For one thing, "It's been very costly for employers to have to comply with affirmative action legislation, and also to have to document and to—the different procedures that need to be in place because of affirmative action. It's a cost." Of the options presented in the interview, the only approach to affirmative action he endorsed was the formally race-neutral reweighting of criteria. His reasons were familiar: Schools seeking to train top-quality lawyers or business executives would do well to pay more attention to "work experience. *Life* experience. . . . What can [other students] learn from this person, what can they add . . . ?" Of course, this kind of policy might also work to the advantage of men like himself.

And like Steve Clayburgh, he understood quite well what was at stake when the top graduate professional schools made their choices. "I know a Harvard grad from law school is very well looked upon in the business world, and usually does great things. . . . They're well paid, they take on the big clients, and they get the complicated [cases]—and it's just because they've been distinguished by going to that school, they've been distinguished as being the best." He was also concerned with the possible impact of any compromise in selectivity on how much students actually learned. "I know that being in the classroom with people of the same . . . caliber . . . you can learn from them, and . . . you can take it farther. But when you're with people that are not as intelligent as you, you're going to bring yourself down."

But if neoclassical economics had transfigured Gil Jarreaux, Drew's close encounter with the KKK at another college he'd attended seemed to have helped jog his perspectives in the opposite direction. Regarding deliberate efforts to enhance racial equity, "I guess my opinions have changed a lot since— just the whole thing with Rodney King and things like that—seeing how bad off and how uneducated a lot of the minorities are. And I think that now that I'm seeing this, I'm more willing to help than I was before."

Not by much, though. For one thing, he felt that the persistence of racism in the 1980s and 1990s was overplayed. "I know the generation . . . is still alive that went through all the racial tensions with Martin Luther King, and all the segregation and stuff. . . . But I think from my generation and those below us—you know, it's still there, obviously. But it's a lot less than it used to be." Like several of his peers, he also downplayed the difficulties minorities would tend to experience as college students.

I don't think they have *more* problems [than whites], it's the same adjustment. Coming in as a freshman you have adjustments to the college atmosphere, just as a black person does. . . . [Blacks and Latinos] have grown up in the same environment . . . they've been educated by the same school systems, mostly, most of the time. They should be able to, at a college level, do it. . . .

I think that a lot of the [racial tensions] are created by the individual blacks themselves. If they see themselves as outcasts, they're gonna act like one. . . . For instance, [when] those white students from the fraternity . . . did a lip sync and painted themselves up, such a major issue was made out of that by faculty and by the board and by the newspaper that I can see racial tensions [coming] out of that, when it was just an innocent thing.

At the same time, Drew shared the view that affirmative action itself generated a good deal of inter-racial hostility. "I have to admit that sometimes I do that myself, not necessarily saying, 'Well, he *must* have gotten there because of affirmative action,' but saying, 'I wonder *if* it was affirmative action,' I gotta admit, 'or if that's person's really capable.'"

Addressing actual differences in achievement levels between members of different racial or ethnic groups, Drew never explicitly linked them to heredity; but he was nonetheless quick to endorse the notion of systematic, inborn differences in capacity. "Just, like, watching the Olympics, you know, there's a lot more blacks that are faster runners. . . . I think it is inherent. I swam most of my life, and I know that blacks cannot swim [competitively]. And it has been proven that it's because of their body chemistry and the amount of white blood cells they have. And I think the same thing goes with intellectual ability as well. . . . They have different abilities."

Much more pertinent, however, to differences in academic outcomes was the psychological and social impact of the very research and rhetoric in which affirmative action was grounded. Blacks and Latinos "may not see themselves as being able to perform as well as whites . . . just because of all the statistical data that's shoved in front of them, showing that they're not—there's not as many representing them in corporations. . . . These [inner-city, minority] seventh- and eighth-graders that [visited his company] were *very* aware of the disparity in the corporate world." Like some of the other men interviewed, moreover, Drew was annoyed by what he considered exaggerated notions of just how special other people's difficulties were. During the same field trip, a black executive

got up and started harping about opportunity and how [the children] deserve this, and how they need to dream and, you know, all this and that. And . . . a [female] eighth-grader [asked] my [white] boss . . . "Being a woman, didn't you feel discriminated against?". . . And [my boss] started talking about, yeah, how she's felt that it's harder to get ahead and stuff like that. My argument [is] that I feel the same pressures as *both* of them. Okay, I'll give 'em—maybe they're *different* pressures, but I do feel a lot of pressure, and it's not [that] different.

Among people of any race, the key to getting ahead was self-reliance, in the face of whatever pressures they faced. "The successful people are very hard-working, very determined, very goal-oriented . . . whereas the people that weren't successful were always looking to be given things . . . complaining about how hard they have it and how rough it is, instead of accepting it and just, you know, looking past it. . . . I think that it's 98 percent attitude." And it was the attitudes of blacks and Latinos, Drew believed, that kept them from making the same progress as other ethnic groups.

You just look at the growth of Chicago, um, the Poles, all the Europeans that im-migrated over here. Um, they had the sweat-shops, they were working for *well* under what minimum wage is today, and they—I know my grandfather worked in a steel mill, and worked 15-, 16-hour days. . . . But . . . I think that *because* of all this affirmative action, and because of all these people telling them . . . "Oh, you don't get as fair a chance as—you should get a better chance," that they think that they deserve to just be given these positions . . . they're not willing to work as hard as those others. . . . You see the Poles, the Italians, they came over and they worked all the way through the cycle. Whereas the blacks have not worked through the cycle, but they've already demanded their equality without serving their time.

There was more than a little hypocrisy, or at least "false consciousness," in Drew's responses. For example, he downplayed the importance of role models but made numerous references to his current supervisor, who clearly served as an effective and valued professional exemplar and mentor. His current position, moreover, was an outgrowth of what must have been a highly selective internship that Drew had been able to take advantage of during his very first semester as a college student in Chicago—at a firm heavily involved in the same industry as Drew's father. It was not prudent to ask, of course, but I could not help wondering if this young man's foothold on the fast track had not been a product of more than luck or talent.

On the other hand, Drew's faith in "the cycle" of upward mobility had clearly been challenged. In contrast to the notion that everyone had grown up in the "same environment," he knew that some of the eighth graders from "the south side somewhere" who had visited his company's offices "had never been downtown. They'd never ridden elevators or escalators, or seen big buildings." He understood, moreover, the powerful influence of parents on their children's performance and aspirations, "Just the way—their characteristics, their drives, you know, their dreams," as well as their own educational backgrounds and economic status. "I know my parents wanted me to go to college since I was born," Drew recalled, and "I always had the track that I was gonna go . . . and I can't imagine having it any other way. . . . Whereas if they . . . didn't care, I might not have cared either."

And thus any baggage minority parents carried might impact their children. "The root of the problem [with minorities in America] goes back into the racial tensions. If a parent grows up feeling *less* [than] another person, it's gonna be shown in a way that they bring up *their* kids." And despite the sharp contrast he cited between race relations now and in decades past, I knew that Drew had to be a good enough mathematician to grasp that the parents and aunts and uncles of his black and Latino contemporaries—people who had come of age during the racially volatile 1960s and 1970s—would not have had the same chance as whites to attend college or otherwise succeed on their merits, and might not have had much faith in the promise of full equality to pass on to their children. "It's hard to put myself in [blacks' or Latinos'] shoes. So I think I would be *somewhat*—maybe it would be *somewhat* acceptable to give them a ch—you know, better chance, or give them a little more of a push."

All of this seemed to have led Drew to a kind of middle ground with respect to race-targeted affirmative action generally. "I don't see a need for blacks and Latinos to go get graduate degrees, so I don't think they *need* to be targeted [at that level]." However, social justice did demand a serious effort to encourage minority youth to attend college and help ensure they had what it takes to earn a degree. "A lot of positions now require undergrad degrees. . . . I feel that to be competitive in the work force, you need to have an undergrad degree for sure." All things considered, he had come to support the sort of outreach to high schools conducted by the company he worked for. High school students, after all, are still "forming their dreams and their careers," and minority youth

> might not even be *thinking* of law school, because they don't see it as a possibility. . . . And if there was an intervention [by a graduate professional school] they would be more encouraged to actually broaden their dreams. . . .
>
> A fellow here . . . goes twice a month to [a ghetto high school], and for about an hour talks about business. And we took [the students] on a tour of our office, and also took 'em downstairs to the bank [in our building], and showed 'em how a bank works, and things like that . . . gearing them to think about—You know, we talk about going to college, and encourage them to do those things. And at that level, it's a lot more important.

LARRY DOBBS: TOO LITTLE, TOO LATE

> I guarantee, you go down to the inner city, and you tell the mothers of all
> those kids . . . that [if the kids take] math and science in their high schools,
> then we can guarantee them a college education, I guarantee you, in five
> years, you're gonna have more than enough [minority] applicant pool. . . .
> Even if he doesn't have [an exceptionally high] math aptitude . . . if he's
> just [fairly] good at math, all's he'd need is practice. . . . You tell a black
> student who lives with his mother who's on welfare and who doesn't want
> to live this life any more . . . [that if you] pass out of [first-year calculus]
> . . . we'll bring you in and put you up . . . [then] you solve the whole prob-
> lem. . . . Now they're wanted. Northwestern, University of Chicago [busi-
> ness schools] will recruit that young man . . . because . . . [he meets] very
> high standards.

Larry Dobbs's own path to graduate school had been a little more cir-
cuitous. Not too long after finishing high school, he'd abandoned college studies in New Jersey for a demanding full-time job that eventually led to several
positions in middle management. At twenty-nine, he was back in school to
complete a BS in business and then an MBA, which he felt would definitely
give him an extra leg up the corporate ladder. For the future, he could see
himself as head of marketing or production for some large corporation—and
later, perhaps, as a college professor, or the head of a federal agency like the
General Accounting Office.

Regarding affirmative action, Larry was a true believer. It was a question of
equity; it was a question of the greater good; it was a question of balancing
meritocratic norms with the weight of history; and attempts to uncouple inequality of outcomes from racial discrimination just wouldn't wash.

> If equal opportunities [were] available, then just by the mere fact of hiring natu-
> rally . . . [minority representation would tend to be] pretty much like the popu-
> lation. . . . The fact that we haven't achieved that shows that . . . there's something
> we're missing along the line. . . . You cannot . . . [in the] long term have a healthy
> society . . . with certain members of the population always deprived of opportu-
> nity, 'cause what will end up happening is you have divisive government, you have
> divisive everything, and it simply does not work. . . .
>   [A policy of no affirmative action] assumes everything else is equal, which I
> don't think you can do. . . . You have to have everybody in the population achiev-
> ing the same level of education in high school. . . . That's what college adminis-
> trators hope for. That's not what happens, and you have to do the other steps . . .
> [to say] "Okay, this person *will* achieve in college. However, we might have to give
> him some back-up courses."

One of the big beefs I have is when I see a Japanese reporter telling an American reporter how upset [the] Japanese are with the racism in America. . . . Well, that comes from having a free society [and] from having a culturally diverse society. If we were a mono white, we wouldn't have all these problems. But at the same time, we wouldn't have the energies we have. . . . If we are indeed becoming a global, quote-unquote, society, [Americans] must become the leaders in showing how a global society has to get along.

In Larry's view, race relations at UIC were relatively amicable—at least on the surface.

Anyone who comes here . . . though they may not like it . . . [knows enough] not to be overtly racist, because . . . it's more of a even-Steven type deal, okay, it's not like four black students and 150 white students. . . . [Racism at UIC is] mainly more covert, more secretive, more writing on the bathroom walls. Not walking down the hallway and saying, "Get out of my way, nigger." You're not gonna see that. But . . . in a closed [rest room] stall . . . [people] can write the little things down they think. . . . And it deals mainly with black [male] members or white members, the size of the p---s. It's amazing. . . . I look at it and I say, "How do you want to be known?"

The simple explanation for the extraordinary persistence of animosity between whites and blacks or Latinos, Larry believed, was their physical appearance. While most ethnic groups had experienced considerable hostility when they first arrived in this country,

Once [any given white ethnic group] became a member of the population and mixed in . . . [so that just] by looking at you, I can't tell if you're Irish or whatever, then the prejudice was eliminated just naturally through the population growth. . . . The only real difference is that blacks and Latinos *carry* their [distinctiveness] from generation to generation. . . . They can't simply just blend in.

Under these circumstances, one of the most immediate benefits of greater diversity among business managers at all levels was that it helped offset white racism and deeply engrained, mutual distrust between whites and blacks. "If I'm a black man, and I walk into a clothing store and I'm dressed like this [in casual college-student garb], I'm gonna get followed around, there's no doubt about it. But if I'm a black male and I walk into an establishment and there's a black male manager there, he's gonna look at me for what I am." Likewise, greater diversity higher up the ladder would help to offset the concerns of black and Latino managerial applicants.

I think a black or Latino person . . . would *say* they have that [necessary] confidence [in themselves], but maybe in the back of their mind, there's that old, you know, feeling too much pressure. They carry a lot of baggage with them. . . . That will change as the work force changes. As more and more examples of what you *can* do are out there, you're gonna think, well, I'm no different than—that goes back to the high school example. . . . [Moreover,] a black male or a black female or a Latino in . . . upper-level management . . . [would] probably not be as racist about it as a white man who stepped over the black man before. So you're gonna see a lot more of a diverse group coming *up* will hook into the upper ranks . . . [where] decisions are made who is and who is not hired.

As for graduate professional school admissions, Larry's endorsement of modified quotas and race-norming was not without qualms—especially with respect to less competitive MBA programs like UIC's. The most prestigious MBA programs—housed almost exclusively in private institutions—could afford to limit enrollment to "the best of the best" of every racial or ethnic group, and so could achieve desirable levels of diversity without significant adjustments in their standards or criteria. Selecting from less competitive pools of applicants to begin with—reviewing application files likely to provide more mixed indicators of executive potential—publicly sponsored MBA programs faced a bigger challenge, balancing racial equity with the quality standards of the job market. But like so many of the other men interviewed, Larry also feared the costs of affirmative action on minority students themselves.

If someone tells a black or Latino, you're only here because of an affirmative action program, then what they did to achieve to get to that level's kind of devalued. It's like saying, you got an A on the test *but* because you're white, we graded it on a little lower scale than everybody else. So, yeah, you got an A . . . but not really. You know, it . . . makes them feel like, well, I really didn't *earn* to get here.

For similar reasons, Larry could not endorse race-targeted academic support services, which were too much like "what special ed was in high school: You get that little stigma attached to you." All in all, affirmative action at the college level was a kind of cop-out.

For some people, it's simply a pill that they can say they agree with it, that they're not racist. . . . If you simply say to the universities, "You have to bring on 20 percent black, 20 percent Latino, and 60 percent white," and they go off and simply do that, you're not going to solve the problem. You're just taking the top 20 percent of each group, you're not expanding [the number of high achievers in] the group. The real goal should be to take that black or Latino population and bring them *up* to the white population, and . . . [not simply to] fill up your racial quota. Then the universities, you know, get out cheap.

A much better solution would be to equalize opportunity among minority schoolchildren.

College is a three-step process. You gotta do well in grade school, so that you're prepared to do well in high school. You got to take the right courses in high school, so that you can go into college prepared. . . . Then . . . college is actually the easy part of it, 'cause [you've already] got all the basic skills. . . . Then you really start to explore things and look at things. . . . [But a great many minority students are] behind when they start [college], okay? If you're struggling with your basic algebra, how can you understand . . . economics? If you're really working hard to put a sentence together, how can you understand literature—what it means, you know? If you're reading at a fifth-grade level, how can you do your assignments at night? . . .

In . . . my last economics class, I had a [black] girl in two of my classes, and we used to sit together, and she'd just never get it. We used to sit and have counseling sessions after every class, we sat for an hour, and I found that the things that she was deficient on were things that *I* knew in high school, and that if you didn't know those . . . simple, basic things, the rest of the course just didn't come into focus. And the professor had no time to take this one person and do [what I was doing]. I feel that once you start behind and you're in college, there's no way you can catch up. There's no way you can . . . learn the basics of the course *and* at the same time review what you should have known in the first place. . . . College builds so much on what high school has taught you, if you're behind when you get to college, you may pass, but you're going to be behind when you get out.

This helped to explain the self-destructive defeatism, exaggerated perceptions of racism, and lower GPAs, on the average, of black and Latino college students. Because inferior schooling had left so many minority youth unprepared to succeed in college, "What invariably happens is, they fall *back* on stereotypes and to, 'Well, I wouldn't achieve anyhow, it doesn't make any difference.' They don't think they have the opportunity, they're not gonna work for it. I wouldn't."

The best way to ensure a plentiful supply of top-drawer minority applicants to MBA programs, then, was for universities and business executives to reach out to "minority-majority" elementary and secondary schools. That was the place not only to reinforce basic skills but to help shape young people's aspirations—just as crucial for white youth as for anyone else, Larry stressed.

In my management class, we brought [business] executives in . . . to talk to the students. I mean, that should go [on] more on the high school level. . . . Talking to [us] college seniors . . . they said, "How many of you have math degrees?" We all said, "No, but it's too late now! We're about to graduate." He says, "Well, there's great opportunity out there, for anybody that's good in math or sciences."

Well, we're not the people to tell! The people to tell that to are seventh, eighth, and ninth graders. Say, "Hey, you, I'm chairman of Dow Chemical. If you get a math or science degree, the odds of you getting a high-paying, good job are about 99.99 percent, as long as you get a good GPA." . . . That's why I think that the whole thing is coming too late, you know, when we tell some [black or Latino] high school senior, here's how you apply to our college. . . . Tell this to the kid down in sixth grade. Make sure they concentrate on their math. Take it home every night; come [to school] on Saturdays and have a college professor here go over assignments. I mean, that's where an intervention has to work.

This kind of thing, moreover, would tend to eliminate what Larry, like Dave Zaluba, viewed as unreasonable demands in some quarters for white professors to adapt more fully to alleged inter-ethnic differences in learning styles. To equalize opportunity,

I think what has to change . . . is not . . . the professor, but change the way— standardize the way people are [prepared for college] . . . [by] taking the college-type atmosphere and putting it into the high schools, [so that blacks and Latinos] get used to working on their own, they get used to being responsible for what they have done. . . . If I was a teacher, I would teach the way I was taught, it's just the way you do it. . . . I mean it's really tough for a professor to teach if he has a white, black, and Latino classroom to teach a white, black, and Latino way. . . .

Maybe in a black culture or a Latino culture, they're used to much more interactive one-on-one. . . . Maybe being in the lecture-hall type atmosphere is very strange to them. . . . [But] that's also a fault with our educa—maybe we should— we have to give them a blending. . . . [Just] one or the other, that's the wrong way to go. . . . You need to integrate everyone into the same society. If you wanna have separate teaching for separate groups, you're always gonna have them separate and you're always gonna have the problems you have.

At least as important to genuine equality of opportunity as more effective teaching, or the dissemination of practical information about college going, was the kind of person-to-person mentoring this sort of outreach could provide, and the sort of work ethic this could help to instill—especially considering the many *negative* influences that minority schoolchildren were likely exposed to.

Somebody who is twelve, thirteen, fourteen years old [is not] going to do what they need to do to achieve [academically] . . . without *somebody* showing them [another way]. . . . All these gangland shootings that you see on TV, I feel so bad, because those children, they didn't make a decision, a decision was forced upon them. . . . They may be bad, they may be terrible kids, they may be murderers. But they didn't decide at eight or nine to be a murderer. . . . Six or seven-year-olds are very susceptible to what they see in their environment. And if the only [black or Latino] people who [they see] get ahead is the one who's down dealin' on the corner, then that's what they're going to do. Economics tells you that you're gonna go for what gets the biggest return to yourself. . . .

I was shown as a child that you have to work for what you want, you have to strive for it. If you don't make it, you have to get back off the deck and try again. . . . Somebody who's been shown the way, who's in college, who simply decides to party instead of to study, all things being equal, that person deserves what they get. . . . I think college education is as close to being equal and unbiased as far as prejudice goes as you can get, currently. . . . Those who want to achieve, will. But a [college student] won't have that unless they're shown that [as a child].

Larry did not stint on the importance of parents to the success or failure of their offspring. His Uncle Bill, for example, was a very successful salesman because he "works very, very hard at it, put in a lot of weekends, he does whatever it takes to get it done. . . . He decided that what he wanted would take *this*, and that he'd have to work hard to get it." The reason that Bill's son-in-law had not yet settled on a career and never held the same kind of job for more than two years was that, "He simply thinks the job should be enjoyable, and a job always is not enjoyable. I mean, one has made the decision to sacrifice." Bill, on the other hand, "doesn't like a lot of the things he has to do, only he knows this is what it takes . . . to succeed and do the other things he wants to do, while the other one . . . still wants to find the perfect love for a job—you know, work three hours a week and get paid $60,000 a year." Bill's son Tony, on the other hand, had profited from his father's influence.

I was [at Bill's home] one Christmas Eve, and Tony had to go to work [at the local factory], so, he goes, "I'm gonna call in sick." And [his father] says, "don't. You get a reputation as someone who calls in. . . . You go to work . . . you grunt it out, and later you'll achieve." Well, next year, he came back in as a foreman. Because he came in, he did that. But he *got* that . . . it goes back to that role model.

Larry faulted Bill and his wife, however, for not encouraging Tony to go to college.

My cousin . . . didn't get real good grades [in high school]. His parents decided, well, you know, not everybody's cut out for college, therefore he's just gonna have to be someone who works with his hands. . . . My mother was so mad at her sister. . . . "How could she make that decision for Tony at fourteen years of age? She is choosing for the rest of his life, because he came home with one bad report card!". . . Tony got into [blue-collar work] and he's done very well. He's worked very hard, and now he's doing better than all of [his siblings]. But . . . if [Tony's mother] had not let him get away with [underachievement] at fourteen—had said, "Young man, you're gonna work and you're gonna work until it hurts," and he's gotten his college education, with the drive he has today . . . what [could] he have achieved?

In Larry's view, the biggest obstacle to academic achievement among blacks and Latinos—more significant than bad schools, or absent fathers, or the lack of good information about college admissions or financial aid—was that centuries of discrimination had quashed the aspirations of a great many minority parents and grandparents, and thus their ability either to model or encourage academic achievement as a route to economic empowerment. Hence the legitimacy as well as the utility of the right sort of affirmative action at the elementary or high school level, which would not simply compensate for unequal educational opportunities after the fact but cancel them out, and at the same time function "in loco parentis" as an immediate counterweight to the culture of poverty.

That was not to discount, however, the value of programs designed to help students already in college stay the course—something young college students of any ethnic background might have trouble doing. "It's real hard to tell somebody eighteen, nineteen that what they did this year is gonna preface the whole rest of their life." That was one of the reasons Larry felt that MBA programs should look more carefully at letters of recommendation, which might tell them, "This person in the first two years . . . just didn't do jack. But in the last two years, [he or she] just kicked, just really went into high gear, decided what they wanted to do, got energized on the system. . . . It's a flowing thing. What is this person like today?" At the same time, race-targeted programs on campus might help to compensate for the relative lack of parental pressure on blacks and Latinos, simply because most of them were first-generation college students, as Larry was.

> So when I went, it was a *big deal*. If I just got out, that was good enough [for] . . . my parents. . . . When my child goes to college, I'll have a much closer idea [of what's involved]. If he comes back with a b.s. story about, "Oh, I couldn't get this because of this," I'll say, "Unh-unh, time out. I went there, buddy. I know that's not how it is. You've gotta do this and this right now, okay?" "Oh, math is so hard, everybody's failin' math." "Unh-unh. Sorry. Time out. That's the biggest excuse in the world."

Upper-middle-class students of any race would already be on the receiving end of that kind of feedback.

> Let's say that the black parents are professional—doctor or lawyer type—and say, nothing less than almost a perfect GPA is acceptable. So, I'm sorry, we can't allow

you to do any less. . . . [Their children] get out [of college], I'm gonna guarantee you they're equal [to whites]. It's just—it's the force that's driving them.

Blacks, however, were far less likely than whites to confront such parental expectations. So on the average,

[Even if] two children come to school equal, a black and a white student. . . . [If] the white's parents tell him he must achieve such and such, or they'll be disappointed . . . whereas the black ones just think, he'll be there, and as long as you graduate, that's good, [then] when they get out, there's gonna be a difference.

As *things were*, then, Larry could not very well approve any MBA admissions policy that *didn't* consider race. "You equate opportunity [in the public schools], and then you try to do as much as you can to alleviate the [psychological] baggage they bring . . . *then* you can start equating those [admissions test] scores."

On the other hand, Larry resisted the notion of any kind of affirmative action as just compensation for slavery or Jim Crow or the historic exploitation of Latinos: Rather, it was compensation for the ways in which *today's* blacks or Latinos had been shortchanged.

We can't make up for what's been done in the [distant] past. The only thing I think this country stands for is, everyone's given the same opportunity to achieve the same thing. If you start saying, "Well, you're owed, and the only reason you got this job is because of the debt we owe to your mother's mother's mother," that's not right. . . . It isn't what happened in 1882, it's what happened to them in 1992 that I'm worried about, okay?

TOM SORBO: YOU'VE GOT TO ADJUST

It's really [black and Latino college students'] responsibility not to allow these other factors to get in the way of the grades or the test scores. . . . You've got to adjust, and if you don't, it's too God-damned bad.

"I'm very argumentative. I'm very arrogant," Tom Sorbo told me, and thus

born to be a lawyer. . . . You've gotta have [enough] confidence . . . [to be] almost oblivious to any type of embarrassment, you see what I'm getting at? . . . Just . . . very aggressive, the kind of person that always thinks that you're the smartest, or at least one of the smartest persons in the room. . . . As far as societal standards are concerned, I think it takes a lack of moral conscience.

At twenty-four, Tom's love of argument and a conscience apparently still intact had generated some heated exchanges with his father, a successful executive in one of Chicago's traditional rust-belt industries, on the issue of corporate culpability for environmental pollution. Following his transfer from another, out-of-state university, one of Tom's UIC professors had sparked his interest in this issue and in a career in environmental law. As a professional, however, Tom anticipated defending alleged polluters at least as often as he spoke for plaintiffs.

On the issue of social justice, Tom was quite skeptical of both the efficacy and the equity of policies aimed to help those in need. For example,

> I saw an interview once . . . [with a black woman] on welfare . . . and they said, "Why don't you go and get a job?" And she said, "Because welfare pays more." And I thought, that's very strange. . . . I mean it almost seems kind of conspiratorial to me. I think maybe there are a lot of white people who would be willing to pay a few extra tax dollars to, you know, keep minorities out of the corporate work place.

Suspect as well was affirmative action hiring for the executive suites of that same workplace.

> [Blacks and Latino] communities should be starting to put their *own* [business ventures] together, if that's possible. . . . In *The Autobiography of Malcolm X* . . . he said, "We don't want the scraps from the white man's table." . . . [Affirmative action] could be looked at as a way of just *keeping* minorities from really achieving something. . . . It might be, "Give them a *little*," without [whites] having to sacrifice a lot in the long run. . . .
>
> It seems to me that in the corporate structure, no matter how high you get, if you're not on the board of directors or lead top guy, it's almost like a token position financially. If you have a corporation of, like, 400 people, 90 percent of your income is going to be going to, like, 5 to 10 people, you know. . . . [If] a few Latinos or a few blacks . . . are suddenly vice presidents, and they then gain, like, $100,000 a year, and the corporation generates, like, $500 *million* a year, what's that?

Affirmative action to graduate professional schools, Tom seemed to view as a kind of transfer of opportunity. "Considering how competitive law school is, and that I am planning on going, it's very hard for me to sit here and say to give something away, you know, if it was my choice." Yet Tom endorsed on principle the legitimacy of race-conscious admissions policies—even of absolute quotas, if that was what it took to achieve a reasonable proportion of blacks, at least. A review of Tom's responses on the issues in play, however, suggests a young man at war with himself, the embodiment of liberal sensibilities doing battle with a more entrenched creed of rugged individualism.

Tom was not unsympathetic, for example, to the special difficulties black and Latino undergraduates might tend to encounter on a majority-white campus.

> Maybe they're just not privy to the information that whites would be, and maybe they just don't feel like it's a world in which they can be as readily accepted as whites. . . . If I [imagine] myself . . . going to a school that has a large majority of a certain race [other than white], I think I would feel uncomfortable. I mean, if I suddenly decided to enroll in Grambling [State University, an historically black institution in Louisiana], I'd feel extremely uncomfortable, I think. And so I can understand, from that standpoint, why they would feel a bit of difficulty. . . . And that just raises problems with speaking out in class, I think. You know, feeling secure in their environment. You know, if you feel completely secure in an environment, I think that that brings out the most in a person. That's when someone *is* the most productive. And so, you know, yeah, maybe, you know—well, not "maybe," I think they *are* at a disadvantage from that viewpoint.

This was, however, a disadvantage that Tom seemed to expect blacks and Latinos to do a better job of overcoming. "I think once you get to [the college] level of academics, there's a certain academic culture to which you should be attuned, by that time, no matter who you are." And did not give much credence to allegations of racism on campus. "If [a] person went to college, you know, they're not doing too bad. I mean, there aren't that many prejudices hitting them." At UIC in particular, "It seems like prejudice and racism are just so taboo. . . . The people on this campus are extremely politically correct, from my experience. I don't think [incidents of racial hostility] would happen." More generally, "I don't think [racism is] really an excuse [for underachievement] anymore, because even if there are white people in high positions who do possess prejudices, I don't think that they're allowed to act on them anymore. I just don't think it would be possible in this day and age, it's sort of taboo."

As much as Gil or Joe, Tom saw blacks' *perceptions* of racism as a more serious problem. "Sometimes, [when] I'm walking through the door and someone bumps into me, I say, 'Watch it,' . . . [or] 'Get out of my way,' or whatever. I'd say that to a white person just as I would say that to a black person, but a black person might take it as a racist comment." And false perceptions could prove a serious obstacle to self-improvement.

> I saw a show on [public television] Channel 11, it was produced by a black woman, and it was about an area that's similar to South Central L.A. [but] in Boston. She was talking to [some] black kids . . . hanging out in this youth center,

and . . . they were talking about not having jobs, and how angry they were, and
she said, "Well, have you looked?" and they said, "No," and she said, "Why not?"
[and they answered,] "Some white boy's gonna get the job." So, I think in a way
minorities are *assuming* prejudice, when perhaps it's not even there, and that hin-
ders their progress.

But Tom failed to recognize for what it was the same kind of everyday discrimination observed by Joe Murtaugh and Larry Dobbs and Steve Clayburgh.

I think it depends a lot on appearance and the way a person carries himself, you
know. The guy comes walking in [to a store or an office] with, like, a baseball cap
tilted to one side and, you know . . . I don't think [Latino actor Jimmy Smits]
would experience any prejudice. . . . I think actually a white kid [dressed the same
way as that black kid] would just be seen as probably . . . an upper-middle-class
white kid who's emulating somebody he saw on MTV. I think the white kid [who]
would experience prejudice because of appearance . . . would have, probably,
long hair and . . . bad clothes, that kind of thing. There's a kind of a redneck look
to 'em.

On the issue of diversity, Tom recognized the benefits of a more multiethnic pool of lawyers to blacks and Latinos caught up in our legal system. White
lawyers working with minority clients might have "a slight problem . . . relat-
ing to their social situation. . . . and perhaps a black client could relate better
to a black lawyer, and trust the black lawyer more, and be able to be more honest with that person and work better with that person to, uh, get the most out
of the legal system." But as for the notion that cultural diversity might enrich
the legal profession overall, "Unh-unh. . . . I mean, if you have other ways of
settling problems, then don't bring them into this system. You know, maybe in
your neighborhood, have an elder who solves the problems or something," but
as for mainstream jurisprudence, "Got to adjust. If you want to live in this
country, you got to adjust your ways to certain ways that are already instituted."
    An exchange on the sources of inequality of outcomes, however, raised the
possibility of inborn constraints on making that adjustment.

Tom Sorbo: I think the problem is starting with the parents, and the way they're
raised, and the schools and the teachers in those schools, because I think that
the people—their minds should be geared at an early age to be able to conform
with what the society demands of one to succeed, instead of completely going
against it, you know. . . . From what I see, there seems to be a resistance to entering society in the American manner as white people know it and as it's been
formed by white people. . . . Actually . . . I think maybe inherently there are differences in the way people do things, like, I mean, white people seem to be
more conservative.

Helen Lipson: You mean morally conservative? or fiscally conservative? or in how they dress? Or—

TS: Yeah. White people I just think are more reserved altogether, more, uh, tight-collared. . . . [But] I do think—I really do believe there is an inborn, inherent difference in people of different ethnicities. . . . I mean, like, just looking at different types of Europeans, there are obvious differences. . . . Or maybe it's just tradition that's passed on; a lot of attitudes and so forth are derived from your parents. . . . It's a little of both.

Like Joe and Dave Zaluba, moreover, Tom also saw significant cultural differences between blacks and Latinos, in that the latter "seem to have *strong* family structures." Living in the ethnically diverse, far northside neighborhood of Rogers Park, "I did make friends with a few of my neighbors who were Latinos, and they had parties and, like, the whole family would be there. And [they] seemed very family-oriented, so, uh, I think it seems to be a real problem in the black communities."

Was Tom a hard-core racist? I'm still not entirely sure. What seemed to trump all of his reservations about blacks and about affirmative action, however, was the history of slavery in the American South, and its impact on his black contemporaries.

They're born with the slavery stigma. . . . To be a child and to go to school and take a history class and hear that your forefathers were slaves, I just think that that would be incredibly demoralizing. . . . I just think it would make me feel secondary on a social level. . . . Although slavery ended, what, 130 years ago?— I don't think that's a long time to rid us of that stigma. . . . You see what I'm saying? . . . Those people *are* owed.

Well, most of them, anyway. "What if a black or Latino gets accepted before a white, and the black or Latino has lower grades, but they grew up in a similar socioeconomic situation, where in fact they weren't disadvantaged at all? I mean . . . I think that's wrong." Clearly, "black" didn't simply refer to skin color or ethnic roots, but to a particular slice of American life and of our socioeconomic pyramid. When I asked if he'd had any black friends or Latino friends in high school, he explained, "I had one black friend. His father played [for one of Chicago's professional sports teams]. I don't think he really counts, you know what I mean? . . . He came from the same background as I did." More generally, "Many blacks and Latinos I know are just, I mean, if you couldn't see the color of their skin, they could very well have, you know, grown up white."

Differences in income between *most* blacks and most whites, on the other hand, helped to justify race conscious outreach as well as admissions. In Tom's view, there was no reverse discrimination involved in special efforts to ensure that black youth in Chicago had both the skills and information they needed to make a go of college, because "I think the kids in [upper-middle-class suburban] Wilmette are going to be getting it anyway." As far as academic support services on college campuses were concerned, Tom was resistant to race targeted programming on the grounds that this promoted a sense of "inferiority— a feeling that—I think there's something going on here, I think it's *very* racist." Any special needs of blacks and Latinos in this regard could be taken care of by targeting low-income students generally. Should family income cutoffs be introduced, I asked him, to determine eligibility? "I think that's fine, because someone who comes from a higher income can afford to take, say, the LSAT intensive review, which costs, like, $695."

Affirmative action admissions, however, Tom wished to limit to blacks still suffering the economic consequences of the "slavery stigma." It ought not be extended, moreover, to Afro-Caribbean immigrants or their descendants, who were after all not descendants of *this* country's slaves. And despite his positive experiences with Latinos, Tom didn't think they deserved affirmative action either.

> I don't, you know, think the Latinos are any different than a Polish immigrant, that's my question. . . . I think any racism a Latino experiences, I think is basically . . . the same type of racism that Irish people experienced when they first came here, or Italians. . . . I think the problem [is] that they're coming *now*, and there's just not that much happening here. I mean, it's not the land of opportunity anymore.

AN ELLIS ISLAND OF THE MIND

Most of the men interviewed shared Tom's concern that collective interventions to reinforce equality of opportunity ought not extend to inappropriate targets. Americans have a soft spot for the very young, and almost everyone I interviewed agreed with Drew Kazinski and Larry Dobbs that minority *children* were by far the most desirable beneficiaries of race-conscious policies, and drew considerably more sympathy than college-educated young adults.

As the reader may already have noticed, moreover, depictions of racism and inequality almost always focused exclusively on African Americans, and especially the so-called black "underclass" inhabiting our urban ghettos. Blacks, it was clear, were viewed as the sole alloy still resistant to the American melting pot, and their experience of prejudice and discrimination, most agreed, was distinct in kind as well as degree from whatever had been visited on my subjects' forebears, and from the experience of Latinos as well.

Roots: *The "white ethnic" experience*

> Actually, I think of myself more as an American. Grabbin' a hold of Irish is nothin' to hold on to. It's a small island, and just about everybody pulled up a boat and conquered it. I think their gene pool would have worn out a long time ago if it wasn't for sailors' holiday.
>
> —Joe Murtaugh

Like the other men I talked to, Joe Murtaugh didn't have much invested in his own ethnic heritage. But he knew his history:

> Every immigrant this country ever had worked like a *mule*. You just point in a direction and tell 'em, "Start working." They don't need to know how many. They aren't gonna stop working until there's no work left for 'em, 'til you come back and tell 'em to stop. Everybody who came to this country did the same thing. . . . When the Irish came here, the last [ethnic group] off the boat is the lowest. . . . They worked in New York. They worked in Chicago in the meat. The Italians worked in Chicago. Where do you think, you know, that the term "dagos," for Christ sake, and "micks" [come from]?! Everybody was trying to put down that last son of a bitch that got off the boat. . . . The Orientals couldn't get a job. Neither could the Irish. The only way the Irish guy got a job was, he was put in charge of the blacks when they were workin' on the plantation. And [the plantation owners] didn't even like the Irish guy. And after that ended, then the Irish were buildin' the railroads with the Chinese.

Likewise, Pat Gaheogan knew the story of how

> my great-great-grandparents came here and they had nothing, and just through the generations, they came up. . . . When they came here, I've heard the stories of burning crosses in front of Catholic churches. They had one down at about 102nd and Longwood, St. Barnabas Catholic Church. Upon it's completion, people burned a cross in front of it. And my mother remembers that vividly. . . . I don't recall any stories about Irishmen being hanged. But also I have heard the stories of Catholics being taken out by the Klan.

Even today, in Jack's neighborhood,

> There's almost like a ranking. . . . [American-born] Caucasians consider themselves the, uh, I don't want to say elite or anything, but it's sort of like the . . . ideal [background], and then you have . . . the immigrants from the European countries, fresh immigrants . . . next in the social ladder, the next rung down. And then, Asian. And then, Latino. And then black was considered the lowest, as far as where I was brought up.

In rural Iowa, assimilation came more slowly. Phil Zeckman's paternal grandparents, second- and third-generation German Americans, "did not speak English until my father and his brother and sisters entered school and taught them." And the German Protestants still thought of themselves as a little smarter, more on the ball, than Roman Catholics like Phil, who in turn still considered the Protestants a bit snobbish. Back in Chicago, Dave told me, it was west-suburban Italian American kids who had earned that stereotype.

> A lot of people . . . still think . . . "I'm better than so and so because of whatever." I think it's very strong in some of the *Italian* neighborhoods. . . . Italians tend to think that they are the ultimate—. . . . They tend to be very conceited about themselves. . . . I knew some in high school. . . . We used to talk about Harlem [Avenue, a dividing line between Chicago and some of its western suburbs], the strip where you see a lot of Italians out there with the cars that Mom and Dad bought them.

Defending affirmative action, then, simply wasn't enough to argue that blacks and Latinos were victims of prejudice, physical exploitation, or economic injustice. Wasn't everybody? Phil cited a larger economic picture put forth by Bayard Rustin in 1965.

> In the 19th and early 20th century, [various] ethnic groups . . . could come to the U.S. and start at a very low poverty level as an unskilled and semi-skilled worker and acquire new skills along the way, and it was possible to end your life maybe two, three . . . income levels higher than what you started at. Even uneducated, that's the case. And really, in today's technological society, unskilled jobs are being cut away. Semi-skilled jobs are leaving; and even [there] you need to be quite educated to [run a machine] in a factory. . . . *What* they're encountering is the same. How they're able to deal with that is different because of the time.

Essential to endorsement of race-conscious policies of any kind was the conviction that members of *some* groups were victims of greater, more persistent discrimination and exploitation than almost anyone else. Like Tom Sorbo, most of those interviewed seemed to feel that African Americans had met that criterion and then some.

Some of Dan Lysenko's ancestors, for example, "had trouble getting jobs in the nineteenth century, but . . . [that was] a long time ago. . . . [Blacks encounter] a different kind of discrimination on a different level. . . . I don't think it's comparable." Matt Vigoda seemed offended by the very attempt to compare the two. "I don't think there was too many times that an Irish [person] or a Jew or whatever were not considered humans." Granted, "The Italians or the Irish were made to work at the sweatshops or whatever," Tim Kovacs pointed out. "There was a slavery there, and [there was] prejudice against [them], but it was not the visible kind of slavery in the sense with the shackles."

Jack recognized, "The time when slavery was abolished 'til now is really a short period of time. . . . In fact, I sit here and think, it's amazing that [blacks have] come this far in a hundred [years], from their being slaves." Like Tom, he was concerned that "there's still that stigma that . . . this person . . . [is] a descendant of a slave, you know." And what helped to stigmatize blacks in that way was the relative ease with which others could pick them out. Whites, on the other hand, "can always take a racial position instead of an ethnic position. . . . When the Irish [Americans] fight the German [Americans]," Doug Peruggia considered, "I don't know if it's [a different] intensity, but . . . it was easier for [the victims] to . . . claim that, 'No, no, I'm white.' . . . Even though they were still at odds with one another, it was covered up by the fact that they had now in common a race that they [both] had something against."

Recognizable differences in skin color and facial features, Len Hellstrom argued, had long served the divide-and-conquer strategies of big business.

> Racism is used by [economic] interests to divide people. . . . So, like, they have all these Polish immigrants or whatever, working in factories, and the Polish people realize that they're getting scammed on. So they start to organize. So the company starts recruiting in Lithuania. And that brings in a wave of Lithuanians to crush the newly organized labor unions set up by the Polish workers. And [when] the Polish people go out on strike . . . they can stay out there, because there's all these Lithuanians'll take their jobs. And they can't communicate because they don't speak the same language, most of them, and they're new here, and they're scared, and everything else.
>
> Wave after wave, that happens. [But] it's not so easy to maintain that on a more or less permanent scale, because [these white ethnics] all look the same. . . . The color barrier is the key to things, it's the key. You can't keep Irish people and French people apart for any length of time. . . . It's . . . difficult to teach children that there's a difference between Polish and Lithuanian. . . . Their kids won't notice the difference. It's easy to teach children that there's a difference between black and white.

Others raised a familiar argument once popular among social scientists and policy makers, directly linking the experience of slavery with what these subjects saw as a critical lack of familial and communal supports for achievement. Joe contrasted Jews' strong sense of their own history as a people with blacks "just grabbin' at this loosely affiliated, 'Well, I know I'm black, and I gotta be comin' from some country.' You know, I think that bollixes the affiliation with maybe heritage." "They were forced to come" to America, Mike Benedetto pointed out, "and then they were also just released. . . . A society, I believe, never, ever really evolved. . . . There's not, like, a sense of community joining together and, you know." Dave was more specific:

> [If] you're being bought and sold like property, can you really *have* . . . close family life, because who knows if you're gonna be here tomorrow? I also know that a lot of children were born . . . [to] black women [who] were, like, raped by [white] men and all that. . . . Well, that's not a very strong family life right there. . . . I do know there were *some* families, or there was some family life. . . . A lot depends on how mean the [white] people were. So that might be where their lack of community comes from. . . . [As a black slave] you relied on the white family you were working with, not on other black people. That's an assumption, you know, 'cause I really don't know . . . [how often] the black mother and black father stuck together, and were *allowed* to live together, allowed to have children, allowed to stay together as a family, and what [proportion of owners] would just sell them off, you know?

Latinos were a different story. On one hand, Mexican Americans—the Latinos the men interviewed were most familiar with—were often seen to conform much more closely to what was once referred to as "the deserving poor," exemplars of the same family values and work ethic as earlier waves of white ethnic immigrants. In Dave's experience, for example,

> From what I understand, from what I've read . . . [Mexican Americans] tend to have the father, they tend to work, you know, sixteen-hour days, [the father] has, like . . . janitorial positions, the mother cleaning lady, seamstress, that type of thing. . . . [They] tend to help each other. They tend to stick together. . . . [Kids] see a mom that works hard and a dad that works hard. Their parents are saying . . . "We don't want you to have to work like we worked. Go to school and get an education so that you can live a better life than us."

For similar reasons, Joe was

> more eager to help the Latinos than . . . the blacks. . . . You pass a black guy's house, he's just workin' to get out and move into something else. He isn't really working to make his lot better where's he's at at a particular time. And I think the Latinos *are*. . . . Outside, the place might be falling down, but you go inside, and there's usually, you know, a coat of paint on the walls, you know. . . .
>
> I've worked with both. . . . I had a job with railroad construction. I worked with Mexicans. Most of them didn't speak English, and my job [was] to communicate the job to 'em, get the job done. And every day you are at work, you know, hard labor, just like the old westerns. . . . Mexicans would try to hurt you and get you injured so you'd be thrown off the job, so that they could bring in their friend, or their brother, or somebody to fill that spot. . . . They knew . . . if they got in a fight,

they were gonna be gone. But there's so many things you can do on a job, just to injure somebody. . . . Whereas it made for a hostile work situation, I would also respect that same thing. You know, he's trying to get his brother a job. He's trying to get things better for this family.

Jeff may have explained it best. A San Diego native with a Chicana wife, he had observed that when Mexican Americans come into this country—legally or not—"They're happy to be here, okay? . . . At least we're not down in Mexico. . . . and that's what they teach their kids, just like my Irish grandparents taught my parents . . . that you should be thankful for what you've got. . . . I don't think it's that way in the black community. . . . They came over from Africa, but I think that's a long, long time ago and, they kind of consider it as, you know, this is theirs."

Most African Americans and perhaps most whites would embrace that logic. Some of the men I interviewed, on the other hand, saw Latinos as *newcomers,* whose underclass status and victimization were therefore business as usual. Only in the last twenty years, Mike Benedetto told me, had Mexicans and Puerto Ricans begun arriving in this country

in the major proportions that they have. . . . I can see Puerto Ricans already gaining more of an acceptability, and I believe within, maybe, twenty years, they will be on the same level. We don't think of Italians as a minority now. We think of them as American. . . . That's something I don't think blacks have ever received.

To a considerable degree, of course, one's "acceptability" was literally a matter of color. Matt's family and friends had "not really" reacted negatively to his African American girlfriend partly because, "She's very light. She's not really dark, and that does matter to other people." Greg Bogosian's geographic origins may have been closer than most whites to the mountain range from which "Caucasians" get their label, but "I've got this [olive] skin color where I feel like, if somebody saw me, they'd say, 'Well, is he really white, or is he, like, Spanish or something?' . . . I'm, like, in a jumbled area where you're not *not* white, but then again you're really not, quote-unquote, blond hair, blue eyes."

But this very variability of "white" skin color and facial features may have made it easier for Latinos to "blend into the culture," as Greg put it, than blacks.

Even in my social group that I go out with, if there are Spanish people there, [my other friends] don't think twice about it. If there are black people there, [the whites] wouldn't say anything, but it wouldn't be socially acceptable. . . . I could be friends with [blacks] but I couldn't really socialize with them to any great extent . . . [whereas] a third of my friends are Latinos. . . .

Even though [whites] might have gotten some dirty looks for [marrying a Latino], you wouldn't have gotten disowned. . . . If I married somebody other than an Armenian, my parents would frown upon it, but they'd live with it. But if it was a black [woman], I mean, they'd just disown me completely. . . . [in the case of a Latina] it would be more how much darker her skin was.

It was an open question, then, whether Latinos were as deserving as blacks of race-conscious affirmative action. And in any case, such policies had to target the deserving *poor.*

Class Matters: *Coping with socioeconomic constraints on achievement*

Like Dave Zaluba, like Larry, everyone seemed to feel that the biggest problem with being black or Latino was that disproportionate numbers of both groups had to deal with poverty and its psychosocial and sociocultural correlates. "Economics," as Matt Vigoda put it, "determines what you put priority on and what you have *time* to put priority on. It determines what you value." Blacks and Latinos were more likely to suffer from a low self-image, a feeling of hopelessness, chemical dependency, and so forth, Len argued, "because there're a higher percentage of blacks and Latinos than whites that are poor. And it's *poorer* people that will encounter those things, regardless of their color. I mean, the people in my [all-white] neighborhood are poor and they're stupid and uneducated and have bad jobs and get hurt a lot."

In any family scrambling to make a living, maximizing school achievement might be that much harder. That helped to explain Jack Uberhof's endorsement of nontraditional admissions criteria.

There *are* obstacles [to academic achievement], in an economic sense. . . . Maybe [more blacks and Latinos] were required to work when they were younger. They had more instability in the family *because* of the economics, there was more stress put on the family relations. A lot of that has a *heavy* impact on academics, and therefore they probably *did* have to try a lot harder *economically.* And in that sense, that's why I favor having a more, um, subjective interviews, and having more variables involved, because it *is* harder for someone from an economically lower background to *get* the higher grades.

Among graduate professional school applicants, however, even nontraditional measures of "merit" might reflect one's economic origins at least as much as motivation or competence. Sean Hanna noted that

You might find some black or Latino [pre-meds] that have done a lot of community volunteer work or something. [But] you might find some that have had to work at McDonald's or something all their summer breaks, in order to keep their heads above water while they're in college, you know what I mean? . . . Myself, I was living at home with my dad, he could support me. I had a part-time job, but I volunteered at the hospital. So I feel like, there might be a built-in-bias.

Asked to explain inequality of outcomes *within* racial or ethnic groups, a great many felt that it had a lot to do with the socioeconomic status of one's parents. Matt's father had been "really, really poor, and now he owns part of a business, but that's rare. . . . I don't think many people have a chance to do that." On the other hand, "Once you have money, you're usually pretty firmly set," Mike Benedetto assured me. "And power. Money *is* power. . . . It's just, you know, you can probably trace George Bush's family down to Pilgrims of the Mayflower." There were really just two criteria for admission to medical school, Len Hellstrom argued, "how good are your grades, and how big is your daddy's bank account . . . George Bush, Jr. . . . Kennedy, Jr. . . . Mellon, Jr., will get in . . . regardless of any of that other stuff."

Dan Lysenko didn't go quite that far. "Once you're old enough, you're kind of on your own, so what you do or don't have is pretty much up to you. But some people are given a much better head start than others." On a personal level, Dan knew people his own age who were already homeowners, and "there's just no way I could do that right now . . . and that's only because their parents helped them get a start." In Sean's view, college students from more affluent families had several advantages. On one hand, "You have a car to get to and from home to college. . . . You [can] call home and say, 'Send me a hundred bucks, I need to buy some socks,' or something. . . . You know, you're not worried about certain things and you can focus your energy and attention towards getting the job done." At the same time, he felt that more affluent students had a better chance of attending top-quality universities, benefiting from "better education . . . [and] better facilities . . . [like] new microscopes. . . . At MIT, you have a Nobel Prize-winning physicist that you can pay $100,000 a year to, as opposed to UIC."

In line with Tom Sorbo's preference for class-targeted academic support services, a general awareness of the import of socioeconomic background seemed to influence the views of several men who were opposed to *racial* preferences. In terms of *under*graduate admissions, Jeff McEwen argued, one's economic origins

shouldn't gauge a whole lot . . . [but] there should be something. I mean, if a person coming out of high school had lower grades, and yet that person had to work all the way through high school, there should be some exception, a slight exception made . . . a couple of extra points on [the] scale . . . because of what a person has had to do while in school.

Jack argued for modified quotas and college-level and high school outreach based not on race or ethnicity but family income. "I'm sure there's a lot of whites that were deprived" of middle-class advantages.

Whatever the poverty level is, I think maybe [the income cut-off should be] somewhat above that. . . . Probably $25,000 to $30,000 with [a two-parent family and] just one child, and then just whatever the increment, whatever you decided about that. . . . Now it may be a higher proportion of blacks and Latinos who are part of that; I don't know, like, two or three whites would be needing the same program . . . but you still [include] the white group . . . in the same category as [blacks and Latinos].

He did not think his own family qualified, however. Although his parents had raised at least three children on a combined income of about $40,000 a year, "I don't think we were necessarily deprived or anything. . . . There was no economic barrier." But Jack was nonetheless familiar with the darker side of some of Chicago's less fashionable suburbs.

I grew up in [west suburban] Cicero. . . . In high school, there was a big gang problem at that time, from '80 to '84. . . . There weren't any shootings, it was mostly fistfights. But it was—there were actually certain sections of the hallways [where] certain gangs . . . would hang out all the time. . . . Cicero was at the time, and probably still is . . . a very prejudicial suburb. . . . The Nazi headquarters was three blocks from my house. . . . There were no blacks, zero, in Cicero . . . [not] one black student in the high school. And we still had the same problems. . . . [My youngest brother] always got . . . straight A's all the way up to about eighth grade. At that point, he turned. I don't know if it had to do with the people that he was associating with or whatever. But there was a bout with drugs and it got really messy for a couple years and the grades went, you know, he didn't go to class, and it just seemed—suddenly it seemed like it was up in the air. . . . It's not a racial thing, it's more of an economic thing, I think.

No one failed to grasp the historic links between these two "things." Like Tom, Matt responded positively to the notion that affirmative action could be justified simply as compensation to blacks or Latinos in general for that history. "White Caucasians have always . . . had affirmative action, if you wanna think of it. We get admitted, get the job before a black person, simply on account of race. So I think if you're gonna make it equal, then it's gonna have to be reversed . . . for a while." But no one else agreed. "Okay, there was slavery . . . so how do you compensate for that?" Pat Geohagan wanted to know. "Thirty percent of all the white people should be slaves for the next fifty or sixty years?" Isaac Fedelovich's problem was that, "Those people were oppressed a while ago; they're not around anymore"; compensating their descendants was beside the point. Most of the men seemed to agree with Larry that to the degree that affirmative action was warranted, this was as compensation for what their black and Latino contemporaries had suffered *themselves* as a consequence of discrimination against their forebears.

That may seem like a distinction without a difference. But if the purpose of affirmative action was to address the consequences of racism for *today's* minorities, and if those consequences were seen to revolve around economic deprivation, this rendered ineligible those blacks and Latinos whose families had managed to surmount those economic barriers to achievement.

Several of the men I interviewed had some firsthand experience with the way that economics could constrain academic performance, and they were concerned that affluent blacks or Latinos might have a better shot than they did at competitive graduate professional schools. Matt might have earned something better than "straight B's," he felt, had family problems and financial pressures not forced him to take a full-time factory job during his senior year of high school. I didn't want to ask Jeff any awkward questions, but it was clear from his children's ages and some comments about high school that he and his wife had started a family before they'd planned to; and he was up front about how the need to support a family had slowed his progress toward a degree. "There might be several affluent black young men, and because they're black, even though they have a better upbringing than *I* did, okay?—they might have had a lot better toys than I had—does that give them the right to get that twenty extra points?"

One of the few members of his extended family to attend college, Phil Zeckman had spent two years at the University of Iowa before "Reagan-era" changes in financial aid guidelines made it impossible to continue. He spent a year at a community college in rural Illinois, then moved in with his brother and sister-in-law in Maryland for a while before deciding that a four-year degree would simply have to be pay-as-you-go. Now a bartender at a Loop social club, he strongly endorsed race-conscious admissions and outreach—for those who needed them.

> So this person may not [otherwise] be able to even finish school because he's having financial problems which hold him back. This student maybe . . . came from a poorer [high] school. . . . [Whereas] if you get a young black junior . . . [who is] a four-point-nine on a five-point scale . . . he's financially stable, either from financial aid, or through his parents . . . he's goin' through school, that person is pretty well set.

Dave, as well, "wasn't from a very rich family. I was lower middle class—if I was middle class." His long-time girlfriend, a college graduate with a full-time job, hoped the two would marry as soon as Dave had earned his bachelor's

degree; and I couldn't help wondering if Dave's reluctance to tie the knot until he'd finished medical school sprang from a fear of falling into the same pattern he'd grown up with. Dad had "jumped around a lot," starting college but
never earning a degree, drifting from job to job and from one line of work to
another, with considerable stretches of unemployment in between. Clearly
more of a go-getter, his mother had earned her bachelor's degree while working full-time and raising a family, and at the time of our interview she was pursuing an MBA. "Now she's doing pretty good. But—I don't know. . . . We're
not making a lot of money, they never really have, and so I was really never that
privileged either. . . . I bet there's a *lot* of blacks out there that make more
money than my parents do." At UIC, Dave's 4.2 grade point average reflected

> progressively better [performance] throughout the years except for when I've
> had to work a lot. . . . One time . . . I can remember that I was gonna get an A in
> a course, and because I work on computers, computers go down, and my clients
> tend to be lawyers and stuff. This lawyer had a case on their hard drive, like, this
> thick, you know . . . a couple of hundred pages. And they needed it printed out
> [but] the hard drive went down, and the case was gonna be in a week, and I spent
> many hours doing it. My grades went dropping from A to a C. And so that's some-
> thing medical schools, when they look at my grades aren't gonna see.

But high-income families could buy their children more than time.

> Obviously, when you go to school, and your parents can afford the Presidential
> Towers [a row of expensive riverfront high-rises a five- or ten-minute drive from
> UIC], you don't have to worry about crime and you have a new car you can drive
> over here. It's a lot easier to do better in school than if you have to take a bus an
> hour and a half and you're driving through a bad part of town, and once you get
> off the bus, you have to watch over your shoulders that no one's shooting, you
> know, and people bothering you with alcohol and drugs.

Unlike Jack, Dave had no problem with race-targeted affirmative action—
but you may recall that this was largely based on his grasp of the dynamics of
the culture of poverty. "When I'm talking about blacks . . . I'm talking [mostly]
about the poorer areas. . . . I mean, I'm not referring to the higher class, because those people have *seen* achievement. They know what it looks like. And
they're being pushed, you know. . . . It's not race, it's class. I think there's poor
white areas, and I think they're in the same situation as poor black areas."
What he found hard to live with was that

> You may get a black who was born in the [very affluent, lakefront] Gold Coast,
> . . . and [his] parents had millions of dollars, and [he's] gonna apply to medical

school, and they're gonna say, "Look, he's black." And [it's] gonna be . . . easier [for him] than me, where . . . I've had it a lot *harder* than they have. And they're gonna [say], "Look, white," and they won't—It's harder to get in. . . . And it's just not fair.

Hal Voorhees's family was more solidly middle-class than Dave's, and he was concerned that affirmative action might benefit blacks and Latinos very like himself. If blacks and Latinos deserved special consideration, it was not simply because of their race, but

because they grew up in a fragmented home, or . . . a community like [the west-side Chicago ghetto of] Austin. Or they went to a poor high school, or a combination of all these things. . . . *And* you've made it through college, but you probably still don't have the same sort of scores on the LSAT or whatever as whites who have gone through, you know, a superior high school and a superior college. . . . I think someone who went through all of that and still shows the will to want to get through law school and shows the desire to be there and to . . . get done what they need to do, I think that ought to be rewarded and encouraged. . . .

But I wonder to what extent those racial set-asides go not to the person who worked to get themselves out of the ghetto or a housing project . . . but instead to suburban blacks or suburban Latinos . . . who have gone to suburban schools and have achieved roughly the same as the whites who have gone [there]. . . . A black or a Latino who grew up in the same community as I did and went to the same school and had a nuclear family and had all the advantages that I did ought *not* to have the advantages that *should* be allocated to someone who is *dis*advantaged.

While the exceptionality of white-on-black or white-on-Latino racism might be the sine qua non of affirmative action, I was getting a clear message that compensation was deserved only to the degree that racist attitudes, behavior, and public policy had constrained economic opportunity.

The argument can be made, of course, that *all* blacks or Latinos have suffered constrained opportunities on account of discrimination, and that those who succeeded in spite of that could have gotten that much further, were it not for their race. Among my subjects, however, *maximizing* opportunity was much less of a concern than making sure everyone had *enough.*

A principle purpose of affirmative action, they seemed to be saying, was to help create some *floor* of achievement and income for Americans generally. While differences in outcomes along racial or ethnic lines might be suspect, inequalities of outcomes per se were simply a fact of life. Rick Skilling was "pretty comfortable" with inequalities of incomes and status "as long as it's not so wide that people are being killed off or anything like that." Isaac was likewise comfortable with inequality unless it "reaches [such] a high degree

... [that] it starts interfering with a person's life, so that person has to struggle to exist."

Part of Pat's objection to affirmative action was what he viewed as an implicit assumption that *without* special consideration, blacks and Latinos could
not get ahead on their own. They could, of course; and the fact that economic
factors or an inferior high school education might keep them out of the higher
education fast track did not concern him. "If you keep working . . . in this day
and age, you have options. You don't have to go to a four-year college, if you
can't go right now. You go to a two-year college. . . . If you're still working at
McDonald's, you might, if you can save up, you might be able to afford it. You
can get loans and grants."

While Mike supported much more affirmative action than Drew Kazinski,
Mike's rationales were similar, sharing the view that a college degree was essential to a reasonable degree of social status and material comfort. "There's a
level of inequality that shouldn't be accepted by anybody . . . a level of living
that . . . everybody should be above. A lot of blacks that are poor," moreover,
"*are* trying to get out of it. . . . If they were . . . trying to make the step [to attend college] . . . they should be rewarded."

As for graduate professional schools, except for absolute quotas, Mike actually approved every form of affirmative action admissions and outreach on the
list. Not only would he restrict eligibility for affirmative action on the basis of
socioeconomic status, however: His endorsement was further limited to medical schools and a handful of other programs whose minority graduates were
essential to ensuring low-income blacks and Latinos adequate access to services he saw as critical to the "level of living" that everyone deserves. On this
basis, Mike felt there was no reason for race-conscious admissions for graduate programs in management, finance, engineering, or architecture, for example. "I mean, there's plenty of people to draw buildings. . . . I believe it should
have a direct societal impact."

Mike was the lone dissenter from the notion that bedside manner might be
almost as critical to professional excellence as scientific and technical expertise. "I don't believe, just because you're a doctor, that you have some social
ramifications that you have to meet up to. . . . You don't expect that from any
engineer, so why should you expect that from a doctor?" What *was* important
about diversifying the pool of doctors, lawyers, and social workers, however,
was not that they would be more simpatico with minority patients or clients,
but that low-income minorities simply would not have enough doctors or
lawyers in their neighborhoods to support an adequate "level of living" unless
there were enough people "from those areas" to serve them.

What Mike also seemed to be targeting, however, were professional services
that involved a good deal of intimate contact with, and perhaps advocacy for,

one's clientele. He seemed to understand intuitively that in this regard, minority professionals might do better by the blacks and Latinos in their care. As
for other professions, however, special consideration of minority graduate professional school applicants was not called for. "Once everybody has risen above
a certain level of living . . . and have the necessities of life, [and are] able to
live comfortably and be happy"—none of which required more than an undergraduate degree—"it's a matter of getting it on your own."

The more so since black and Latino graduate professional school applicants
might be several years *too old* to deserve special consideration.

Growing Seasons: *The advantages of race-conscious interventions with the very young*

> In the country, when you grow corn, if you don't take care of the plant when
> it's young, what good is it when it grows up?
>
> —Phil Zeckman

Phil's metaphor may have betrayed his Iowa roots, but his message was the
same as Larry Dobbs's and essentially repeated by most of the men I interviewed. In the most practical sense, getting kids to focus their ambitions early
was at least as important to pre-meds as to business students. For a black and
Latino applicant to be fully competitive with whites, Zack Pritchard argued,
they needed to start thinking about medical school "when they're younger,
while they've still got a chance to do something about it." With med school in
view, they could hit the ground running as undergraduates. "If you know that
[medical school] is what you want to do the first day you walk on campus" as
an undergraduate, Sean Hanna pointed out, "you can start with your general
chem and your general bio and have a logical and coherent four-year program."

Earlier outreach was not only more efficient than interventions with undergraduates but was also more consistent with shared notions of equity. For one
thing, it would allow *more* of our real target population to benefit. College-
level interventions were "good for those students that are [attending college],"
Len Hellstrom explained. "But a lot of students *aren't* there that might be
there if there was intervention at the high school level . . . [on the part of] those
schools. A lot of those students won't end up in medical school. But they'd end
up in something else" better than what they'd be doing without a degree.

And this kind of outreach could also help blacks and Latinos achieve a solid
enough foundation for success in college that by the time they applied to graduate schools, they could be fully competitive with white candidates. Steve
Clayburgh sounded very much like Larry: "You're *enticing* students to work at
something and to really make a decision for themselves. . . . [not just] saying,

'Hey, come to us,' . . . [but] 'This is what you need to do: You need to take math, sciences, and a foreign language.' . . . I like that better than—I guess this sounds like a typical white male kind of thing to say, but [better than] a 'free meal' for someone." The goal was to instill "a greater desire for—a work ethic that they might not have had" otherwise. And the earlier this work ethic was acquired, "the more productive they become in school, and elevate *themselves* to a higher platform. So that *they* are doing the work because of a thought process that you've put in their heads." Charlie Kilgallen, too, preferred that racial equity be achieved without having to resort to affirmative action admissions at the graduate level. "If things were started off earlier, maybe . . . in twenty, thirty years . . . there'll no longer be past injustices that need to be taken care of."

One of the problems with affirmative action admissions, as discussed earlier, was that marginal equality was thereby abandoned in favor of *cumulative equality*—compensating for past injustices in the opposite direction. By contrast, outreach to schoolchildren could help to eliminate marginal inequality by fostering great parity among contemporaries of diverse ethnic and economic backgrounds. If far too many black and Latino kids aren't learning "what their potential is . . . [or] how to put their best efforts forth," as Jack Uberhof put it, if they "come from backgrounds that don't really teach them about how to channel their energy," university outreach could help ensure that those gaps in their preparation were filled.

Perhaps the most important way in which university outreach could help further marginal equality at the grade school or high school level was to introduce students to black and Latino professional-managerial role models. That was something schools serving whites needn't be so concerned about: "If you're Irish or you're Italian or whatever else you are," as Matt Vigoda put it, "you're still Caucasian and you look at people in power and they look like you, you turn on the TV and people look like you. And you can strive to be that." Without role models who "look like you," Jack argued,

> Whether they consciously think of it that way or not, [black and Latino kids] see the better people or the good people as being white, then they just assimilate that because [they're] black, [they're] obviously not gonna be . . . the good people, or whatever. . . . So they need people of their race [to look up to], just so they don't believe that . . . because of their race, they can't get to where they want to be.

Through their neighbors and families, moreover, white children and teenagers were more likely to have personal contact with successful executives and professionals—something Steve urged outreach programs to provide to blacks and Latinos.

You know, show me, don't tell me. Let me see somebody with an IBM button on his lapel, and a blue suit and a white shirt and a drab tie. Let me *see this happen.* Let me have somebody I can talk to, not only on an academic sense, but also just shoot the shit with, and find out what he *really* did, what he *really* thought about growing up, what his real problems were and his real obstacles. . . . That is really where the learning takes place, I think, and it really allows you to form your ideas in a more concrete way than just sitting in the classroom, or being recruited by a university and having the administrators throw it at you.

Also in line with the ethic of marginal equality, outreach to Chicago's minority-majority public schools would also help to redress the imbalance in per-pupil spending or teachers' salaries. Targeting those inner-city schools didn't really count as reverse discrimination because it wasn't giving minorities anything whites didn't already have: In "more white affluent areas," said Jeff Ewen, "high schools get more funding, they have better facilities, everything's better, and there's more opportunity for [the high schools] to bring in the lawyers and doctors [as speakers or role models]. So the opportunity's [already] there for whites." Given Chicago's racially and economically segregated neighborhoods, moreover, by attacking the problem of inequality "from the other end," as Dave put it, "you *know* the people you're helping are the people that need to get help."

In contrast to race-conscious interventions at a multiracial university, moreover, high school outreach would avoid the problem of unequal treatment of students in the same setting. As Doug Peruggia described it,

The law school could target, say, specific schools where the higher minority population is, but everyone still participates. Say, you were to take a sophomore or junior class out, but instead of going to [well-to-do, suburban] Winnetka . . . go down to, you know, [inner-city, largely Latino] Juarez High School. . . . [So] they're not picking . . . specific people out of the group . . . but the group just happens to be Latino. . . . It's not racial, you know, picking and choosing. More or less, people in *your* situation, where *you* live.

On the other hand, the argument could be made that colleges and universities had *more* of an obligation to help their own, current constituencies than to help mere aspirants. Chris Feraios, for example, found race-targeted interventions with college students less distasteful than outreach to schoolchildren, because the former had "been admitted into the college . . . [so] the college should give you some means to get some help or whatever." For similar reasons, if Joe Murtaugh was in charge, he would never push for pump-priming initiatives of any kind. "I'm the dean of the grad business school? Definitely not. 'Til they reach my door, they're nobody."

Nonetheless, Joe did not really oppose race-targeted outreach to grade schools or high schools. At that level, it would do some good for minority kids while helping to recruit future students, without thereby putting whites at any disadvantage. A paid internship, for example, would

give a kid a chance to get a job in high school, probably, being involved with a program like that. But in college and after college, an employer's not gonna care what you did in high school. . . . Doesn't mean anything after he's out and finished his masters'. . . . All you're doing is you're telling a kid, "Hey, you get this clean environment to work in, and you won't be swinging a pickax or anything" . . . [and] offering the, uh, mental drive that's wanted.

Maybe, you know, from that point on, after *getting* that mental drive through the program, he'll always think, "Gosh, Michigan State." I don't have any problem with that, because what you're doing with that is, you're almost inspiring somebody to continue, or [to recognize] that this option's available. . . . [provided that] if there's a white guy going to that [high] school, because of the plague of busing, that white guy should be able to go into this program too.

Joe did have some personal beefs. Because he's dyslexic, staffers at UIC and one other school had discouraged him from enrolling. That other school eventually allowed him to enroll in a dyslexics-only course sequence that not only failed to meet his real needs but crowded his schedule, making it more difficult to pursue his major. At UIC, the foreign language requirement was waived for Joe—but only if he agreed to complete seven quarters of history courses.

They asked me to leave the [other] school twice, because they weren't prepared to deal with it. If I was a black guy, it would have been no problem. . . . Nobody walks around saying, "Oh, poor boy. You know, we're gonna test you at a different time." You know, "Your grade was a little bit low, I'm gonna set you up with this internship with this company, that's gonna help you get a job later on. It's gonna be a *paying* internship, did I mention that?" There's all these special benies [for blacks and Latinos].

Joe recognized that on the average, whites were more likely than minorities to have access to good jobs, positive role models, or other kinds of real-world experience pertinent to professional-managerial careers. Nonetheless,

I'm [still] not given that same chance. Or, only a small percentage of you white people would get that chance. That's ridiculous. I mean, that's the kind of thing that people should be grabbing torches and chasing [the university administration] down the street, you know? . . . If I'm able to say, I had an internship, that means something to a business when I go in there. . . . Going on a field trip, it's a different experience. This guy gets to spend a weekend, you know, at some accounting firm . . . he's gonna meet people while he's there . . . he's gonna be up a little bit [in the job market].

Displaced Persons: *Diversity and the college experience*

While some campus-based programs are designed to give blacks or Latinos the sort of "leg up" that Joe Murtaugh was concerned about, most race-conscious initiatives on campus are geared primarily to help them succeed as college students in a setting more intellectually challenging than most are accustomed to, and in which they are in a distinct minority, subject not only to some inevitable racism but perhaps also to culture shock or a severe sense of dislocation. Is this experience exceptional enough, however, to merit such programming—and perhaps to help rationalize special consideration for minority graduates?

Like Tom Sorbo, Jack Uberoff thought about what it might be like if the tables were turned. At a predominantly black school, "I think [it] would be a little bit more difficult to interact in an open way. . . . I'd just assume offhand that they wouldn't understand my background or whatever." Hal Voorhees imagined how he would feel "if I walked into an all-girls school. . . . I think maybe there'd be a female perspective on everything; then I would feel somewhat disenfranchised." Len Hellstrom compared the minority experience at UIC to attending college in France. "I'd have a hell of a time, even though I speak French fairly well. . . . If they're feeling very uncomfortable, out of place, or putting a lot of—at least a certain amount of effort into [that], rather than studying and paying attention in class . . . that would be a problem."

Even laudable efforts to pay more attention to the minority experience in humanities and social science courses had their downside, Doug Peruggia pointed out, when attention turned to slavery and interracial violence.

> Some things are just offensive. . . . It's a historical fact that certain things were this way, and maybe you embarrass [African Americans]. I would say I was even embarrassed at times, being in Professor _____'s . . . race-relations class. [Enrollment is] basically fifty-fifty white-black, a couple of Latinos here and there, and some of things that he talked about . . . are just offensive to say to a black person. . . . At times, he was almost apologetic, being a white professor from Oxford [University in England].

In the pre-med and pre-allied health courses, on the other hand, blacks or Latinos might feel especially isolated simply because their numbers were especially low. "There's not as many blacks to socialize with," Dave Zaluba explained, "[so] it's harder for them. . . . Whites can get together in their groups, and study and communicate and share ideas, and that helps them. The blacks, they don't have such a big community to gather with." Dave compared this to his own experience "when I transferred . . . from that one grade school to the other grade school. . . . That was the worst year of school of my life, 'cause I was so different. . . . Most of the people . . . we really didn't mesh. . . . [So] I didn't want to think about school. I didn't want to go there, didn't want to be there, I didn't want to do the homework." Dave had tried and failed to make friends with an Afro-Caribbean student who'd been his lab partner.

> He was Jamaican, I think. But he was very much to himself. I mean I tried talking to him . . . he seems to be a real nice guy but, you know, I just—he wouldn't talk to me. . . . I don't know, see, I don't know if it was just because I was white . . . [but] it was, like, basically one-word answers. . . . he wasn't going out of his way to be friendly, so I would think it's . . . more like maybe he couldn't identify. . . . I don't know. . . . But I think they *have* that problem.

The link between these kinds of discomfort and college achievement has long been an argument not only for race-targeted programming but also for affirmative action admissions on behalf of black and Latino applicants to graduate programs. But several of those I interviewed took exception to the assumption of such a dynamic at UIC. "If there was, you know, maybe a group of ten blacks in a school of sixteen thousand students," as Jeff McEwen put it, "then I could see there'd be a problem." But outside the sciences and engineering, there were more than enough blacks to make each other feel at home. Matt Vigoda had "seen plenty of kids feeling that they don't belong here just because they're far away from home, drop out or flunk out"; but while he assumed some minority students felt that way, that was not what he'd observed among the many blacks and Latinos he'd met through his African American girlfriend. "At some schools, they'd be such an extreme minority that it might be quite ostracizing to even go to school there, and then of course there's an effect on their performance. Here, I think they do fine. I think there might not have been any problems because they probably tend to stick together—you know, just like white people'll stick together."

For several men, however, the real issue was not whether or not blacks or Latinos had a negative experience at UIC, but whether it was *more* negative than that of other students. This was, after all, a high-enrollment, mostly commuter campus: Indeed, much of its attraction was that what ran through it was not a river but an eight-lane interstate, as well as two of Chicago's rapid transit lines, making it easily accessible not only to most urban neighborhoods and the Chicago suburbs but also to the commercial districts in which many of its students worked. This sort of campus, however, is not necessarily conducive to building a real community, to a sense of "belonging." As Jeff put it, "I study here and I go home." He hadn't made more than one or two friends on campus "because of having to work full time, you know, I'm in and out real quick." His research position and the demands of the pre-med curriculum had lengthened Dave's hours on campus but had little consequence socially.

> During lecture, you don't really get to *talk* to many people 'cause you're watching the lecture. . . . You tend to meet people in your labs, and then when you're *in* lecture, you tend to sit with them. . . . [Even] if there is no lab, every now and then, you do get to meet people, and you tend to, like, sit next to the person throughout the rest of the [term], and you . . . talk to them in the hall, [but] you don't really get close to the people there, you know?

Perhaps because he had transferred to UIC from a very different campus at the other end of the state, this lack of community really bothered Joe Murtaugh and helped him decide on a second major.

> I took [an arts] class. And I liked it, it made me feel better about myself, I mean, just changing schools, you know, you need a little bit of an "up," and in most fields, you don't—like in business. I joined the [club for students in his business major]. Nobody knows anybody's name in that club. They *try* to get some stuff going . . . but the problem is, that there's no central location that people can just go back to and hang out. And [the arts program] offered a chance to meet people. . . . This is a commuter school, for all practical purposes. . . . People come here, they take their classes, and they're out of here at 10:30[A.M.], you know. . . . The nationals [of his fraternity at the school previously attended] contacted me, they wanted me to get a fraternity [chapter] started here, and—I don't think so. . . . The rest of the country would look at [UIC's fraternity chapters] and go, you aren't a fraternity, you know. If there's no physical building, there's no identity. Part of the reason I'm in [this arts major] is because [the physical facilities required for this major provide] somewhere you can go, they have a physical place where they belong. Having a table across the street over at [UIC's principal student center] is *not* a place to belong, you know? Playing a couple of football games does not make a unity; mostly those are just drinking buddies, there's not more of a unity beyond that. But being involved in [the arts] gave a chance to meet people, and people were friendly over there. You'd walk in, "Oh, what's your name," you know, and you'd be meeting people every day. Whereas in the [business] department, you know, you meet the guy sittin' next to you in class . . . and you know the teacher's name, and you know the person the teacher always talks to, and you might know four people in a class.

In this setting, the very best black students might in some ways be at an advantage, to the degree that they had long since learned to tune out elements of their environment not related to school achievement. Mel Gibran had a different take on the kind of experience Dave had had with the Jamaican in his lab section.

A couple [of blacks] . . . that I've met [at UIC] . . . just seemed to be very serious and, like, goal-oriented. They want to, you know, understand and everything. . . . They're actually *more* serious than a lot of the [white] students that I even hang around with. . . . They're very focused. . . . [It's] like [a] tunnel vision type thing, which I have [myself] . . . and . . . I admire that. . . . Maybe that's . . . because . . . [people] expect minority students not to do as well as [whites], and these people are so focused [on] proving them wrong. . . . Like, when somebody tells me I can't do something, I *wanna* do it, and I just wanna say, "Here, take that."

And while racism might make it harder for blacks or Latinos to feel at home at UIC, several of the men interviewed had observed a good deal of white-on-white tension as well. Asked if he'd had any firsthand experience with interracial animosity at the school, Marc Huston talked about the tensions between Jews and Palestinians.

The only thing I've ever been a part of on this campus that was racially motivated was at a Palestinian birthday party—or an Israeli birthday party—[where] I was a body-guard to one of the shahs who came in. . . . It wasn't really a bodyguard, we just had to sit on stage and make sure none of these Palestinian people charged the stage. . . . And then they came outside and there were all these Palestinians chanting and they're all wearing turbans and dark sun glasses and they were throwing rocks.

Rick Skilling tried to put a more positive spin on things.

All that stuff you see over at the [student center]. . . . You've got the Palestinians on one side, the Jews on the other. . . . You go over there some time; it's usually in the fall, when they got all the newbies, all the little freshmen and everything. . . . They got nine or ten different ethnic groups there trying to recruit everyone, you know. . . . I've had a couple of [white supremacist groups] try to recruit me 'cause of my [blond, flat-top] haircut. It's just kind of funny, 'cause one time . . . [there was] the PLO, or some sort of Palestinian organization . . . [with] a Jewish organization about two booths away from 'em. I thought they were gonna start throwing Molotov cocktails at each other. . . . It was actually kind of nice to see that everyone would get their two cents in, but. . . .

Greg Bogosian had found one of the student center's dining facilities "very cliquish." With few identifiable fellow-ethnics—"There's not an Armenian *anything* on this campus"—he had apparently been adopted by one of Chicago's largest ethnic groups.

> There's, like, certain parts of the room where, if you're not black, you just don't sit in. And vice versa. I mean, if you're not white—generally, if you're not Polish— which I'm not, but I just happen to be part of the group—if you're not Polish . . . everybody, like, looks at you funny. . . . And then, along the entire wall . . . 90 percent are just Hispanic, Latino. And then, on the opposite side, you've got the— I don't want to say Palestinian, but the Middle Eastern ethnic groups sitting over there. . . . I mean, it's something that an anthropologist or a sociologist would, like, love.

And it was Steve Clayburgh's perception that

> *Every* person here is likely to encounter [hostility], not just centered around black and Latino . . . [but involving] every sex and ethnic background that you have on campus—everyone. . . . Everybody has segregated themselves so much on this campus, everyone is open, I think, to an equal extent. . . . I've seen it on campus with Lithuanians and Italians. . . . Not to the large extent that I've seen it between blacks and whites. . . . They didn't come to fisticuffs or anything. But there has been some resentment. That's why . . . there's so many segmentations, Polish, Lithuanian, Palestinian, Jewish, black, Latino.

So even if blacks and Latinos were likely to experience some degree of hostility from students of other backgrounds, or to have to work somewhat harder to adapt to college life, *anyone* might have the same problems fitting in and feeling accepted in this new environment. Life was like that. If you were old enough to go to college, weren't you old enough to cope with that? Shouldn't college-age blacks and Latinos be able to unload any emotional baggage they'd brought with them and not let it compromise their performance or stunt their aspirations?

On one hand, Hal's support for race-conscious admissions seemed to flow in part from a more tolerant attitude toward adjustment problems among young people generally. "There are always some, you know, uncalculated and incalculable factors you just work in. . . . Like maybe they've just gotten their act together, and they discover that in law school, instead of getting their act together in junior high or whatever most people do." Likewise, Phil Zeckman was sympathetic to what students fresh out of high school might be up against, and compared blacks' and Latinos' situation with his own. Like most rural, working class, German Catholic Iowans, Phil explained, his extended family had little experience with higher education and he knew firsthand how hard it could be to overcome childhood conditioning not to broaden one's vocational horizons too far. In Phil's case, some of his customers at the social club where he worked had encouraged him to aim higher. Likewise, race-targeted outreach to black or Latino undergraduates could be

> very important. . . . If they're still very young in college, they're still developing, [and such a program] gives them a sense of hope, as in, yes, they *can* achieve this. I never thought I could get into law school, 'til recently, [when] people started talking to me, you should go to this school, you could do well, you know. . . . It's letting those students who may be struggling, who may think, well, I'm not gonna get there, I might as well just give up, that, well, maybe they *can* get there.

Closer to graduation, however, there was a general expectation that the most deserving blacks and Latinos would have gotten past such barriers. Isaac Fedelovich, for example, allowed that

> There are some programs provided for minorities to help them go through these [college] years. Well, they're not available to whites. . . . It's fine. It helps [blacks and Latinos] go through some hard times. . . . [But] by the time they're done with college, they're pretty much at the same—they have an opportunity to be at pretty much the same level as whites. And that's why I wouldn't . . . pay too much attention to their ethnic background when they go to graduate school.

Willing to pay substantially more attention to race than Isaac was, Matt nonetheless raised a similar argument when I raised the question of test bias. Cultural bias might be difficult to avoid at grade-school level, he reasoned,

> because *then* the child is only pretty much subjected to, you could say, his own little world of family, whatever . . . [which] might be vastly different from the way a test is written. . . but I don't know if [cultural differences] would have as large an effect . . . [on] the LSAT. . . . There's cultural differences, especially in language, between blacks and whites. But by the time someone's twenty-two, twenty-three, they're at least familiar with, you know, quote-unquote standard English.

He was also concerned that minority applicants with *excessively* low grades might nonetheless be admitted to law school, even though they obviously

> weren't very serious academically . . . [and] might not make the best of the opportunity. . . . We're talking about people that are probably twenty-two, twenty-three years old. And they should be trying to get good grades in their undergraduate work. And if they haven't, then . . . regardless of their color . . . going to law school wasn't really a priority to them.

Opponents of race-conscious admissions, of course, were less generous and less ambivalent. Pat Gaheogan recognized that blacks and Latinos might have special needs as college freshman; but "after the freshman year, you know how to take college classes, and you know where to go for help," obviating the need for many kinds of race-targeted interventions, including outreach by graduate professional schools. "In high school, I had no idea what I wanted to do," Pat conceded; but once in college, "I guess by then you know what you want to do. And if you don't, you're spending a lot of money to find out." Jack Uberhof questioned even race-targeted recruiting by graduate business schools. "I think if the person wants the education, and is really serious about the education, he's gonna look for it. I don't think you need to find these people." Likewise, Jeff found affirmative action admissions completely unnecessary because, "If anybody has what it takes, at that point [in his or her life], they're gonna get there."

Do Unto Others: *The delicate balance between individualism and empathy*

Can every college student who "has what it takes," as Jeff McEwen put it—the brains, the energy, the commitment to succeed in an extremely demanding, high-status profession—actually "get there"? Just how autonomous are we? Talking about success and failure, Dan Lysenko sounded very much like Ralph Waldo Emerson or Rudyard Kipling:

> I guess the people that I think are real successful didn't expect anything automatically to come to them, they didn't feel they were owed anything, and they just—they risked [losing] everything to get something more, and they repeatedly did this. [The less successful would say,] "I expect this promotion to come," and it would never come, and then they'd get upset, they'd get bitter, I guess it would snowball from there. . . . [The key element] is kind of, like, the willingness to accept the risk and be responsible for yourself, and that's it.

Success, in other words, and the potential for future achievement were very much a matter of individual willpower. For affirmative action advocates as well, this individualistic worldview was not easy to breach; but they nonetheless made greater concession to the weight of so many blacks' and Latinos' past experience on their perceptions of the present and future.

Rick Skilling, for example, made some interesting observations about the degree of substance abuse and gang violence in a Chicago Housing Authority complex adjacent to campus:

> Sometimes I don't understand where they get that from; they're in a bad position and . . . they make it worse. . . . I think the violence is part of the position they're in. They don't have much, so if they see something that they want, what have they

got to lose, really? To go to jail and watch cable TV? . . . Drive down Roosevelt Road here [just south of campus] . . . and [you] wonder what makes people do what they're doin', you know, five o'clock in the afternoon, drinkin' a bottle of malt liquor.

I don't know. I often think to myself, if I was in that position, what would I do? I'd wanna get the heck out of there. But then again, like I said, they might not *know* any other way. To them it's all concrete and buildings, projects. . . . People have to overcome where they come from, whatever their situation is, but, to be honest, I don't know if I could make it out of somethin' like some of the projects and everything. . . . I don't know if I could make a judgment like that, 'cause I haven't really been there.

Doug agreed, "It's easy for me to sit here [and say], 'Pick yourself up by your bootstraps and get going.' But it's hard for—if I was in a different person's situation, you know. . . . We [whites] have sort of a privileged [life]." Mike explained further,

Just coming from my own experience, I know that if you push hard enough, you can get stuff done. . . . But then again, you have to have that in your mind*set*, that you can do it. I mean, if you're not accustomed to that way of thinking, you're not going to think that way. I mean, I know people who have, you know, the first thing goes wrong and they go, "Hell, it's not gonna work," you know. . . . I think to a certain age . . . the environment that you're set in will *form* the way that you think.

Opponents, moreover, seemed less sensitive than advocates to individual differences between one black or Latino and another, and to the need to pay attention to those who lacked *extraordinary* resilience to what might be going on around them. Sam Turner, for example, argued,

When in society has it ever been different? There's always been a group that has been, you know, there's *tons*, hundreds, especially in American . . . of rags to riches stories, where everything was stacked against this person, but they tried to make a difference, and they gave it their best shot. And that's all you can ask, really.

But Joe Murtaugh—no slouch on self-reliance—took a different tack.

Everybody has obstacles [to overcome], but I think some of the obstacles that people overcome are unduly forced on them. I mean, people look at Whoopi Goldberg. She was on welfare at one time. . . . I think she did a really great job getting everything together. . . . [But] comin' out of that slime pit's a heck of a journey, you know. Not everybody's gonna make it who *could* make it. . . . I think it's right that we throw a rope in there and help pull them out.

Regarding the need for same-race role models or service providers, opponents were once again often unable or unwilling to take psychosocial factors into account. "I just don't understand," Bill Sajak told me, "why a black person or a Latino needs a role model like that. I don't know why everybody has to feel so different about themselves." Asked to consider the advantages to blacks and Latinos of access to more minority doctors, Zack Pritchard acknowledged, "It's true that the patients and doctors might respond better to each other. . . . [But] the job is, the patient's sick, you want to get them better. Whether it *feels* nice [to the patient] is not a real big question for me."

Advocates, by contrast, were more likely to take other people's perspectives into account. Sean Hanna explained that for black or Latino patients, the advantage of better access to minority physicians was "very subtle. In terms of better care, it may be marginal. . . . I don't think there would be a vast difference, but there could be. . . . [And] who's to say that's a marginal difference for the patient?"

As for minority encounters with racist whites, advocates and opponents were in agreement that blacks' and Latinos' *perceptions* of racism often seemed exaggerated in relation to its objective manifestations. But the staunchest advocates nonetheless seemed much more willing to *legitimize* those minority perspectives. Past experience had made blacks and Latinos "more sensitive" than whites to interethnic hostility, Matt Vigoda argued, "and I think a lot of white people don't understand it, 'cause they haven't gone through it." On the job, Mel Gibran explained, racial discrimination "might not be something [that] an employer . . . realizes that they're doing. Like . . . they might just be favoring people and not be realizing it." In college classrooms as well, "I'm sure there are a lot of things . . . that . . . we [whites] probably wouldn't notice . . . [that] a minority student might take objection to." From this perspective,

> racism is very prevalent. . . . It might not always be, you know, . . . stated outright. . . . It would probably be one of those indirect things . . . but I'm sure they feel it—looks, things like that. . . . Some black people tell me about certain things that . . . offend them. . . . A few incidents [that] have happened at school and . . . that seemed minor, you know, to somebody else, maybe to a black person or a Hispanic person . . . are very offensive. And, you know, we might not be able to understand it, but we should try to, anyway, at least listen to their point of view.
>
> It wouldn't be, like, . . . somebody gave you a look or something . . . and you go home and, like, feel sorry for yourself the rest of the semester and have horrible grades. But I'm sure . . . [that] indirectly, it probably affects somebody. . . . Psychologically, things bother people. Things that I've encountered have bothered me, and I can't say they affected my grades or affected any aspect of my life . . . [but] maybe . . . they did, and . . . I never realized it.

Indeed, minority *perceptions* of fairness were one of Hal Voorhees's criteria for the achievement of racial equity generally.

> If another white male . . . gets into graduate school [and] I don't, I don't think they were culturally biased . . . they simply chose him 'cause he had better results. . . . [But if] the white gets in and the black doesn't, even though I may have had better scores, [the black] may believe it was simply because he was black. We have to get beyond that point. If blacks believe that they lost out . . . [only] because they just weren't as [qualified] as the person next to them, that's your ultimate goal.

Were some of the affirmative action opponents I talked to simply less empathetic, less good at putting themselves in another person's shoes, so to speak? Much more likely, I think, they simply didn't feel that they *had* to. As just cause for race-conscious policies, opponents seemed to make much more of a distinction between relatively concrete barriers to achievement—for example, lack of access to good schools, or bias in hiring or promotions—and the *internal*, psychological barriers to achievement that followed from a history of these insults. To the degree that they recognized the need for some collective effort to correct for barriers of either sort, opponents were also more likely to question whether colleges, universities, and their graduate professional schools should be expected to take that burden on.

4

WHITE MEN'S BURDENS

Allocating Affirmative Action's Costs

PETER GALOSZY: THE INVISIBLE HAND

I say, let the market prevail. . . . Whatever happens out there in the market when you let it run would be the best distribution ever. . . . If it happens [that] the smallest . . . group of this earth ends up with 99.9 percent of the wealth . . . because of their capabilities in a free-market system, then let it be so.

The most ardent free-marketeer in the bunch had spent a working-class childhood in what was then a communist country in Eastern Europe. At fourteen, Peter Galoszy had immigrated with his family to Chicago, where he'd attended one of its most multiracial, multi-ethnic, public high schools. For reasons he didn't care to go into, Peter had been on his own since his midteens, supporting himself as a carpenter and carpet layer, among other things. At the time of our interview, he was a twenty-five-year-old business major, employed by a Chicago consulting firm and looking forward to a career in hotel and resort management.

As for affirmative action, Peter actually thought of himself as a potential beneficiary, one reason he had checked off "other" as his racial/ethnic background on my questionnaire. Swarthier than Greg Bogosian, Peter argued that he was of a darker hue even than most Americans of Mediterranean or West Asian descent; so

> To categorize myself as to a certain race . . . [is] kind of weird for me. . . . My family is much lighter-skinned. . . . My mother is probably as white as any Irish lady would be; [but] to categorize *myself* as "white" or "Caucasian" would not do me justice. . . . By not . . . checking . . . [that] box, that might have some businessperson say, "Okay, we have an opportunity to hire a minority other than black or Hispanic." . . . I can always take the argument I am a smaller minority than [they are].

His experience as an immigrant, moreover, had left him with a good deal of empathy for the special difficulties blacks and Latinos might face as college students.

> Of course. It's part of the cultural—it's part of the style of the classroom and the culture. I cannot expect every time my wife of two years [says] something to me, to completely understand *her*. Because she *does* come from a different cultural background, even though . . . I do have pretty good command of the English language. . . . [Sometimes] friends . . . maybe, like, sixth, seventh generation Americans . . . would say something to me, and I would have to sit there and think, "Now, what did that person mean when that person said that?"
>   I recognize how special a problem it was for *me*, and not only the language. . . . One [feels] pretty awkward whenever the environment is different than what the person's used to. The manner of speaking, the tone of voice in conversations, the way people look at each other, the way people dress, the way people do things—everything is different. . . . It is pretty hard for *every* [new student] . . . and especially for those [minorities] that come from predominantly black or predominantly Latino high schools. Where they have probably never had . . . students in the classroom [from a different background], now they come to a university that is so diverse, that covers almost every country from the globe.

Outside the classroom as well, they might have a greater problems than most whites with

> the way *things work* in a university, the way you have to go to . . . Admissions and Registration in order to register for a course. And the way that you even have to approach a professor or an instructor. . . . I think that this would be a bit harder for *any* student . . . if the student did not have any training, or did not have any experience, in *change*. If things were so constant in their life that they did not experience much change at all, the period of adjustment . . . is that much harder. . . . Things in [black and Latino] communities are pretty *constant*, and they do not endeavor out of their community too much.

Likewise, he had little doubt that the GMAT might contain enough cultural bias to disadvantage blacks or Latino with less of a general knowledge of middle-class, mainstream American culture.

> When [my wife] reads certain novels that are written here in the United States, she tends to understand them better [than I] . . . maybe . . . because of the total of her experiences . . . the books she has read, the stories she's been told, the whole life experience that she's had. If I would be pinned against her in a . . . competition . . . on these type of novels, *of course* I would feel that it is biased against me. Because why are you giving me a test about this type of stuff? . . . That's what I would probably *feel*.

But Peter was a champion of self-reliance. Among successful people of any race, "the will to do any one thing or to achieve any one thing is so strong that you can overcome whatever barriers come in the way. If the will is there, the person succeeds." While attending college

> *might* be harder [for blacks or Latinos], I think it is one thing that each student has to brace him- or herself [for] when they start . . . at a university. . . . I'm pretty sure there are students that are deeply affected by [racism] in a negative way, and I'm pretty sure that there are quite a few that would rise up to the challenge. . . . Because it is a challenge. You know, whatever your goal is, whatever obstacles come in the way, if you are willing to achieve that goal, you will try harder.

And while blacks or Latinos might indeed require special incentives or special help to meet that challenge, top-down efforts to reallocate opportunity were unfair and ill-founded. "You're [making a] special effort to recruit a certain group, you are incurring a special cost in doing so. . . . To take the tax-payers' money or the tuition money that's being paid and to say, 'Okay, we're going to *favor* a particular group,' seems pretty bad to me." If the goal was to undo the economic and social consequences of generations of interethnic hostility, then top-down solutions were just as counterproductive in the United States as they had been in Eastern Europe.

> What we've been calling Yugoslavia, ever since the end of World War II, it's not "Yugoslavia." It's a whole bunch of different countries . . . different people with different cultures and different religions. . . . We *forced* these people . . . to be one country, and that is the same way we are doing it in the United States right now. We are *forcing* [people] . . . to tolerate and not distrust others. And that cannot be *forced*, that cannot be put into *law*. It has to come from within. And if we're going to suppress people's feelings and attitudes about each other, to the degree that they have been suppressed in Yugoslavia, we can expect to have the same kind of outbursts in the future that we see right now in Yugoslavia.

Besides, top-down affirmative action was simply not needed. Peter did not object in theory to a concentration of wealth and power in the hands of a single ethnic race or ethnic group; but now that official barriers to greater equality of outcomes had been set aside, the very diversity of America's consumers and its workforce virtually guaranteed a growing proportion of graduate-trained black and Latino business executives. The invisible hand of the free market would set things right.

Peter agreed with Joe Murtaugh that maximizing morale and productivity among a multi-ethnic workforce more or less demanded greater numbers of minority managers at every level. Peter could certainly see himself taking ethnicity into account when it came time to hire managers for one of the heavily minority departments of a hotel or resort, "if I have . . . two individuals with equal footing, equal standards, everything else is equal, *but* I can reasonably and logically say that one of them is going to work with these people better." As businesses sought to hire more graduate-trained black and Latino executives— whether to enhance productivity, or for other sound business reasons—they might push MBA programs to further diversify their enrollments. "I'm the business person that's telling the MBA program, 'Hey, get some black people into the program, 'cause I need a black person to head my construction site,' or whatever." But business schools did not need a double standard to do the job. "If there is a big enough demand in the market for [black MBAs], then this will work itself [out] *in the market*, and there *will* be [black] people coming out for the MBA program. Because I know, as a black person, if I try my *hardest* to get into an MBA program and to complete the MBA program, I *know* that I am in high demand, and I will be paid well."

Of course, that might take more than raw ability and hard work. MBA programs were subject to market forces, just like their applicants, and that meant turning out graduates able to hit the ground running for whatever firm hired them. From this perspective, familiarity with the dominant culture was certainly a valuable asset, and thus any cultural bias in the GMAT was not necessarily an illegitimate measure of MBA applicants' potential, "If that *is* what the school is [deliberately] testing . . . if that is their choice."

On the other hand, as long as their criteria remained formally race-neutral, business schools had every right to adjust their criteria in a manner that tended to increase diversity. "If the school itself . . . comes to the decision that they would prepare students better for the work force through a certain type of education, and . . . they would be better [off] screening candidates [a different way] for the type of education that the school would like to provide . . . *then* it would be fair," as long as "it would be implemented in an acceptable way." For Peter, as for Pat Gaheogan, that meant rigorous quantification—taking into account the difficulty of one's previous jobs, for example, as well as the number of years and months and hours-per-week worked.

That is after all consistent with the free-market principle of transparency—that is, the free flow of accurate information. Peter wanted the line between admits and rejects to be perfectly clear; in fact, if Peter was in charge, standards on each of several criteria would be specified in such a way that *all* applicants who met those standards were admitted, and all others refused. Likewise, he felt that any changes in the weighting of criteria must be made

> with enough advance time for those students who are thinking . . . of attending that school to say [to themselves] . . . "This *is* a better choice than the other choices that are available, and now I will concentrate on those things that are required to get admitted" . . . [or] "That is not anymore . . . what I want, how I want to prepare myself." In that case, Don't apply *there*. Go to a school that does not give priority to that. . . . If you let the free market prevail, and if there is a demand for a different approach, then a supplier will come along.

To considerable degree, Peter's was the neoclassical economist's universe of autonomous "rational actors," responding to the inexorable laws of supply and demand. Differences in achievement motivation, he attributed to "individual differences . . . in personality." But he also understood the role parents played in their children's achievements. "Sure, there are instances—and I know people that sort of had it made throughout their lives, in that all doors were open and things were pretty much handed to them." But much more commonly, it was a matter of molding one's children's work habits and aspirations. From what Peter had learned of his Scandinavian American wife's upbringing,

> Nobody in her family ever said [it] to her directly, but . . . what she understood was expected of her . . . [was that] after high school, you go to college. . . . [Maybe] in a different culture . . . even if it's not spoken . . . [children get the message,] "Well, just don't get caught by the truancy officer, 'cause I don't want to see him, but otherwise you can do whatever you want to do."

In a sense, though, families and even ethnic communities were also players in this free market, so there was nothing unfair about a system that tended to favor the offspring of those families or communities that did a better job. If "the strength of one's honor in an Oriental culture definitely is higher than . . . in . . . any other group in the United States," and if this and other values tended to inspire exceptional performance, then "to *not* discriminate" in favor of those imbued with those values at an early age, "to not say that, 'Yes, that *is* a better value system than not caring *anything* about positive values' . . . would be [like saying,] 'Well, you know, who's to say your values are better than mine? . . . But, you know, give me half of what you make, because you make more money than I.'"

Considering the possibility of race-targeted university outreach to school-children, Peter was willing to bend the rules—just a little. "I do believe that the children at a very young age that have, maybe, some backgrounds that are not very competitive with the rest of the children their age, maybe they should be helped to get out of poverty." Keeping that going through high school, let alone college, however, Peter saw as reverse discrimination. The real burden lay with the black and Latino communities to reverse the vicious cycle of despair and underachievement. "If [a minority students'] organization arises out of [their interest in] a better adjustment for entry-level students, and is supported and managed and administered *by* the students," for example, "it is wonderful."

And they wouldn't have to go it alone. "Private donors . . . is really the way to go for all these programs. You will always find private benefactors that would be glad to promote the same things that the group is promoting. And they would be willing to give up a good portion of their salaries on an annual basis or on a monthly basis to promote those things."

As for Americans in general, "We have to take into account that we *are* human beings, and we are not perfect in being able to *not* discriminate." It was not the place of governments or universities, moreover, to enact policies that essentially *demanded* from Americans generally some compensatory action for a long history of racial injustice. What was a legitimate demand was simply for everyone to follow, *henceforth*, the Biblical edict of the Golden Rule. "If I treat each and every person that I come in contact with, no matter where and how, as I would want that person to treat me, then I don't need affirmative action laws. I don't need some weird admission practices in order for [blacks and Latinos] to have an education."

For along with a free market for goods and services, capital and labor, was a free market of ideas and ideals, whereby the actions of morally autonomous *individuals* would inevitably move things closer to a vision of social justice most consistent with the community's bedrock values. So we needn't worry, for example, that inner-city youth might not even *know* about those free-market incentives for blacks to earn MBAs. "Whoever would be the person that would give me that argument . . . [I would tell them], 'You don't need to get paid by anybody, you don't need to be supported by anybody; if you are that concerned about that, you would take the bus to that neighborhood, and you would tell that person yourself.'"

ROB INGRAHAM: A THOUSAND POINTS OF LIGHT

I'd like to be actively involved in a lot of things in the community . . . medical things, everything. If I could do it all, I'd run for mayor. . . . Maybe it's because I'm young and inexperienced . . . [but] there's a lot of things that need to be straightened up—things that don't seem right to me. . . . I would like to see . . . why [certain] things are happening . . . and if I don't like it . . . work with others . . . [to] change things.

Rob Ingraham had chosen UIC for the quality of its pharmacy program but, after working part-time as a pharmacy technician, had switched to pre-med. Twenty at the time of our interview, Rob had grown up in a small Illinois town about two-and-a-half hours southwest of Chicago, where he was still involved in the volunteer ambulance corps, and where he eventually hoped to establish a practice, either as a GP, internist, or general surgeon.

I could picture Rob ten years later, say, as something like Dr. Brock in the television series *Picket Fences*—or like Dr. Torvalsen, railing against the powers that be in Henrik Ibsen's *An Enemy of the People*. While he seemed unwilling to go into detail, I doubted he was as confident as Peter Galoszy in the benevolence of an unconstrained free market, which might help to explain his desire to be involved in government along with other kinds of community service. But *big* government, he didn't trust. "If I was president of the United States," moreover, "if I was dictator of this country, I would outlaw quotas and things. . . . Two wrongs don't make a right. You can't sit there and preach about being victimized and . . . downtrodden and . . . discriminated against, and then turn around and do it to someone else."

As for medical schools, "When you look at the grand scheme of things and social justice and the whole society, I don't think that that should be an obligation for the medical school admissions committee." It's only real concern should be, "Who is gonna make the best doctor. . . . [Blacks and Latinos] *earn* their way in. . . . That way . . . it's fair, and you don't have to worry about incompetence. I mean, survival of the fittest."

Fitness, of course, was not just a question of grades and test scores. "There's more to being a doctor than simply having all the statistics logged in your head, and being able to remember everything that you've learned." It was Rob's understanding that admissions committees had already broadened their criteria, "because they're finding that they're getting doctors who get up and . . . can't communicate with people, and yet they're supposed to be someone that deals with people every day." Moreover, "There may be a reason that my grade point's lower than Joe Schmoe over here: Because I work forty hours a week when I'm in school, I have three kids, and who knows what. And actually that type of person may be more desirable for med school because they're more mature, they've seen more, you know? I mean they're more likely to succeed. They're more motivated. . . . And if [such criteria] happen to bring in more minorities, then that's great."

But Rob shared Len Hellstrom and Steve Clayburgh's concern that the use of criteria not easily quantified would hardly eliminate the question of racial bias.

Really, the problem just goes down the line. Now the pressure's gonna be on what kind of people are gonna be on that board that decides [who is admitted]. . . . Now, do we have an even split up of the different groups in this board? Because really, then, it's becoming an opinion type of issue, and people are gonna say, "No, that was an all-white board, there's no way that's gonna be fair." And they'll argue that forever.

Rob was not unsympathetic to the social benefits of enrolling more students from low-income communities. "There's underserved communities every-where, and maybe if you can get your generally more poorer society into med-ical school . . . encourage them to work hard and work for it, then they would go back and give to the community, you know?" And he had no objection to medical school outreach designed to provide kids in those communities with more information about their options, since "your upper class, whether it be black or white, they've been exposed to it through their parents." But he wasn't very optimistic about how much outreach could do. "Sometimes, I mean, what are you gonna do when—You can talk 'til you're blue in the face to a kid, and he's gonna do what he wants to do. It's up to the person to make their decision. If their priorities are messed up, then their priorities are messed up."

Would increased numbers of minority physicians help to provide com-pelling role models? That depended on how visible they were. An MD would give a ghetto or barrio native the financial wherewithal to move someplace better; so "what are the chances of this black physician being involved in a [low income,] predominantly black neighborhood here? . . . His kids aren't going to that school; he's not gonna be actively involved in that school, in the commu-nity in that sense." And society at large no longer owed blacks or Latinos pref-erential treatment.

[Before] we got rid of segregation . . . blacks weren't treated equally. They didn't have the opportunity to go to school. They weren't giving them equal opportu-nity, okay? . . . As far as blacks are concerned, the sixties weren't too long ago, when you had all those problems. . . . And so you had a generation of blacks who weren't given that opportunity, okay, and then they grow up and they have kids, and their children are higher up, but not quite there yet, you know? But now, I think that the black people my age, I think that it's—we're even. I think we're fair, you know?

Likewise, there was no reason for minorities to seek black or Latino physicians, since whites could be counted on to provide them with first-rate care. "It wouldn't matter who walks into the office . . . and I would expect it wouldn't to my doctor. I mean, when you get to that professional level, you know. . . . I can't see that that has anything to do with medicine."

And if blacks and Latinos *were* to receive special treatment, Rob himself certainly didn't deserve to have his own chances compromised on that account. If there was more of a tendency for minority youth to experience family problems, for example, "then *I* am a minority, then I should be given a special consideration, too, because my parents are divorced, you know?" Programs designed to help blacks and Latinos become more competitive were at least preferable to any form of target or quota because "I at least do have a shot" at besting them in that competition. But

> When you're talking about reserving a spot in a class for a minority student . . . I don't have an opportunity for that spot. I don't even have a chance for it. . . .
>
> I've had to work every day since I've been in school. . . . I've had no special breaks, no special privileges. And there's more of me than there are of the [white] guys that have had [them]. . . . And I'm the guy when you—whom you let them in for, you know? And that's my concern.

NICK DELEO: MARRIED TO THE MOB

> This is not an equal society we're living in. I have advantages that I know some other people don't. . . . [Blacks and Latinos] don't have the same chances that are afforded to myself and people of my race. . . . Inner-city schools are just substandard to those in the suburbs. . . . For the last two years, I've lived right on Racine . . . two doors away from Robert Taylor Homes [public housing project]. I know what goes on . . . around there . . . [and] a lot of it has to do with white suburbanites like myself being apathetic.

The day of our interview, things were looking up for Nick deLeo. Currently employed as a bouncer at a campus-area watering hole, just a few days earlier the twenty-two-year-old senior had accepted a promising management-track job at a major pharmaceuticals house. But while he was looking forward to taking a year or so off from his studies, Nick still hoped to become a physician. "I don't really ever remember wanting to be anything else."

At sixteen, Nick had been "taken under the wing" of an MD geneticist treating his cousin. He'd worked part-time in his mentor's lab for a few years and could see his own future in genetics research, although sports medicine and trauma surgery interested him as well. Despite some useful contacts, however—in addition to the geneticist, "my mother's friend's sister is good friends with somebody on the admissions board at Columbia University in New York"—medical school was hardly a sure thing.

Clearly more sympathetic than Peter Galoszy or Rob Ingraham to the obstacles facing black and Latino medical school aspirants, Nick opposed race-conscious *admissions* of any kind but approved interventions with minority undergraduates and strongly endorsed outreach to minority-majority public schools. "It's not, like, we're coming down for you," which is how Nick viewed race-conscious admissions; "It's, like, we're bringing you up to us. And that way it's gonna make for a better—you know, more competition is better for everyone concerned."

It might also help to dissipate both black insecurity and white racism, which Nick had encountered literally in his own back yard.

> I won't let it go on in front of me. . . . I would never let somebody, you know, start doin' that to another person while I'm around. . . . Last week, we had a [high school] graduation party for my sister, and it happened. . . . I dealt with it. . . . There was a black DJ, and [a white boy] yelled something and I grabbed him. . . . The kid was told in no uncertain terms that that was not tolerated in our house.

Race-targeted interventions, however, could have positive social as well as educational outcomes. "That's when this whole racism thing is gonna end. Once the [minorities] start thinkin' that, 'Hey, I'm just as good' . . . and then the white believin', 'Hey, I'm no *better* than,' that's when it's gonna change." In contrast to Peter and Rob, Nick saw such changes as a legitimate function of higher education.

> This is supposed to be getting us ready for the real world. I think part of the real world is that everybody is gonna have to learn to get over this color barrier thing. . . . One of the nice things about being [at UIC] is that I was exposed to cultures that I never was, you know, in my suburban [upbringing]. . . . There's been a few [racial] incidents in the dorms in the past couple years. . . . But I think this campus is a lot more tolerant than other campuses that . . . my friends go to. . . . Just because we're . . . where we are. . . . It's accessible to so many different neighborhoods, and it's not expensive, and . . . you can commute, so it's kind of like a big melting pot.

Diversity on campus was clearly a good thing, and in Nick's view, so was greater diversity in medicine. On the question of whether it would help to ensure better care for minority patients, however, Nick seemed to make a fuzzy distinction between how things were and how things ought to be: "I don't believe that at all," he insisted. "You take that oath that says you treat everybody equally. Those people—and there are doctors out there that do—that give less—that aren't, you know, comprehensive to blacks—they should be *out* [of the profession], outright." The argument for a more diverse pool of positive, professional role models, Nick saw as ultimately counterproductive. "I can see where . . . young people are gonna look up to somebody their color. But that's gotta be overcome. You know, they should look up to somebody not just because they're the same skin color; it should be because of they want to do what [the role model is] doin'."

But more generally, Nick was all for intra-ethnic self-help. "There're certain black neighborhoods that are, you know, just real respectable . . . that are . . . being taken back by the people that live there . . . [because] people are tired of seeing gangs and everything." And while he endorsed outside interventions, he also told me that it was "up to the individual cultures . . . to get to that standard" of excellence required to expand entrée to the profession *without* race-conscious admissions to medical school. He had mixed feelings about certain groups who had achieved this: "From the [Asian American] people I know, they're pressed more. . . . It's a high stress, living in those families." But he couldn't quarrel with the results, even if it led to *over*–representation in medical school: "They've got . . . drive . . . more of it than the average white person. They're doin' what it takes. . . . So I don't see any problem with that."

Nick himself was half Sicilian and half Tuscan; and in contrast to the largely positive stereotypes that East Asians had acquired in the second half of the twentieth century, Nick felt trapped by some very negative stereotypes that his own ethnic group couldn't seem to shake. Early on, "pretty much the same" as Latinos, Italian Americans has suffered discrimination largely because of "the color thing" and some distinctive facial features, although "I *really* don't think [it was] to the same extent as a black person has to [deal with]." These days, however, it was Italian Americans' behavior that drew ridicule—from Mel Gibran and Dave Zaluba, for example, and even from Nick himself. "Down here," on a campus adjacent to a largely blue-collar Sicilian American neighborhood, "I'm almost ashamed to admit I'm Italian, because these people are not the same kind of Italian. . . . They're the Taylor Street Dagos . . . they're looked down on by—See, they're almost like an undesirable." I tried unsuccessfully to get Nick to be more specific.

It's just the way they act, the way they—You know, it's just not representative of what—An Italian heritage is very proud, culturally rich, not, you know, it's not *like* that. . . . And they, like, *espouse* that they're Italian. I lived with the [the son of an Italian Consul] to Chicago . . . for two years, and he's embarrassed to even *think* that these people call themselves Italian. He's from Rome and he's, like, my God, I can't believe this.

Despite evidence to the contrary, moreover, Nick insisted that Italian Americans' connections to organized crime might seriously compromise his own career.

Nick deLeo: There's still jobs that I'm locked out of. I certainly am not gonna go east and be a part of anything of importance out there, that's for certain, not with my last name.
Helen Lipson: What do you mean? The president of Yale [Bart Giamatti] is Italian American.
ND: But look at [former New York State governor] Mario Cuomo. He could never be in the White House. . . . Na-a-ah. They would never let him in.
HL: There was an Irish American president.
ND: And they were goin' crazy over that.
HL: You don't think an Italian American could be elected president?
ND: Not for a while. No. Because there's such—there's that strong thing that every Italian is a gangster. You still hear it, to this day. . . . I get it in my [suburban] neighborhood now, that my dad's a gangster. If he were a gangster, we wouldn't be living in this neighborhood! You know, I could never be in the FBI, or anything like that. You know . . . maybe . . . way back, my family was. . . . I don't know, but that's being prejudicial against me, though, isn't it?

Relative to other whites, moreover, Nick felt he was also disadvantaged by geography. "I could have pulled A's throughout the whole, you know, 5.0s through every semester . . . with an incredibly high MCAT score, [and still] wouldn't have got into anywhere out east, for the simple fact that I'm going to a midwestern university, and they can't have any of that over there." But his biggest problem with getting into medical school, Nick freely admitted, was his own GPA.

Nick seemed to have mixed feelings about the importance to medical schools of quantifiable criteria, including MCAT scores based largely on the knowledge base acquired in one's pre-med courses. On one hand,

I'd be real scrupulous [as to] the person that had the real high [MCAT score]. I'd want to make sure that they were a *real* well-rounded individual, that that's not all they know. If I brought up, "Who's Babe Ruth?" at this interview and somebody that got [perfect] scores on their MCAT, they go, "U-u-uh," you know. If you're [just] locked in a room [studying], you're not gonna know very much about people.

And that could be disastrous.

> I have a seven-year-old brother. Two weeks ago, he had a pain in his leg, [and] be-
> fore my mother even left [his office], the doctor told my mother that my brother
> might have leukemia, before he did any tests, anything at all. . . . It was on a Fri-
> day, and she was an absolute wreck all weekend. . . . I'm, like, you're never tak-
> ing him back there again. . . . [The test] came up negative. Everything was fine.
> He had, like, pulled a groin muscle, and this guy was diagnosing leukemia. . . .
> They're around it so much, they just turn it off, and you have to turn it off, as far
> as yourself goes, but when you're presenting it to the family of the person, you
> *can't* be unsympathetic, you can't be cold, you gotta be, you know.

I was sure one of the reasons those pharmaceuticals people hired him was
that Nick seemed to have people skills to spare, along with a lot of energy, a
keen mind, and all that lab experience—things that should help to make him
an excellent doctor. Nonetheless, "I was never really good at just sitting down
and memorizing everything," which explained his lackluster 3.4-out-of-5 gpa.
    I was that kind of student myself and was ready to be genuinely sympa-
thetic. But Nick *refused to complain* that this emphasis on rote memorization
might have dimmed his chances. At the end of the day, in fact, everything he
understood about ethnicity and any other influences on achievement seemed
to fall by the wayside.

> I would think the person who's gonna do the best [in medical school] is gonna be
> the person that wants it the most. . . . Evidently I didn't have the drive enough,
> or else my grades would have been better. I was brought up—I was taught that I
> could do anything I want, if I want it bad enough. You know, that's idealistic,
> whatever, but I believe it's true . . . and if I don't get it, it's 'cause I didn't want it
> bad enough.

Likewise, even white-on-black racism "*could* have an effect" on academic performance, but "they shouldn't let it. . . . If it does, then . . . it's a problem with
the student. . . . Their drive isn't there."
    This disjunction in Nick's view of things was too obvious and Nick too sharp
for him not to notice it himself. "As far as I'm concerned, everybody's got the
chance [to succeed]. *But* I don't know, maybe they don't, you know?" Equality
of opportunity "would be, everyone gets the same chance from the time they're
born until the time they die. . . . I don't know how it would happen. . . . It's
an impossibility, really." Real merit was not always rewarded. "I know [white]
people that are hardworking as anything, and they can't get a break, and then
there's the people that just, you know, come out smelling like a rose every
time."

Nick knew, moreover, "I'm not comin' from the point of a black American, or a South African black. You know, they're *not* accorded everything that a white person is." *But that wasn't Nick's fault.*

John Smith, way back when, or whoever it was, they've [discriminated] for centuries and centuries. . . . [But] I wasn't brought up that way. I don't want to be punished for it. . . . My mother and father have never discriminated against anybody, okay? . . . I was brought up that everybody's equal, and that's the way . . . I treat people . . . and that's . . . [how] I want to be treated.

The bottom line? "In my world," at least, "everybody's got a chance." And that meant taking your lumps—be they race, ethnicity, region, or even an excessive demand for memorization—*as long as everyone else did, too.*

I'm not saying, *I* should be the white guy that's gonna get in. . . . [But] If I'm gonna get beat for something, I don't care if you're black, blue, brown, green, purple, whatever, if you're smarter than me, if you're more qualified, then, fine. . . . but the color of your skin should have no bearing. . . . That's why I wanted to do this interview.

THE BUCK STOPS WHERE?

Peter Galoszy, Rob Ingraham, and Nick deLeo were very different men, with disparate frames of reference for tallying affirmative action's pluses and minuses. But their bottom lines weren't too far apart: Whatever exceptional obstacles to achievement a long history of discrimination had placed in blacks' or Latinos' paths, these had already been overcome, *or could be*, without any special costs to whites like themselves, in terms of opportunities that were rightfully theirs.

Nick's rationalizations and outright hypocrisy may strike liberal readers as more disturbing, in some way, than someone who—like Peter Galoszy or Rob Ingraham, perhaps—"just doesn't get it," or quite honestly doesn't give a damn about equality of opportunity in a diverse society. For me, though, Nick conveys with especial clarity the kind of ideological juggling these interviews seemed to evoke from at least a dozen of the most thoughtful, most articulate men interviewed—up and down the policy preference spectrum— in their efforts to square their all-American sympathies for the downtrodden, and what they had already begun to learn about the "real world" they would inhabit as grown men, with what they'd been brought up to believe about open competition, fair redress, and the payoffs of talent, self-discipline, and hard work.

Some of these three men's principal concerns, moreover, were shared by most of the others: All thirty-two had come to resent what they saw as a common assumption that white males are by definition liable for keeping women and minorities down. And few failed to point to *self*-help—on the part of families, communities, and ethnic-specific organizations—as especially crucial to minority advancement. At the same time, there was a good deal of concern that affirmative action might entail unacceptable costs to white-majority institutions, whether in terms of monetary expenditures, human resources, or campus climate.

Mission Control: *What is college for?*

> If you walk ten minutes away, you could be killed for your wallet by people who would want your wallet because they're feeding their kids. I don't know what [the University of Chicago's] Pritzger Medical School's *doing* about that. Maybe they're trying to recruit some minorities. . . . Maybe they just tell everybody where they can park their car safely. . . . Probably more like that.
>
> —Len Hellstrom

I doubt Len had ever had the patience to read word for word the first few pages of any college or university's catalogue. Somewhere in those first few pages, virtually every school in the country says something about its commitment to public service, to the community in which it was located, and perhaps even to a better world. This has always been part of the justification for diversity, affirmative action, and related policies; and most of the men I talked to seemed to regard the advancement of racial equity as an entirely appropriate objective.

Like Len, Doug Peruggia seemed to feel that an urban university's very proximity to an urban underclass made it intolerable not to work for change.

> [Minorities] may have resentment. I can imagine being—having spite. And— I mean, [UIC's] neighborhood is—it's ridiculous. . . . Look at this university, world-class university, standing here. You have some of the smartest people in the [academic] profession in this neighborhood. And yet some of the poorest people in the country, two blocks away. The guy that lives across the street is making, you know, six digits. Now, how would you feel if you were that child living in the ghetto?

Dave Zaluba spoke to the broad-scale, salutary influence of a school's general commitment to social justice in its classrooms and elsewhere. "The people who are going to help represent the country . . . [are] being groomed by these universities," and one's moral and political perspectives "tend to grab the flavor

of wherever you are." Matt Vigoda agreed, and felt that "People are most impressionable, most likely to learn the most when they're in college. So I think
it's the perfect place" to expand their perspectives. Rick Skilling suggested,

> Actually, we could have a whole class on what took place in L.A. [after the ac-
> quittal of white police officers who had beaten Rodney King] or you could study
> that for a whole semester. . . . Let it be known that [discrimination] is taking
> place. You know, I came from a pretty nice white suburb and everything, and I
> always thought—I took it for granted that everything was equal, but I've since
> found out that it really isn't.

Like Nick deLeo, several men stressed the positive influence on race relations of university students' first-hand exposure to members of different
ethnic groups and socioeconomic strata. Jack Uberhof's class-targeted model
of affirmative action, he pointed out, would not just benefit those from less
privileged backgrounds. "The ones . . . from the silver-spoon background
could also benefit by having someone from a different ethnic or black—you
know, something that they might not be accustomed to or familiar with, and
that would broaden their horizons, too." Like the time Phil Zeckman had
spent living in inner-city Baltimore with his brother and African American
sister-in-law, a diverse campus was "a learning experience . . . you just can't
get from reading a book." For similar reasons, Len thought "medical students of all kinds" should have some of their clinical training "in the worst
ghettos in the country."

But not everyone regarded racial amity or the advancement of social justice
generally as appropriate goals. Greg Bogosian, for example, felt that marginal
equality of access to what teachers and textbooks could offer was as much social justice as colleges and universities should provide: "What schools are there
for is education . . . for everyone that wants it . . . across the board. . . . I'm not
here because I want to become more—because I want to achieve a higher
level of social equality with my fellow student. I could care less about that. I'm
here to learn." Like many state and federal justices addressing the issue over
the past three decades, Dan Lysenko was a strict constructionist, with no patience for admissions policies designed to advance equality of outcomes in the
larger society unless one could "prove that there was systematic denial" on the
part of *that* school, *in the recent past.* Gil Jarreaux felt that college students
and graduates of color had no right to expect the same concern for their special circumstances that they might have enjoyed in high school.

> In America, at least, I think that's a *right* to, you know, go to four years worth of
> high school. . . . [But] when you're talking college and graduate school, that is
> something you pay for, that is something which comes down to the line of money,

and, you know, it's cutthroat. High school is not cutthroat. College and graduate school I think have to be a little more cutthroat.

Race-targeted outreach was a somewhat different matter. Even Gil had no problem with pure-and-simple recruiting of black or Latino applicants and was obviously less convinced than Peter Galoszy that the free market ideal of "perfect information" was being met.

> On [broadcast television] channel 32, there's, like . . . some secretarial school, and they target toward blacks. And they say, 'Yes, you too can be a secretary,' and they show this white man in the background looking approvingly at this black secretary. And that makes me sick. . . . I wish Harvard . . . could target [commercials] toward black female students and say, "Hey, you get your MBA from Harvard, and you can run your own company." But . . . Harvard wouldn't advertise on 32.

Larry Dobbs, of course, didn't see the distinction Gil did between primary, secondary, and tertiary education, and felt that the latter, "because they are the end of the chain, and they rely so much on what is produced from the beginning . . . have a responsibility to go backwards—the same as businesses have responsibilities to promote colleges and high schools, because those are [educating] the workers of the future."

On the other hand, several other hard-core advocates of affirmative action admissions questioned the expenditures that such supply-side initiatives might require. "With the money crunch," Phil explained, "there's a lot of things you can't do that we would like to do." Likewise, Isaac Fedelovich endorsed such medical school outreach in theory; but as for whether he'd go ahead with it, if he were Dean, he admitted, "It's really hard to tell. . . . I don't know what kinds of problems the deans face. . . . Probably money's the first one."

Unless private donors could foot the bill—donors who would not have contributed the same amount of money for other purposes—it was difficult to argue with Greg's assertion that any outreach programs would to some extent be "something that was *paid for* by . . . tuition from whites, blacks, Spanish, and everybody else." Like staffing its classrooms or equipping its computer labs, social justice had a dollars-and-sense price tag, and medical schools, law schools, and business school would inevitably pass those costs along, either by taking more out of the pockets of students, parents, and taxpayers, or by transferring away from other uses some of the money that those parties or private donors had already contributed, along with some of the talent, technology, and other resources that their money had purchased. Even Len recognized that medical schools are "designed for a particular purpose . . . and there isn't any more effort left, any more resources . . . if they're doing their best job of turning out good doctors."

While it won more endorsements than any other policy I presented, technically race-neutral changes in admissions criteria, or in their weighting, might be too costly as well. Sean Hanna, for example, understood that the model of admissions he'd proposed—observing each medical school applicant in some clinical setting for a period of time—"would be very expensive. I mean . . . [we're talking about] this ultimate or whatever, but I don't know that that would be feasible." Any substantial shift away from quantitative criteria toward life histories, interviews, work histories, references, and so forth, Steve argued, entailed "an administrative cost of saying, 'How the hell are we going to handle all these different variables in there?' . . . You could detract from the graduate education process . . . and . . . neglect the actual teaching of the student . . . because of resources are tied up in something that they don't need to be tied up in."

A handful of race-conscious admissions advocates agreed with Peter that private institutions deserved more leeway than public ones to set their own agendas, which might or might not include social justice generally or racial equity in particular. For Joe Murtaugh, "Private institution? I don't care what they do. I mean, they can make all their own rules." That didn't change when I reminded them that even private universities receive a good deal of government funding, in the form of student aid, research grants, and other assistance. Phil considered,

> It really depends upon the extent of aid they get from the government. I mean, if it's *super, heavily* subsidized, the government should demand some—it's, like, you don't contract something out to a known, like, racial bigot. You know, if [Louisiana politician and former KKK member] David Duke owned his own construction company. . . .Whereas state universities, being a public agent, they have the responsibility to look after the overall—I don't want to say welfare, [but] the overall *care* of the society that they are serving, and therefore . . . to help those who cannot—who [are] otherwise unable to help themselves.

Larry felt that "universities as a whole neglected the responsibility" to advance social and economic justice. But because public primary schools, high schools, and universities were "all paid for by the same people," those universities had a special obligation to engage in affirmative action outreach. Hal Voorhees, on the other hand, raised an interesting question as to just how public institutions' social missions were decided—and whether there was enough of a consensus behind them to justify doing much of anything of consequence.

> As far as private colleges go . . . they can make their own choices. But . . . public colleges—using, you know, my money and your money—I mean, whose social justice, really, are we gonna use? Will we use Jesse Jackson's or David Duke's? . . .

You would need to boil it down to some sort of consensus . . . [which is] either gonna be one so general you can't do anything specific about it, or, 2, it'll be so specific and so benign.

Common Ground: *The perils of marginal inequality*

The problem was that the closer one looked at the specifics of any given policy, the less "benign" it appeared to be. Race-conscious admissions and off-campus outreach involved some serious trade-offs, not only with respect to access—How far should strict, marginal equality be compromised in favor of cumulative equality, or the long-term benefits of diversity?—but also with respect to the diversion of resources away from direct services to a given school's own student body.

In neither case, however, was any current student actually denied anything offered to other students enrolled at the same school. That was precisely the case, however, with much of the race-conscious programming that might be employed to help prime the pump for graduate professional study. Not only might this be inequitable on its face, but such efforts could work against just the sort of long-term objectives that a diverse campus was supposed to promote.

Several men alluded positively to ethnic-specific organizations and related cultural programming at UIC. Having gotten to know a good many blacks and Latinos through his involvement in campus organizations, Steve Clayburgh felt that

Blacks [and] Latinos being more involved with their culture . . . [will] do better [academically] *because* they're aware of their culture, and they'll carry the burden on their shoulders of *proving* their culture. . . . I have met a disproportionate [number] . . . that do strive to achieve an academic background *because* of the color of their skin, because historically they have not been able to do that.

Jack Uberhof had grown more sympathetic to black and Latino separatism after listening to a classmate in his honors seminar on moral reasoning.

This black guy mentioned that *he* favored an isolationism type of thing. . . . Because of what's going on [inside them] . . . the inner hatred, inner self-destruction . . . they needed to break away from [white] society that imposed these innuendos . . . to regain their respect for their heritage. Because once they regain respect for themselves, then they'll be able to—not *assimilate* into the [mainstream] culture, but . . . be able to work along with [that] culture. Because you can't really respect anything else until you respect yourself.

But outreach or interventions targeting minority undergraduates on the same campus was something else again. Doug Peruggia found such programs "fairly acceptable" in theory, "[but] then—I just—it's inviting problems. You know, little things here and there. . . . What if I wanna go, too, and I'm not Latino?" Steve was concerned with "programs even *inside* law schools here in Chicago . . . that are not open to white students. Things like, [minorities] have private tutors. You have special meeting sessions with professors. That is not fair to the [white] student that is . . . at the same level as a black student." Pat Gaheogan's brother-in-law was a good example. "As a law student, he asked for help. And to go into the study groups. But because he was white, he was not allowed, until he failed. . . . The white students there just did their own thing." He attended some of the voluntary, self-run white study groups, "but when he started having more individual problems and you're falling behind, you can't drag those other people along with you."

One of the celebrated advantages of campus diversity was to bring whites and minorities together, to help bridge the barriers of race and class that had helped to block minorities' opportunities for so long. Having achieved diversity, however, if a school were *then* to target blacks or Latinos for the sorts of "special benies" Joe Murtaugh referred to, that would simply "promote splits," as Pat argued, and thus in the long term defeat the school's purpose in doing so. "It doesn't bring anybody together. It just says, 'Okay, you're black' . . . or, 'You're Hispanic, and now you get this stuff. You're white, you don't get it.' What's gonna happen? Everyone's gonna break up into little groups."

On similar grounds, Dave felt that race-specific student organizations as well were, to some degree,

> counterproductive . . . to [their members], to the whites, to the culture as a whole, if you're forcing that—that difference, that being separate, and you're not sharing. . . . I don't believe that they should *have* to get together in their own black groups. . . . There's a bunch of black organizations [outside of academia] . . . and I feel a lot of them are good, especially when you look in their neighborhoods. . . . But when you start looking into this college . . . and there's these groups . . . like the black student government group or something . . . they're making so many segregations that they're *drawing* these differences, they're drawing things apart. I don't think it's good. . . . I think that's in every culture . . . but the ideal is that you don't *want* that to happen. . . . These groups should be out there helping them intermix and getting *over* these barriers and getting to know each other.

Bill Sajak had a more distinctive viewpoint on "intermixing" as the solution to racist inequities.

> For as long as we have affirmative action, then everyone will feel themselves as a separate race, okay? Someday, we're all going to be the same race. . . . I think it's gonna be more than a hundred years, but . . . the world's getting smaller, and

everyone's, uh, finally mixing. But for as long as we have affirmative action or things of that nature, then we're going to have racism, prejudicedness, and people wanting to stay within their own race, and people thinking differently about each other. So the sooner we take away special treatment to minorities, the sooner they will not be considered minorities.

Full equality, in other words, could not be built on anything less than genuine fellow feeling, the perception of "them" *as part of* "us." So the proliferation of race-targeted solutions could easily become part of the problem. Ghetto and barrio kids, Sam Turner observed, "don't grow up naturally" as underachievers, suspicious of whites. "They're taught what the real world is by the people that bring them up. . . . [And] if there's somebody saying that the real world is a black and white issue, then they're going to be growing up in anger, you know, forever, and they'll never be open to change." Even Len Hellstrom was not entirely comfortable with any of the affirmative action policies he endorsed partly because, "People learn to be good, you know? They learn to look at each other . . . as this group or that group, as my people and those people over there; or they look at each individual more or less evenly, and I'm being treated fairly on the basis of my abilities and qualities."

That was one of the reasons Steve regarded affirmative action as "a necessary evil," given "the incredible amount of problems that quotas present for people" and the degree of "animosity" race-targeting programming evoke. For that reason,

> Whatever type of affirmative action plan you have . . . [the school] should have an education program that's just as strong, directed towards everyone, that says why we are doing this. . . . Because if you do not say that. . . . If you don't educate people on *why* it is you are giving [members of certain groups] special privileges, then you are doing more of a harm because of the attitudes that are perpetuated through white students being neglected. . . .
>
> I don't think it should be in one particular class, but that might be an answer. Equal opportunity class. Pluralism class. Whatever you want to call it. But I think a *better* way is to meld that into people's educations, like it has been in my curriculum [in the College of Business]. And you do not do this on the basis of lecturing; you allow exchange of ideas. Which most of the classes I've been in, you know, we have some pretty informative discussions, that I've learned from somebody who's black and who's Latino views that I never even knew about. But I think you need to provide an opportunity for that exchange to take place.

There is still the question, however, of just *who* should be expected to foster that sort of exchange or to follow through on other facets of on-campus efforts toward greater diversity.

Do Your Own Thing: *Recognizing the rights of faculty and the obligations of minority communities and families*

Critical to the kind of interracial classroom exchange Steve Clayburgh had in mind, obviously, were university faculty. They might also be major players in on-campus or off-campus efforts to "prime the pump"—if, that is, they chose to get involved. Clark Kerr's famous caveat about the difficulties of "herding cats" is often borrowed to describe other kinds of organizations, but it still applies best to universities, whose faculty are notoriously jealous of their autonomy and their time. Len Hellstrom's biggest concern with the viability of many kinds of race-targeted interventions with undergraduates—for example, special presentations, research internships, or field trips to various units of teaching hospitals—was that those favoring such programs "would have to get the [medical school faculty] to do it. If you [could] . . . organize the people and go out and do it, that'd be one of the best things about it, and it's the most difficult. I don't know many professors who would be *willing* to do that."

Just as different schools had different missions, different individuals within any given institution might have somewhat different missions, and these were to be respected. Pat Gaheogan had no problem with recruiting law school faculty to get involved in race-targeted interventions or outreach, "as long as it doesn't affect their job." Whether the issue was racial equity or some other social justice issue like homelessness or world hunger, Sam Turner saw the university's proper role as providing *opportunities* for student, faculty, or staff involvement. "You can't force it, but if you make that possibility available, it's really up to the person, how they're going to react."

As Sam saw things, this was not simply a question of freedom of action; for like Peter Galoszy, he drew an explicit connection between his policy preferences and his religious faith. The son of overseas missionaries and a self-described born-again Christian, Sam felt that the salvation of societies, as of individuals, lay in spiritual rebirth, a shedding of old skins and old habits. "Maybe it's idealistic, but I think it would be great if we could look at it from the perspective that every day is a new day." And "it's never a new day" as long as public policy and the public conscience remained focused on past sins. Not every serious Christian I talked to agreed: It was Hal's reading of scripture, for example, that encouraged a more liberal stance on affirmative action than most of his conservative Republican idols. To Sam, however, marginal equality on the part of the state, at least, was not simply good social policy but *God's law*.

Greg Bogosian, too, saw individual virtue as the solution to social injustice, and like Peter, he faulted affirmative action advocates for imposing their agenda on others. "If every single person just was fair and nondiscriminatory, you wouldn't have any of these problems. Everybody's saying, well, 'What can *you* do to help?' They're not saying, 'What should *I* do?' . . . Everybody's sitting here pointing their finger when, you know, the first person they should point at is the person in the mirror."

Less for ethical than for political and economic reasons, Steve felt that certain kinds of special opportunities for future black or Latino lawyers and MBAs should be sponsored by the private sector. A mentor program, for example,

> would still need a particular budget, but the majority of it, which would be *donated* time, donated effort, corporations I would think would do nothing but target these things, maybe pay for it outright just for corporate good will. . . . And it does more to enhance society . . . [if] people are willing to spend private dollars on this. . . . [showing that] people are willing to do this outside of an academic environment. It's the *essence* of it really, really working.

But "self-help" on the part of minority students or off-campus fraternal organizations won especial praise. "I know there are black engineering societies that [students] started," Pat recalled, "they asked faculty to come in and help them, I think that's great." Once again, part of the problem was money. Phil Zeckman, for example, felt that blacks' and Latinos' biggest source of frustration at UIC was that they lacked the resources to "maintain an identity they would like to maintain"—but that this was unavoidable, since those running the university "don't have the ability to cater to everyone's cultural background."

Steve Clayburgh agreed that each racial or ethnic minority had a right to "a certain place" on campus in which to maintain their identity, but he felt that it was up to ethnic-specific fraternal, religious, or community organizations to help make that happen. Hillel House and the Newman Center, for example, were on campus because the larger Jewish and Roman Catholic communities

> have chosen to have that. They've made the effort to get that. . . . I don't think the responsibility is on the university. To some extent I do, provided you can release certain resources, yes, I do. Because when they do that, it starts to erode some of the stereotypes and feelings that people have of racism, and [improves] the social environment as a whole. But I think the majority of the onus should be on their own people that would like to have that . . . like the American Negro College Fund, and the Latino Centro Corporale. . . . The biggest extent of [the responsibility], I think, falls on those groups themselves.

Elsewhere in these interviews, several other men emphasized the role of ethnic communities in fighting discrimination against their own members. Like the Asian-Americans cited in chapter 3, Jewish Americans had been able to "foster themselves along," Jack Uberhof noted, despite persistent, ubiquitous anti-Semitism, through a degree of "synergism" that black and Latino communities lacked. "You gotta fight [discrimination] by any means necessary," Tom Sorbo argued, even if that meant a "Mafia type structure," which (out of earshot of Nick deLeo, fortunately) he cited as a mode of communal advancement among Italian Americans. Mike Benedetto explained,

> When Italians came over, Polish came over, you could say now that the Arabs are coming over, they tend to band together very tightly. When an Arab guy owns a store, he hires Arab people to work in that store. His brothers come over, he lets them work in his store, he helps them set up for a while, and there's a sense of strong community. . . . When blacks make money, they move *out* of the black community . . . they don't pump their money back in to the society which they came from.

Of course, successful fellow-ethnics could supply not only seed money for business ventures, but models for academic achievement. With this in mind, Phil was concerned that a growing number of black and Latino lawyers would have little influence unless they

> keep their own heritage. . . . If you go into the Jackson Park-Englewood district on the south side, look how many law offices there are: relatively zero. And a lot of these kids don't come up to the north side, they don't come downtown, and if they see a law offices building, they don't know that there's any blacks inside that building. . . . I myself, if anyone from that region [of rural Iowa] I grew up in . . . wanted to get out . . . [and] come to Chicago, I would be more than happy to . . . not necessarily lift them up and take them by the hand, but at least show them which street to walk down. . . . A lot of blacks making it out of so-called ghetto communities in the inner cities aren't giving back *to* their community. . . . A lot of it may be just economics. Maybe they just spent all this time to . . . "beat the system". . . and if they moved back, they would be negating all that. . . . [But blacks and Latinos who] grew up in these streets [and] were able to overcome, like, the poverty cycle . . . should help others.

As cited in chapter 3, a handful of men argued that the race of kids' role models was immaterial; but others argued that the direct participation of black or Latino professionals was critical to maximizing the impact of any sort of outreach to schoolchildren. Tim Kovacs, for example, agreed with Steve that it wasn't nearly enough to *tell* kids how to get ahead, without adults from the same kinds of communities "that they can look up to . . . instead of drug dealers . . . [so] that . . . they're able to say, you know, 'I would like to be a doctor, 'cause I see . . . Dr. Smith, he's somebody I can respect and . . . he's doing well.'" Larry Dobbs stressed that high-visibility black or Latino athletes or entertainers weren't nearly enough:

Michael Jordan going into an inner-city neighborhood, telling black kids to study hard is a moot process. . . . He's one of the finest basketball players to ever live. [But] a black kid that looks at him is not gonna say, "Well, Michael got to where he is because he studied," you know? . . . Michael Jordan *can't* say . . . "You can be like me, if you work hard." That's not true. That a purely physical talent. . . . [But when] a black lawyer comes in and says, "If you do these things, you too can achieve what I have achieved," it's a true statement. One look at that, then you put the effort into it.

In Larry's view, seasoned executives and professionals who had benefited from race-targeted policies themselves "owe it back to the society that put them through school" to get involved in that kind of outreach, "especially if they went on student aid, or if they went on a grant." Likewise, black and Latino schoolteachers in the inner city should do more than "just . . . get everybody to the next level." He especially admired Jaime Escalante, whose work as a math teacher in the East Los Angeles barrio was depicted in the film *Stand and Deliver.*

> He *expected* his students to do this, this, this, and this, and changed the system to accommodate *them.* . . . Each [student] had their own problems . . . not all of [their parents] supported what they did. But there was this one [teacher], this one driving force that said you *do* this, you achieve this, I'll get you a college education. And it worked for all of them. It was a tough struggle for him . . . and [involved sacrificing] a lot of his own personal well-being . . . but he nailed himself to do it. That's what I think the whole system is lacking, that kind of drive and leadership.

Current college students from those neighborhoods might be especially effective role models, in Larry's view, and should be expected to do their part.

> How're they gonna pay for themselves when they get [to college]? Well, you simply have to go *back* to the same high school they came from and have *them* teach that math course to those seventh and eighth graders. . . . And this is how they make their money going to college. . . . It's much better than that person working at JC Penney's ringing a register. . . . [This way,] nobody's getting a free ride. I mean, they're getting a student loan, yes, but they're giving something back to the same society that gave it to them.

Phil as well felt that community service was "something that you could maybe tie to financial aid." Black and Latino applicants might be offered a quid pro quo: "Hey, we'll give you a scholarship as long as you promise to do so much community service in these communities that need services." While he knew that "the volunteer army fights harder," Len jokingly suggested making community service a requirement for any university subsidies to black or Latino pre-med societies. "Do you want to form an organization? You have to go to a high school and talk to students."

Ideally, though, the strongest motivation would come from those students' own families. When I asked these men why they thought some ethnic groups tended to be overrepresented in the best graduate professional schools, I also asked them if they thought this was fair, or if they felt that some *upper* limits should be established. As I'd expected, no one did: Rather, they saw the success rates Jewish Americans and Chinese Americans, for example, as object lessons in how to succeed. "If they spent, you know, 90 percent of their childhood life and adolescent life . . . studying," as Dave Zaluba put it, "and they worked that hard, they should be able to get in, you know? And if you're gonna have blacks that are gonna spend that much time, good, more power to you, you can get in, you know, and there should be no limit." Larry was adamant:

> You have a member of the population that is achieving above and beyond another group, then you don't take *away* from that group. You look at what they're doing. . . . You'll see Asian Americans very, very adamant about their children doing very well in school. You don't take away from that. You simply tell the rest of the population, if you want to achieve the same way—Society only gets better as it's forced to change.

As I note in chapter 2, Larry's prescriptions for advancing equality of opportunity focused largely on parental influences on school achievement. But he never offered this linkage as a reason for educational institutions or society at large to back off from affirmative action. Others, however, seemed to suggest exactly that. Hal acknowledged,

> There's real validity in saying, "We're going to allow you in here and let you have a chance.". . . On the other hand, though, . . . it seems like the rewards of clean living are being diffused. . . . Why should a nuclear family work to stay together, when, you know, any social benefits or whatever are only going to be compensated for later if they were not together?

Joe Murtaugh seemed to be on the same wavelength.

> Maybe the reason I did better [in school] was that my parents would beat me when I walked in with bad grades. . . . They didn't beat the hell out of me, but, you know, I was *in trouble*. . . . So my parents took more of an active—My parents were doing things to . . . increase where I was gonna be in life, and what the quality of my life would be. They spent that time, I spent that time, and I think that [under affirmative action] . . . I think I'm gonna wind up with somebody in class next to me, who's not prepared to compete with me.

It is often argued that opposition to affirmative action is rooted largely in an excess of "individualism"—that is, the belief in "making it on your own," climbing out of poverty "by your own bootstraps." What I was hearing from some of these men, however, was something else: an acknowledgment that individuals were indeed the products of their environments, including their families and ethnic communities—along with the view that it was counterproductive, or even unfair, to strip these *smaller* collectives of *their* accountability for the life chances of their members. As Greg put it,

> That's your *personal* family. I've seen black families—I have seen friends that happened to be black, and their grades are, like, far and above my own. This one guy . . . I didn't know him too well, but he always ranked in the top four people in my [high school] class. He was black. He was in a bad neighborhood. But the point was, he *wanted* to do the good grades, his parents wanted him to do it. You know, they're just using, well, "I was black, it's not fair," that's just an excuse for not wanting to try hard enough.
> [Conversely] you can't punish [a white student] for having a good home life. . . . If [blacks and Latinos are] going to blame anybody . . . don't blame us [whites], blame your parents. They were the ones that didn't care enough about you. Or maybe not that they didn't care enough, but, didn't put forth the effort, you know. . . . It's like you're taxing white students because of the fact that their parents tried harder.

What Color Is Your Bootstrap? *How much should affirmative action cost individual, nonracist whites?*

Whatever its costs to the schools that practiced affirmative action, the men I talked to seemed to take for granted that, not unlike sales tax, most of that cost would be passed along to students, their parents, and other taxpayers, in the form of dollars and cents and in the form of lost opportunities. Most advocates of affirmative action would point out that these places never belonged to whites to begin with, and that it was several generations of ill treatment at the hands of whites that kept a larger proportion of blacks and Latinos from being *able* to "earn their way in" *without* any special consideration: Thus any costs to whites of race-conscious policies might be justified in part as fair compensation for what whites' behavior and past policies have cost minorities. Indeed, a number of white and minority academics have written books and offered courses designed to raise whites' consciousness of the privileges they have enjoyed by virtue of their race, and hence their complicity in a racist economic and political system.[1] Did the men I was talking to think of themselves as privileged in this way?

Although obviously not "advantaged" in the usual sense of the word, when Dave Zaluba considered the question "from their point of view, you know, you [white] guys have so many more advantages up front. . . . Yes, I [had] more advantages." Attending an all-boys Catholic high school, "I know I got a better education than some people in the Chicago public school system," Charlie Kilgallen told me. "And I think I was fortunate enough to have a dual-parent household, dual wage earners . . . and I know a lot of people that didn't have that. So I consider myself lucky. . . . I'm not sure if it gives *me* a leg up, [but] I think it might actually detract from people that *didn't* have that." Also a Catholic high school graduate, Pat Gaheogan explained,

> What [affirmative action admissions is] doing . . . is saying, "Okay, you have to be better than the next guy, but in certain ways you can't compete with the next guy." . . . I may have gotten a better education than someone in a Chicago public high school. I took all my sciences. I took four years of English, and then I went to college, and I've had no real problems, and I've worked hard. But other people who don't have those tools may not be able to compete this way.

Those "other people" arguably included other whites—among them, perhaps, men like Rob Ingraham, whose concerns about being "the guy . . . whom you let them in for" might be right on target. As mentioned in my introduction, one likely consequence of affirmative action is a transfer of some quantity of opportunity away from the *least* privileged members of the dominant ethnic group. Some of those with relatively affluent backgrounds, however, seemed to be in denial regarding their own reliance on the advantages that had conferred. Zack Pritchard, for example, was majoring in the same field that his father worked in, but he insisted, "If I let my dad help me get through college, my degree would be worth less to me, knowing that . . . I didn't do it on my own." On the other hand, he seemed to have no compunctions about using his connections to medical school. "I think I'll get accepted at more than Rush [University], but . . . that's the one place where I do know one of the doctors. . . . My chances are better there than anywhere else, I think." Despite his arguments for "survival of the fittest," you may recall that Gil expressed no sense of guilt at working the system to his advantage, notwithstanding his own upper-middle-class background and no real *visible* markers of racial minority status. Drew Kazinksi, as suggested in chapter 3, may very well have benefited a good deal from his father's professional connections; and while he downplayed the importance of role models, numerous references to his current supervisor made it clear that the man was a valued exemplar and mentor.

A few men seemed to more or less equate the legacy of racism with other kinds of handicaps that got in the way of their own progress in certain areas of endeavor. "Everyone has things that give them a hard time," Zack pointed out. "Like, there may be some things I can't do at 5'8" I wish I could do. I have to deal with that." Two inches shorter than Zack, Greg Bogosian may also have been a frustrated NBA'er.

> Your problems may be a different *type* of problems than mine are. . . . [I could say] "I want to be six foot, so you *have* to let me play basketball on your all-black, six-foot-nine basketball team." . . . Tough luck. You know, if I was good enough, if I could make the shots, I could jump as high as them, great, you know? Just because we have problems, you can't go crying, "You have to take care of it for me."

Certainly, none of the affirmative action advocates interviewed would have thought much of Greg's comparison. But whatever advantages they had enjoyed relative to blacks or Latinos, however extraordinary the barriers those groups had encountered, not one of the men I interviewed felt that affirmative action could be justified simply on the basis of unfair treatment to generations past. Neither did any of them regard himself as party to collective guilt in that regard; none seemed to view himself as liable for whatever advantages his own racial identity might have bestowed, or what his quality of life might owe to the exploitation of other racial or ethnic groups.

For Bill Sajak, the question of collective guilt as a basis for collective accountability was very simple: "I don't agree, because *I* don't discriminate." The notion of affirmative action as fair redress for white racism Greg found "totally horrible, because they're going to discriminate against me . . . just because of somebody else's racist activity five years ago, or even six months ago." "Things like the Civil War," Sam Turner told me, "I had nothing to do with that. I wasn't the one with the slaves or anything, and I don't think you can just keep holding that against people and—I mean, where's it gonna stop? When are they gonna be satisfied? . . . Let's put it to rest."

Clearly, most of the men had heard this sort of argument before. Dave was tired of hearing, "'You *owe* me because of the slavery.' . . . I'll tell you, my ancestors . . . came *way* after that." He was impatient with "blacks' attitude of white original sin. If you're born in America, you have the original sin where you are responsible. And even people that root back to the beginning of America. . . . I mean, it's so many times removed, these people [alive today] had nothing to do with it." While some of Hal's ancestors had helped to colonize Massachusetts, none of them had been slaveholders, as far as he knew. "Very likely, there has been plenty of discrimination in my family since then," Hal admitted; but "racism is absolutely heinous to me," and he objected to any rationale for affirmative action that made it sound like, "I'm being punished for the sins of my father."

For Steve Clayburgh, the notion of guilt by association hit a little closer to home. "My family roots go back into America in the 1740s. . . . My family fought the Revolutionary War." Distant relatives included James Madison and Patrick Henry. "And my grandmother can remember playing with her great-grandfather's Confederate war uniform." Like most middle-class southern families, Steve's forebears had owned slaves before Emancipation, one reason "that I was ashamed of being a Southerner" growing up. But none of that baggage gave him any personal sense of guilt, or in his view, any greater responsibility for righting past wrongs than other Americans. "*I* am not responsible for my *father's* attitudes . . . [or] my *brother's* attitude, and [they're still] alive. And they are four generations removed from people that owned slaves in our family." Moreover,

> Because I am a white male . . . I take offense at being considered the one, uh, white sexist pig that kept somebody down. . . . I pride myself on *not* being racist. I pride myself on not being sexist—and I might have to work at that, because I was brought up in a racist white society . . . but to deny *me* something for the sins of, say, my grandfathers . . . I think is wrong.

But this sense of personal innocence did not keep Steve or fifteen others from embracing affirmative action even when the stakes were at their highest. Liability lay with a political, economic, and educational system that, in turn, rested on an implicit social contract whereby *Americans in general* were accountable for making good on. Given *their part* in this social contract—regardless of their own innocence with respect to ways it had broken down—they saw no reason for colleges and universities or other government agencies not to enforce policies that might demand the sacrifice of some opportunities that might otherwise have been theirs.

Even Joe Murtaugh, at his most racist, seemed to allude to this kind of collective when he argued that since blacks lacked an adequate work ethic, "*We* need to find a way to get black people to work" [italics added]. Dave was as leery of the efficacy of public school reform initiatives as any conservative, and all for self-help—in conjunction with a healthy dose of public funding.

> Throwing money at [elementary] schools isn't gonna do it. . . . You walk outside [those schools] and what do you see? You see rundown buildings, you see empty lots, you see litter all over the place, graffiti all over the place, I mean, what kind of impression—What kind of hope do you have in this kind of upbringing, you know? You can do *so* much with getting people together, pull money to groups that'll clean that up . . . get the kids who are out there gang-banging—or get 'em before they start gang-banging, and pay *them* to start cleaning this place up. And now not only [does] . . . funneling money into their pockets keep them off the street selling drugs . . . you're also making the community they live in more positive . . . and it feeds on itself. . . .

You know, we send billions of dollars into other countries. We put billions and billions of dollars into defense, and into politicians' pockets. . . . They're [always] playing with the laws to benefit big businesses and stuff like that, and . . . doing things that are unconstitutional. Com Ed [Commonwealth Edison, Chicago's supplier of electric power] . . . you know, they lose a . . . fair increase one day, they file for another one the next day . . . figuring . . . eventually the increase is gonna be passed. . . . [If] these politicians worked . . . as hard [for] these neighborhoods . . . it'd be a lot better right there, you know. But, no, they don't *give* money to these depressed neighborhoods, they give the money to big businesses. [People in these neighborhoods] got so many things stacked against them, and you just wanna, like, just scream or just jump on and strangle these politicians, or slap people and wake them up.

But this assumption of collective accountability demanded that one set aside his everyday notions of just deserts.

A Notion at Risk: *Juggling affirmative action, individualism, and the social contract*

> See how the fates their gifts allot: When A is happy, B is not.
> Yet B's deserving, I dare say, of more prosperity than A. . . .
> If I were fortune, which I'm not, B should enjoy A's happy lot,
> And A should die in misery—That is, assuming *I* am B.
>
> —W. S. Gilbert, The Mikado[2]

Most of us have little trouble finding a rationale for policies that benefit *us*. What affirmative action required of young white male advocates, on the other hand, was some rationale for approving policies that, *in the short run at least*, not only offered them no benefits but might very well exact some costs, at least in relation to the everyday conventions of fair play they'd grown up with. But advocates' judgments on fairness—and what fairness demanded of *them*—weren't about the short run. And despite their allegiance to the same norms of procedural fairness as opponents, their calculations of fair play were much more complex than that, and they saw the urgency of those procedural norms as much more contingent on real-world conditions and the competing claims of marginal and cumulative equality.

One way some opponents may have sidestepped those complexities was to calculate their own "fair shares" in upholding the social contract without regard to the failure of so many other people, past and present, to hold up their end of the bargain as well. It may have been more than a turn of phrase when Nick talked about affirmative action in terms of how people were treated "in my world": For despite his obvious familiarity with racism, and what struck me as a sincere desire to counter its impact, when it came to race-conscious admissions, Nick seemed to limit his own obligations to the sort of simple, Golden Rule reciprocity that would be demanded of him in a better world.

In like manner, two other opponents seemed to address the benefits of diversity in a similar manner: that is, in terms of what *ought* to be needed. "I think there's jerks out there who have problems with—between races," Zack admitted, "but . . . I don't think it has to be that way. . . . I don't think they have to get worse care. . . . I can treat a black person just as well as a white person." Sam's response was a bit gentler and more evenhanded. "Idealistically, I would say that I don't think it should matter [how many physicians are African American or Latino]. . . . In all the education that a doctor's had, [I hope] that they can view their patient as a patient and not as a color. . . . I'm not into the medical profession right now, so I haven't seen a lot of what would be my peers. But I'm optimistic, I would hope that would not be the case."

But advocates and even some of the more moderate opponents would have none of this. Hal Voorhees was right on point: "No affirmative action is the ideal, you know, some abstract ideal, at least . . . in a case where you could legitimately say that [blacks and Latinos] can always at all times compete on an equal footing, equal ground with people of white or Asian or whatever background." It is worth noting that the same reasoning seemed to explain a couple of borderline ratings from opponents. "It'd be nice to live in an ideal world," Jack Uberhof told me, "where there wasn't any prejudice, and to hell with all of these policies," but as things were, he did condone the formally race-neutral, class-based model of affirmative action discussed in chapter 3. For Tim Kovacs,

> It's kind of—'cause I'm looking at [this policy] in a theoretical world and I'm looking at it in the real world. In the theoretical world . . . there is no prejudice, and I think that everybody should be judged equally. But I know that in the real world . . . there are sometimes prejudices and sometimes that does get in the way. So I would say, in a theoretical world, I would say a [rating of] 1 . . . [But in the real world] I guess I would give it a 3.

Advocate Mike Benedetto seemed to follow the same logic, although he found this way of thinking

> very hard to explain. You just can't put down some set standards, because everybody didn't grow up in the same surroundings, same standards, and everybody doesn't have the same background, so, um . . . you should have an equal opportunity to do things, but then certain concessions should be made for those that have . . . had a harder time. It's hard to put my finger on.

For Steve Clayburgh, as well, *"Fairness* is so damn hard to define." But he did as good a job as anyone of explaining just how far he was willing to push aside commonplace, everyday dictums on fairness—and the feelings evoked when those dictums were compromised—to make room for a more nuanced conception of justice.

> Let's say I have a dollar from the state, and I have the opportunity to put this in [a general] instructional fund *or* [one] that is divided on the basis of color. . . . It sucks being a white male and having somebody say that we're tearing this dollar in half . . . giving you forty cents of it and giving this black student over here sixty cents of it. . . . It would be hard to me to make that decision [one way or the other]. . . . I think "equity" is a weighted type of fairness. Where "fairness" [means splitting things] down the middle . . . this person would get 50 percent, and this person would get 50 percent. . . . I view equity as a weighted type of fairness, to make up more [for] certain *in*equities that have happened in other places.

As for race-conscious allocations of opportunity in particular, the big picture did not necessarily make things clearer. On one hand, Steve agreed with Drew Kazinski and Gil Jarreaux that mandates for affirmative action hiring by public contractors "involves too much government in the private sector . . . inside the workings of things that government doesn't belong in. If they can do this, then where does that put . . . the freedom to hire and fire at will?" "Total fairness" on the part of graduate professional schools "would be to set a minimum standard [and] if you don't make it, then you don't progress." Moreover, "If you do [affirmative action] all at once and . . . don't accept any whites to graduate college . . . [then] *moderate* whites, whites that might have views that are similar to mine . . . are gonna [have] more animosity towards them and try to keep blacks and Latinos out of those [professional/managerial] realms." On the other hand,

> If you are less aggressive [than you should be] and less willing . . . to compensate for the past inequities, and take away from whites . . . you're gonna prolong the period of time . . . [in which] blacks and Latinos [are kept] out of particular power positions. . . . I don't know what the perfect balance is, but you have to balance the two to create a better good.

By contrast, opponents of affirmative action admissions often seemed to agree with Nick deLeo and Peter Galoszy that the "better good" to be derived from full equality of opportunity was simply unattainable—perhaps a handy way to suppress any instincts they might have to compromise marginal equality to any serious degree. Midway through Zack Pritchard's interview, he recalled,

> I've said a lot of stuff about "same footing." Everyone starts off with equal footing, right, the day they're born. . . . [But] then they start to have these factors flung at them in their lives. . . . Nothing's equal . . . *there's no such thing* [as equality of opportunity], it's really hard to think about. . . . I'm trying to imagine a situation where there *would* be equal opportunity; there *is* none.

Pat Gaheogan, too, understood that "life isn't fair." No matter how hard they worked, for example, those whose talents lay in less lucrative professions would earn less money than those who were no more ambitious, and worked no harder, but whose specific talents yielded higher paychecks. Or it could simply be a matter of timing.

> Let's just say I graduate in an environment where the economy is not that great. I tried all the way through school, I got good grades, I could be accepted anywhere, whatever. And in a different time period, I would probably be able to excel *more* [in the business world], or more quickly, than in this one. So in a way, it's not because of ability or effort, but it's just because of circumstances that are beyond your control. . . .
>
> You could get into a discussion of salaries . . . and why should [basketball star] Michael Jordan make thirty million dollars a year, when his contribution to society . . . is, you know, a couple of hours enjoying watching a basketball game. Or endorsement of products, and does that really benefit society? Then you have teachers, who are . . . bringing up the next generation . . . pretty much affecting the whole future of the country, or . . . the world . . . getting paid fifteen, twenty, twenty-five thousand a year.

One might argue that such arguments were simply self-serving, or that opponents sought simpler solutions to the problem of fair allocation of opportunity. Some, however, engaged in their own form of double-think: Life *in general* is unfair, but *I myself* will nonetheless succeed or fail on my merits. Not even race-conscious admissions or hiring would get in Pat Gaheogan's way.

> The things I'm going for [professionally], they're looking for more Hispanics and blacks and women now. Me, I'm a white male. I'm one of the things they just don't want right now. . . . So what I do is, I go, "All right, you don't want me? I'm gonna make myself better than the rest of them. You'll have no *choice* but to take me."

To a considerable degree, this was the same kind of "true grit" individualism I'd heard from several advocates—for example, when Mel Gibran talked about the possible loss of a service academy appointment to a minority competitor.

So, you know, I got shot down in that respect, but I just went elsewhere and looked for another opportunity or, you know, pursued other interests. . . . That's a fact of life, anyway, you get shot down and you get tripped up, you get back up and look for the next best thing and maybe something better, who knows? I mean, in this case, at this point in time, I think I made a better decision. . . . It's not fair, but . . . I don't know how to put it . . . I'm, like, you know . . . that happens. You've gotta pick up the pieces and go on.

But while Mel could cope with adversity, he did *not* claim to have neutralized it. Jack, on the other hand, was almost as certain as Pat that he was simply unstoppable. He had spoken at length on the advantages of coming from a well-to-do family; but as for reaching his own goals,

It may take longer, but I think that someone who has the strong inner drive can still succeed. It's a little bit harder—I'm not saying that it's ideal, and . . . there are extremes where economics just—no matter how hard a person tries . . . they just don't [make it]. . . . [But] there *are* ways to get around things for most people. . . . Inner drive has a lot more to do with it than economics. I see the people . . . that *don't* have to [hold a job] when they're going to school, you have someone [else] who's paying for it, and I don't think [most of them] appreciate it. . . .
In the short run . . . it'd be [easier] for them to get good grades. But . . . the person who's *had* it all, and never really had to strive for anything, they have *less* motivation and drive, on the average, than the person that didn't. . . . Once life throws them a curve ball, if it ever does, I don't think that they would have the ability to deal with that as well as a person that had it harder getting there. . . .
In *that* way, it's easier for the person that *had* the obstacles to succeed, because he's always gonna have that drive, no matter what comes up. . . . The more obstacles that *I've* been faced with, the harder I've tried. . . . I wouldn't have had it any other way.

In other words, *absolute* equality of opportunity is simply not a reasonable expectation; but if one tried hard enough to succeed in some area of endeavor congenial to his talents, then some significant lapses in equality of opportunity *would not matter.*

But if that was true, then what was Jack or Pat Gaheogan's problem, anyway? How could affirmative action constitute reverse discrimination, if in fact it had no ill effects on men like themselves? What about Nick, who did fear affirmative action, and recounted in detail all the other strikes against him that had little to do with real merit—yet insisted, nonetheless, that "in his world" things were fair, and still saw his own questionable prospects very much in terms of his own talents and effort?

It all begins to make sense, however, if we consider that what these men were up against was not simply "reverse discrimination" but the reasoning behind it. If blacks' and Latinos' achievements had so much to do with socioeconomic status, ethnic rivalries, parental programming, community norms, and so forth, *why not whites' achievements as well?* Even as it empowers blacks and Latinos, affirmative action could *dis*empower whites, not only by allocating to others specific opportunities that would otherwise have been theirs, but also, by its very logic, robbing whites of the cherished notion that, *sans* affirmative action, success or failure was truly in their own hands—that the game is not so rigged or the playing field so poorly tended that the best men are not especially likely to be the winners.

NOTES

1. See, for example, chapters by Woody Doane, Margaret Anderson, and Mark Chesler et al. in Ashley W. Doane and Eduardo Bonilla-Silva, *White Out: The Continuing Significance of Racism,* New York: Routledge, 2003.

2. Among the most recent published editions of the operetta, first performed in 1885, is W. S. Gilbert and Arthur Sullivan, *The Mikado in Full Score,* Dover, England: Dover Publications, 1999.

❺

TAKING STOCK

Everyday Ideology and
Affirmative Action's Future

Any time that someone tries to—to make up for any kind of societal discrimination by giving a perk or bonus, it's human nature to say, "Great! Stick
up for the little guy, for the underdog!" And I think that's why, like, maybe
at first glance, my reaction [to absolute quotas was], well, I think that's a
good idea.

—Dan Lysenko

Looking back on my thirty-two interviews, what is perhaps most striking is what
the subjects had in common, in terms of values, experiences, and concerns,
helping to inform a pervasive ambivalence toward affirmative action as a whole.

Across the board, the men I talked to seemed to view demonstrable merit as
the *sine qua non* for the just allocation of places in law schools, medical schools,
and the more competitive MBA programs. *Merit*, of course, referred to *individual* effort, individual competence and achievement; but to a very considerable degree, these were the products of one's rearing, one's schooling, one's
day-to-day life experience. To the degree that blacks and Latinos were seen to
deserve special consideration or assistance—if not as graduate professional
school applicants, then as schoolchildren or college students—this was not for
the sake of diversity per se, or to compensate blacks and Latinos in general for
a long history of discrimination against their forebears: Rather, affirmative action was a necessary corrective for unjust constraints on achievement among
my subjects' black and Latino contemporaries—"unjust" because they were
imposed either through racist discrimination against present-day blacks and

Latinos themselves, or as a consequence of racist discrimination against the families and communities by which their values, self-concepts, and aspirations had been shaped. Economic marginalization, moreover, was viewed as a critical link in the chain of causality between discrimination and unequal attainments: So to the degree that blacks and Latinos had managed to attain upper-middle-class status for themselves, *their* children were not fitting candidates for special consideration. On the contrary, there was concern that not enough of these successful blacks and Latinos were committed to "giving something back" to their fellow ethnics.

As to how merit should be assessed, most of the men I talked to felt that standardized tests were poor measures of *anyone's* potential, regardless of race. Partly for this reason, a serious reweighting of admissions criteria was more popular than any other policy options I put forward. Endorsements were qualified, however, by considerable concern for the financial costs involved, for the difficulty of weighing less-quantifiable criteria against each other in a consistent manner, and hence for the possibility of intentional or unintentional bias. Racially targeted outreach and campus programs might also be too costly. Such programs were, moreover, viewed as threats to campus race relations.

The same could be said, of course, for race-conscious admissions policies. Support for them, nonetheless, seemed to follow from a set of assumptions that, the data suggests, every advocate took for granted and every opponent challenged.

POLICY PREFERENCES, RACISM, AND TRADITIONAL VALUES

Comparing the views of advocates and opponents of race-conscious admissions to graduate professional schools, I found no *categorical* differences between them: Even if we eliminate those in the middle, so to speak—advocates like Joe Murtaugh who would not go as far as race-norming, and opponents like Nick deLeo who nonetheless endorsed graduate professional school interventions with prospective applicants—there was nothing to distinguish the perspectives of all of the staunchest advocates from *all* of the most die-hard opponents. But a close reading of the data does suggest a cluster of assumptions critical to the endorsement of race conscious admissions at the most competitive levels of the American educational system. All of the advocates interviewed were certain enough of the inherent equality of different races and ethnic groups to reject even the possibility of serious, group-wise hereditary differences in physical or mental capacities. All acknowledged the value of diversity, whether on campus or in the professional/managerial workforce. Collective accountability for equality of opportunity and for serious, conspicuous

lapses from cumulative procedural equality were in their view sufficient justification for systematic departures from marginal equality—and not only on behalf of children, or to compensate for concrete barriers to achievement, but
also on behalf of college students and college graduates, and as compensation
for relatively subjective, psychosocial barriers to achievement. "Top-down" efforts toward these ends—enlisting public as well as private organizations and
institutions—were a necessary complement to voluntary, grass-roots activism
and self-help. However innocent of wrongdoing they saw themselves to be,
moreover, these men seemed to take it for granted that this earned them no
personal exemptions from whatever costs those efforts toward a more just society appeared to impose on whites.

Put it all together, and this package of beliefs makes for a compelling argument in affirmative action's favor—compelling enough to explain why so many
advocates find it difficult to understand how anyone can, in good conscience,
oppose it. One or more of those assumptions, however, was made by each opponent of race-conscious graduate-professional admissions I interviewed. No
one had anything against professional-managerial diversity; but several challenged the need for any deliberate efforts to advance it. Most grasped the psychosocial impact of racism and poverty, but several were unwilling to extend
collective accountability that far—especially to members of that collective who
had had "nothing to do with" racist oppression themselves. Not that any of
them wished to place an entire ban on race-conscious efforts to advance opportunity, or to limit inequality of outcomes—but several made the point that
this should remain the province of individuals or voluntary organizations,
rather than state-sponsored or state-subsidized institutions. And when I asked
whether they thought there were any *inherent* differences between racial or
ethnic groups, other than certain aspects of their physical appearance, several
opponents took the bait.

To a very limited degree, so did Dave Zaluba, considering the possibility
of subtle differences in brain function; while Tom Sorbo thought whites
might be inherently more "conservative" than other races. Tom's equation of
"conservative" with "tight collared," however, and Dave's speculation that
blacks might naturally be better surgeons make it hard to view either man's
comments as assertions of white superiority. But some opponents' allegations were much more substantial. Chris Feraios, for example, put forward
the time-honored theory that blacks were by nature more violent than
whites. Drew Kazinski was quite certain of both intellectual and physical differences between different racial groups and felt that the latter explained
why blacks did not excel at swimming. And Gil Jarreaux wouldn't rule out
the possibility that blacks are simply "not as capable of learning." In the
realm of long-standing *cultural* differences, moreover—predating extensive

contact with whites—Bill Sajak seemed quite certain that blacks' and Latinos' ancestors simply had not established a serious work ethic.

Findings like these certainly point to a strong link between "old-fashioned" racism and opposition to affirmative action. Regarding the link between a much more pervasive "modern racism" and *widespread* resistance to such policies, however, the evidence is much less compelling. To be sure, there are plenty of examples of "modern racism" in this book, including a variety of common stereotypes concerning behavioral patterns and cultural norms: Latinos are characterized as clannish, for example, and as not putting much stock in formal education; while blacks are often seen as dangerous, lazy, unmotivated, and quick to blame their problems on others. But this kind of modern racism cropped up repeatedly *among advocate and opponent alike*. From this perspective, was Gil Jarreaux any more racist than Joe Murtaugh? Was Bill Sajak's portrayal of blacks really more damning than Dave Zaluba's?

Even when conspicuous racists resist affirmative action, moreover, we cannot assume that in every case, or even in most, negative perceptions of minorities are the "real" sources of that resistance. A great many whites may grab racist attitudes off the shelves of today's supermarket of ideas because these ways of looking at blacks or Latinos help them come to terms with the paradoxical implications of Americans' "traditional values."

We Hold These Truths . . .

Just as opponents of affirmative action are often branded "racist," advocates are often accused of betraying this country's most fundamental sociopolitical norms. What my interviews suggest, however, is a striking degree of unanimity on that score. All of the men I interviewed not only affirmed the importance of equality of opportunity but also described it in remarkably similar ways. All endorsed meritocratic allocation of scarce opportunities, emphasizing its collective benefits in terms of the quality of goods, services, and leadership this would yield, and its benefits to individuals encouraged by meritocratic competition to fulfill their potentials.

Were opponents nonetheless more "individualistic" in their worldviews? That would certainly be a reasonable conclusion, if the kind of individual autonomy Americans prize meant nothing more than self-reliance. But it also means self-fulfillment, the right to make our own choices, follow our own paths, *achieve* self-reliance, and realize our full potentials—what humanistic psychologists mean by "self-actualization," left-wing activists mean by "empowerment," and part of what Thomas Jefferson meant by "the pursuit of happiness." Both aspects of individualism lie at the heart of Americans' commitment to equality of opportunity, to the belief that, as Jack Uberhof put it, "if you *want* to develop [your] talents . . . there won't be any barriers based on anything except their abilities." But enabling this sort of individual opportunity—and refereeing an inevitably intense competition for top-dog status in any area of endeavor—requires a good deal of collective effort, in terms of schooling, market regulation, the due process of law, and even transportation and health care. From this perspective, advocates of the most aggressive forms of affirmative action might arguably be viewed as *more* individualistic in their worldviews than opponents, in terms of their commitment to the collective facilitation of individual self-fulfillment.

Both advocates and opponents, however, face the same paradox. On one hand, few Americans—however leery of "communism" or "social engineering"—would challenge the role of families, communities, schools, and other arms of the government in facilitating self-actualization. On the other hand, few if any Americans would challenge the importance of self-reliance, which is after all essential to progressivist constructions of self-fulfillment and empowerment. Indeed, one of the ways American families, schools, and other institutions help to promote individual self-fulfillment is by encouraging people to believe that they *can* fend for themselves, and helping them to acquire the skills and attitudes to do so.[1] Pushed to their logical limits, however, the mandates for self-reliance and collective facilitation essentially cancel each other out. Given the delicate balancing act our two-headed ethos of individualism requires, we should not be surprised that some of the strongest affirmative action advocates interviewed were hard-pressed to articulate fully their points of view, or that opponents sometimes split the difference, so to speak, by consigning those above a certain age or a certain level of schooling to a less vigorous collective effort on their behalf.

The paradoxical dictates of individualism may also help to explain the mixed response to diversity, and the ambivalence of several subjects toward holistic assessment. On one hand, we are taught to respect individual differences, and to recognize each man's or woman's unique mix of strengths and perspectives. A respect for individual differences, in turn, supports America's openness to cultural diversity: Men and women are freer to "be themselves" when they are not forced to choose between full acceptance as Americans and enduring links to particular ethnic groups or nations of origin. When it comes to the distribution of scarce opportunities, however, our rights as individuals also mandate fair competition—that is, on the basis of a *common* standard by which individual talents and interests are to be judged. Hence the concern of several subjects that any changes in admissions criteria leave them sufficiently transparent that it's possible to ascertain how consistently they are being applied—something Michigan's "holistic assessment" and UC Berkeley's free-form "comprehensive review" do not necessarily allow.

But affirmative action is up against something much older than individualistic commitments to self-sufficiency or procedural equality: an eons-old mandate to "take care of your own," wherein "your own" is defined much less broadly than advocates of progressive social policies would like.[2] This may be what conservatives really mean by "family values," and among other things, it renders problematic Americans' simultaneous commitment to equality of opportunity and to the substantial *in*equalities of outcomes that the assumption of equality of opportunity helps to legitimize. As social animals, human beings devote a great deal of time, effort, and other resources to mating and offspring, and some of the most prized payoffs of individual success are the tangible and intangible benefits this allows us to bestow—that we are in fact *expected* to bestow—on our own families. Hal Voorhees and Joe Murtaugh and Greg Bogosian ask a legitimate question: In the name of equality of opportunity, how far should we be expected to go toward neutralizing the consequences for *other* people's children of gaps in parental achievement or commitment?

One of the lessons, moreover, of communal responses to terrorist attacks, destructive acts of nature, and extraordinary medical expenses—one persistent message of country western lyrics no less than philosophers like Edmund Burke—is that universally acknowledged obligations to one's immediate family are much more readily extended to relatives and friends, fellow congregants or fellow ethnics, than to each and every constituent of a much larger polity. Even the behavioral proscriptions of some of the Ten Commandments concern inappropriate behavior toward "thy neighbor," translated from a Hebrew word variously interpreted as "neighbor," "kinsman," or perhaps even "fellow-Jew" or "fellow-Israelite," but never as a reference to human beings in general.

Likewise, recent scientific evidence for the deep roots of human altruism in the behavior of other species does not suggest any inherent impulse for caring or sharing beyond one's immediate band or troop. It is no accident that a national chain of Italian restaurants tells us, "When you're here, you're family"; that an insurance company assures us that its agents will treat us "just like a good neighbor"; that many African Americans refer to all apparent fellow-ethnics as "brother" and "sister." Neither is it mere coincidence that so many appeals for broad-scale solidarity talk about *brotherhood*, or extol *fraternity* as well as liberty and equality; or that our own country's motto, *E pluribus unum*—"From many, one"—suggests a simultaneous commitment to diversity *and* the dissolution of any boundaries between us. Affirmative action and other progressive initiatives may not, strictly speaking, demand greater collective accountability than their opponents are willing to accept, but rather a greater degree of accountability in relation to a *larger collective*. It may be tempting to characterize such limits on accountability as yet another facet of racism; but in this regard, the boundaries between "us" and "them" may have at least as much to do with economic achievement, region, sexual preferences, political philosophy, or religious faith as with color or national origin.

All of this may shed some new light on plentiful evidence that familial and communal contributions to one's accomplishments do not necessarily preclude referring to those accomplishments in highly individualistic terms.[3] In my own study, Dan Lysenko's views on affirmative action did not seem to take into account how much of a leg up corporate largesse toward his suburban high school had given him in the world of computers. Likewise, the sort of help or advice Drew was likely to have been offered by his industry-insider father, regarding how to secure or succeed in a top-drawer internship, may give the lie to Drew's self-portrayal as a self-made man up against the dog-eat-dog world of business. What "individual" achievement probably means to these men, however, is simply taking full advantage of whatever opportunities had been open to them— obviously not something everyone in their positions would have done—and not using personal connections *in place of* demonstrable talent and "gumption." In their view, a fair distribution of outcomes did *not* require some larger collective to guarantee every American the same level of support for individual achievement that these men's families and communities had offered *them*.

A good many readers are likely to regard these observations, and the data on which they are based, simply as further evidence of white hypocrisy, and the ways in which ideological arguments are employed as window dressing for whites' selfish but perfectly rational desire to maintain their traditional advantages. Certainly, most of my interview subjects were up-front with their concerns about how race-conscious policies might affect them. If opponents sometimes appeared to discount their own privileges relative to most young people of any race, several advocates seemed to "protest too much" that the long-term, big picture benefits of affirmative action managed to outweigh any short-term costs. But in either case, the principal audience for this sleight-of-hand was very likely the subject himself, too much of a true believer in the idea of equality of opportunity to recognize when the rules he *thought* he lived by were routinely broken. What some have labeled "modern racism" might just as often be symptomatic of an anxious retreat from class-consciousness—so eager are a great many whites to see themselves as self-made men and women with the liberty to rise as far, but *only* as far, as their individual talents and efforts can take them. Just as Dan Lysenko, Drew Kazinski, Gil Jarreaux, and Nick deLeo did not want to see themselves as having had *too* good a chance to succeed in life, opponents from less affluent backgrounds seemed reluctant to acknowledge that their own life chances were not *good enough*, in relation to consensual notions of equity.

Reviewing some of my interviews, I was reminded of one of Sigmund Freud's more useful forays into social theory, wherein he traces our fundamental sense of justice *qua* equal treatment to the way we come to terms, in our earliest years, with the conflict between our boundless wants, our sibling rivalries, and what our parents can realistically be expected to provide: "Social justice means that we deny ourselves many things so that others may have to do without them as well, or what is the same thing, may not be able to ask for them."[4] Perhaps part of what I was hearing was a good deal of resentment of minorities' seeming demand for a *degree* of equality of opportunity that most whites have long since learned to live without.

All in all, the more closely we examine the controversy over affirmative action, the less it suggests a clash of antithetical values, and the more it resembles those sorts of interpretive disputes one finds among theologians working from the same scripture. That, of course, has never precluded schism, or the kind of mutual distrust that the Supreme Court's recent decisions have done little to mitigate.

BY THE SKIN OF OUR TEETH: A CLOSER LOOK AT THE RAMIFICATIONS OF *GRATZ* AND *GRUTTER*

> The court . . . ruled 5 to 4 that the law school's more nuanced, less mechanical weighting of race passes constitutional muster because it . . . provides "a meaningful individualized review of applicants." Those six words . . . are pregnant with burdensome future litigation.
>
> —George F. Will, *Washington Post*[5]

As discussed in the introduction, the Supreme Court's most recent decisions on the matter leave race-conscious admissions still in place, but perhaps on more precarious footing than it had been in the 1980s and early 1990s. My own data suggests broad assent in principle to increased reliance on nontraditional assessments of applicants' qualifications, partly to advance equality of opportunity in relation to socioeconomic status. In conjunction with recent Supreme Court opinions, however, the same findings point to escalating battles over precisely how "holistic" or "comprehensive" assessment ought to work.

Talent Scouting: *Holistic assessment of diverse expressions of "merit"*

Writing the majority opinion on *Grutter*, Justice Sandra Day O'Connor hailed the capacity of holistic assessment to optimize diversity, in contrast to alternative admissions models that "may preclude . . . the individualized assessments necessary to assemble a student body . . . diverse along all the qualities [sic] valued by the university."[6] Not unlike the appeal of alternative criteria to the men I interviewed, holistic assessment's greatest appeal to the American public may be that it encourages schools to pay attention to alternate indicators of *merit*—alternate forms of evidence, that is, of the knowledge, capacities, and motivations thought to correlate closely with academic and professional excellence.

At the graduate professional level, for example, an applicant's experience as a corporate employee, hospital volunteer, or campaign worker would not only enrich her classmates' learning experience but would presumably have taught her some useful skills, while helping to demonstrate and to build the discipline, tenacity, or other traits of character demanded of graduate-educated professionals and managers.

Academics often pooh-pooh the special breaks given to varsity-level athletes; but here, too, we can argue that top-drawer performance reflects much more than brawn or quick reflexes, while one's experience on the playing field is likely to yield perspectives on competition, teamwork, and human motivation very pertinent to a variety of disciplines and fields of endeavor. Likewise, an undergraduate drama major might bring to the courtroom, emergency room, or ad agency bullpen an exceptionally well-honed sensitivity to vocal inflection, facial expressions, body language, and how to employ them to the advantage of one's customers, clients, and colleagues. The varsity basketball player, the journeyman research technician, the honorably discharged NCO, the intern who has won a permanent position with the same firm—all of these candidates for admission have not only enjoyed valuable, out-of-the-classroom opportunities for learning but already provided strong evidence that they profited from these experiences, simply by virtue of their staying power and, in some cases, their ability to start climbing up the relevant career ladder.

Other differences in "background" as well, as the University of Michigan argued, can make "classroom discussion . . . livelier, more spirited, and simply more enlightening and interesting"[7] precisely because of the special knowledge and insights those backgrounds have afforded. The son of a Montana rancher or a New Bedford fisherman, for example, might bring with him some insights on the American food chain of considerable interest to his big-city B-school or med school classmates. In the same way, growing up in an inner-city ghetto or barrio might ensure insider knowledge worth sharing on street gangs, folk remedies, the practical consequences of welfare reform, or just why those home shopping networks are able to offer us such low, low prices on designer sportswear.

Indeed, the Supreme Court's *Grutter* decision was of a piece with a general movement, among this country's most progressive educators and educational theorists, away from what they view as excessive reliance on traditional methods of assessment at every level. Letter grades, grade point averages, and one or two standardized test scores—the latter based mostly on answers to multiple choice questions—cannot possibly capture the full spectrum of students' talents and achievements, or the depth of understanding and insight they have attained. This is a rather compelling argument, especially in the case of thumbs up/thumbs down decisions concerning whether or not a student or group of students have performed at an acceptable level. A review of portfolios of students' work, for example—their history essays, their solutions to math problems, their artwork, and so forth—may be the fairest indicator of which ones have what it takes to succeed at the next grade level. Likewise, interviews with her students and a review of their portfolios may tell us more about whether, say, an eighth-grade teacher's approach to English composition is delivering the goods than the scores her students earn on the typical standardized test of verbal skills.

We want more from assessments of educational outcomes, however, than yes-or-no, pass-or-fail judgments in relation to one or another criterion: For the numerous students or applicants or programs that have met that criterion must then be ranked *against each other*. If a gifted program can only accept twenty students, then *which* twenty are *most* deserving? At the other end of the educational pipeline, which 150 of 5,000 medical school applicants shall we admit to the class of 2009? Inescapably, distinctions between good, better, and best—or in some cases, between talent, exceptional talent, and genius—involve some kind of quantification, some way of assessing who has *more* of something than someone else. And the more high-stakes the decision, the more important it is to judge *fairly*, to apply our criteria in a visibly consistent manner—something holistic assessment makes it much harder to do, or perhaps just as important, makes it much harder to *demonstrate* that we have done.

Hence the enduring appeal of inherently quantitative measures. Taking into account, moreover, all of the differences in curriculum, teaching styles, and approaches to evaluation among different teachers, it's hard to say how much grades or rank in class tell us about the relative performance of students at the same school, let alone graduates of thousands of different high schools or colleges across the country. Therein lies the beauty of the SAT, the MCAT, and so forth: Everyone sitting for the same test in the same year is assessed in an identical manner, on the very same set of tasks. What could be fairer than that?

By Their Scores, Ye Shall Know Them: *A closer look at standardized testing*

Whenever frustrated applicants have complained that "less qualified" blacks and Latinos have been admitted to one school or another, "less qualified" invariably refers in large part to their lower scores on standardized tests. As noted in the introduction, affirmative action by means of holistic assessment could well draw the same scrutiny that comprehensive review did at UC Berkeley in 2002, and similar complaints as to "why students with seemingly outstanding grades *and* admission test scores were unable to gain admission to the University or to a particularly competitive campus."[8]

In his lengthy report on the issue, Board of Regents Chairman John Moores did not argue that applicants should be ranked *strictly* on the basis of test scores, or that less traditional, less quantifiable criteria should not be considered as well. Like so many other observers, however, Moores did seem to suggest that no other dimensions of applicants' records justify veering *too* far from whoever the SAT identifies as "the best."

But are the SAT and similar tests really that useful a gauge? Experts in the field of test construction are as divided as my interview subjects over how good an estimate of intellectual, academic, or professional potential any test of this sort can provide. But we needn't simply take their word for it. These days, sample items for most standardized admissions tests are readily available on the Internet. On my own visit to the pertinent websites,[9] I found an SAT very much like the one I remember taking back in high school, emphasizing vocabulary, sentence construction, and reading comprehension, as well as arithmetic, algebra, geometry, and related content. The GMAT and the LSAT were, as advertised, extremely challenging tests of critical thinking skills, including deductive and inductive reasoning, the ability to analyze and critique other people's arguments, and one's grasp of more than one side of contentious economic, political, or ethical questions. As expected, the MCAT demanded considerable rote knowledge of the natural sciences (never my strongest suit), but also the ability to plug that knowledge into critical thinking and practical problem solving.

Most readers would likely agree that these tests are tapping into abilities critical to top-drawer performance in a variety of settings, and that those who do well on these tests would tend to be good students and good prospects for a variety of professional and managerial career tracks. But the real question is not, Are these tests useful? but rather, Just *how* useful are they? As useful as much of the criticism of holistic assessment and comprehensive review seem to imply? As several of my interview subjects cautioned, those who do well on these sorts of tests may nonetheless lack the drive, the strength of character, the street smarts, or the people skills to go the distance in the most competitive strata of the American job market. Hence the vital importance of balancing test scores against other assessment criteria, so as to eliminate as much as possible what research scientists might call "false positives"—that is, those whose test results are better than they ought to be, providing exaggerated measures of their true potential.

A thornier problem, however, is "false negatives"—that is, those with much more of just the sorts of capacities these tests are supposed to tap than their scores give them credit for. On a case-by-case basis, of course, this might simply reflect lack of effort, or "test anxiety," or (as in the case of one of my own brightest students) getting drunk the night before the test is taken. In the case of blacks and Latinos, however, there is also the possibility of systematic cultural bias. Several studies suggest that standardized test scores actually tend to *over*predict the performance of both groups; but it can also be argued that some of the outcome measures to which test scores are compared—college or law school grades, for example—likewise reflect discriminatory practices, so the relationship between scores and outcomes proves nothing about each group's rightful place in the pecking order.

Regarding the SAT, at least, the research suggests that some specific *items* are biased against them, in the sense that whites tend to do significantly better on those items than blacks and Latinos whose overall performance on the test is just as good. On some other items, however, blacks or Latinos seem to do better than whites. Human variability more or less guarantees that any definable subgroup of test-takers—Norwegian Americans, trombone players, those with dimpled chins, you name it—will tend to perform better or worse on some items than test-takers generally. Jay Rosner, an expert witness for the University of Michigan, referred to systematic differences in certain aspects of test performance not only between different racial or ethnic groups, but in relation to region, religious affiliation, and other demographic variables.[10] Most experts agree, however, that to a very considerable degree, at least, the gap in test scores between blacks, Latinos, and whites reflects genuine differences in how well they have mastered the knowledge and skills most critical to academic achievement.[11]

But that may be just the point. Ideally, admissions candidates are selected— and scarce opportunities allocated—on the basis of candidates' relative *potential* for high levels of academic or professional achievement in the future. As a practical matter, however, that potential is inevitably inferred from here-and-now performance of one sort or another. But that *achieved* level of understanding or know-how is at least as much a product of formal instruction and overall life experience as of innate talent or capacity. And on both counts—the kind of book learning and the kind of life experiences likely to enhance academic achievement—blacks and Latinos are likely to be shortchanged in comparison to whites. But neither genetics nor cultural heritage nor even racism need have anything to do with it: Just follow the money.

The Cash Nexus: *Cornering the market on opportunity*

Whether or not they approved of race-conscious admissions, a good majority of my interview subjects looked favorably on policies that took socioeconomic background into account to some degree. They might challenge the notion that poverty or economic uncertainty posed a significant barrier to academic achievement, or the reach of our collective obligation to take such barriers down; but almost everyone seemed to acknowledge the ways in which affluence opens the doors to opportunity.

One of the distinctive features of modern capitalist democracies is that opportunity is not only bought and sold but aggressively marketed to all comers, like cheeseburgers and floor-care products. When parents are willing and able to purchase homes in good school districts, furnish those homes with at least a couple of computers, pay for music lessons, hockey equipment, specialty summer camps, and foreign travel, or perhaps help their children find relatively well-paid, stimulating part-time or summer jobs, they are not only buying the good life in the short run but putting a down payment on their children's futures. Money can also buy physical safety—one reason that black parents are eager to move out of low-income ghettos as soon as they're able—as well as expensive test-prep courses which, contrary to the dogma of the test-construction companies, have been shown to significantly improve most people's scores.

Of course, it's not just a matter of what money can buy. Parents with more money are also likely to be better educated themselves, exemplars of reading for pleasure, more effective coaches of their children's studies, more competent guides to the college and financial aid application process, and perhaps more beneficent sources of financial support. If, as Hillary Clinton put it, "it takes a village to raise a child,"[12] then it's fair to say that more affluent parents also tend to provide their children with a better informed, more sophisticated village, full of adults who not only model achievement but who, through hundreds of casual interchanges with the offspring of their relatives, friends, neighbors, and colleagues, year by formative year, help to educate and nurture those children, boost their vocabularies, hone their reasoning skills, excite their curiosity, channel their ambitions, and eventually offer some very practical advice and some extremely useful contacts.

Having observed all of this firsthand, I find it hard to dispute Nick deLeo's assertion that *absolute* equality of opportunity is difficult even to imagine. As things are, persistent findings of *class* differences in grades and test scores, even when we control for race, help to explain why such a large proportion of places in top schools are allocated to the children of the well-to-do, while low-income youth in general are even less well represented than young people of color.[13] Could standardized admissions tests be modified in some way to lessen the impact of socioeconomic status and of the relative quality of prior schooling? It is difficult to imagine a valid test of teenagers' or adults' quantitative reasoning that was not *also* a test of their mastery of algebra, geometry, and related subjects, and hence their access to quality instruction in these areas. On the other hand, some of the SAT's verbal sections might be modified to make performance less dependent on the sort of vocabulary one is more likely to encounter in the classrooms, homes, and social circles of the well-to-do. The verbal analogies section might have been worth saving, as a useful test of reasoning skills, had its vocabulary not included words like *atrophe, ponder, skittish, stanza,* or *tiresome.*[14]

Judging by the sample exercises provided to help people prepare for the 2006 Reasoning Test, the verbal sections of the SAT still favor the children of America's educated upper and upper middle classes. For example, more affluent teens are, on the average, more likely to have attended plays and visited museums on a regular basis; so reading comprehension segments about paintings and live theater are likely to be more familiar territory—and familiar territory makes for less stress and more self-confidence. Relatively privileged teens are also more likely to have encountered in everyday conversations much of the vocabulary they will encounter in the SAT—to have participated in discussions of *paleontology*, for example; to have heard things described as *furtive* or *subtle*; to have heard people referred to as *dilettantes* or *devotees,* as *rationalists* or *raconteurs.*[15] Perhaps the most promising change in the SAT is the addition of the essay-style writing test which, as the *New York Times* noted, offers colleges "easy access to an undoctored writing sample" for each applicant,[16] as opposed to the essays typically submitted with applications, often the product of extensive collaboration among students, educated parents, and the professional admissions consultants affluent families can afford to hire. Other substantial advances in admissions testing may be in the works as well. Over the past several years, for example, a team of researchers led by Yale University psychologist Robert Sternberg has been working on measures of "creative intelligence" and "practical intelligence" designed to supplement measures of "analytical intelligence" currently captured by the SAT and the GMAT. Results so far suggest that this approach to testing shortens the gaps in scores among different racial and ethnic groups and predicts undergraduate GPA better than the SAT alone.[17]

It is an open question, however, just how well or how quickly these findings will translate into serious changes in the SAT or other standardized admissions tests. For one thing, these new measures are composed largely of open-ended questions, answers to which (like the new SAT writing section) must be scored one at a time by specially trained scorers. This inevitably makes for a more time-consuming, more costly test than the largely multiple choice tests we're accustomed to; and both open-ended and multiple-choice items in these tests are bound to induce public controversy concerning the nature of "creativity" and "practical intelligence" and just how they are being measured.[18] And in any case, any full-scale movement in this direction on the part of the SAT, the

GMAT, or other tests is bound to influence the test-prep industry, high school curricula, and the kinds of less-formal instruction parents provide directly—all of which may tend, once again, to favor the children of more well-to-do, better educated parents.

All in all, it is unlikely that any modifications in the SAT—or any substitute for it—could eliminate entirely the influence of socioeconomic status on performance. Those taking graduate admissions tests, of course, will have spent at least a few years in more diverse educational settings; but that may not always be long enough to "catch up" with more privileged peers whose long-term potential is nonetheless no greater than their own. Standardized admissions tests, then, are likely to remain a more accurate gauge of how much academic potential has already been realized—and perhaps how well prepared one is *right now* to meet the demands of undergraduate or graduate study—than of how much potential *might* be tapped in the future, provided optimal encouragement, instruction, and academic support were available.

Neither will those aspects of holistic assessment discussed above necessarily be of much help in equalizing opportunity, since whatever achievements or experiences admissions officers start paying attention to, affluent parents and their children will almost always be in a better position to achieve or acquire them.

Almost but not always: For one of the few things that money doesn't buy is the experience of not having much money, other sorts of life experience that tend to come with that, and the kind of inner strength that it can help to build—one of Jack Uberhof's sources of self-confidence, you may recall, in the face of potential competition with men and women of more affluent backgrounds. Making admissions more genuinely meritocratic, then, would seem to demand greater consideration of applicants' socioeconomic origins. And compared with explicitly race-conscious policies, such *class*-based affirmative action may be especially advantageous to low-income Latinos.

North of the Border: *Race, class, and the Latino question*

Of late, public discourse surrounding affirmative action has not echoed the questions raised in my interviews regarding Latinos' right to affirmative action on their behalf. But it may be no accident that formally race-conscious policies have been set aside in three states with especially large Latino populations, in relation to blacks as well as whites. Texas and California, moreover, are home to some of the most prestigious, selective state schools in the country; while Florida's Cubans, its most prominent Latino population, do not fit the stereotype of a downtrodden minority group. These states' rejection of race-conscious admissions may stem in part from a concern that affirmative action not target the "wrong" people.

"Latinos," a.k.a. "Hispanics," are not really an ethnic or racial group at all, in the usual sense. It was not until the late 1960s that these terms came into general use in connection with activists' efforts to enhance educational, economic, and political equity among them, and with government efforts to keep track of their status and progress. Generally speaking, we find both terms applied to anyone born in a Spanish-speaking, Latin American country, or their American-born descendants, although the terms often embrace those with roots in Portuguese-speaking Brazil, and depending on whom you talk to, may or may not include anyone with roots in Spain itself.

A great many Latinos do not think of themselves as such, but as Mexican Americans, Dominican Americans, *Cubanos*, or what have you. Within their countries of origin, moreover, we find the same sorts of social, cultural, economic, and in some cases political divisions between whites, blacks, and "Indios" as one finds in the United States. In recent years, however, the term *Latino* has gained greater currency, both as a reflection of linguistic and cultural commonalities (most conspicuously in the realm of cuisine and dance rhythms) and as an expression of political solidarity. As a group, Latinos now comprise the United States' largest ethnic minority.

I was rather taken aback by pre-med Mike Benedetto's reference to Latinos as *newcomers* who simply hadn't been around long enough to make it up the ladder. Didn't he know that *West Side Story*'s story—with Anita's humorous prediction that very soon, everyone in San Juan would have moved to New York City—took place in the 1950s, decades before he was born? Even in Chicago, there have been Mexican Americans since at least the 1920s, and I cannot help wondering how many more whites have simply forgotten how much of this country was originally in Spanish hands, or in the hands of native tribes from which many of today's Mexicans could trace their descent. It is hard to dismiss the argument of some Chicano activists that the people of Mexico have at least as legitimate a claim to the American Southwest as the *gringos* whose ancestors won it either from the Mexican government or directly from Spain. In many ways, the "commonwealth" of Puerto Rico remains one of the United States' last colonies, while the nations of Central America are arguably no less a part of our economic and political empire.

As a rationale for special consideration on the basis of race or ethnicity, however, the intertwined histories of the United States and Latin America are simply no match, in the public mind, for the certainties of slavery and Jim Crow, or the outright massacre of North America's native peoples by the U.S. military. However many ancestors of today's Latinos were on hand to greet their Spanish, British, or American invaders, most white Americans—and most blacks and Asian Americans, for that matter—probably view "Latinos" as immigrants, or the descendants of immigrants, whose history of economic exploitation and political marginalization is of a piece with the experience of other immigrant ethnic groups.

Helping to explain the economic and educational statistics on U.S. Latinos, moreover, is the flood of *new* Latino immigrants over the past three decades. By 2000, 40 percent of U.S. Latinos were foreign-born, and 28 percent of those born here had at least one immigrant parent. A great many of those immigrants, moreover, were here illegally, which has tended to guarantee a lower standard of living and is often associated with irregular school attendance and other distractions from academic attainment. Close to 60 percent of U.S. Latinos are of Mexican origin, and in 2001, about one in six of *all* U.S. residents of Mexican origin were living here illegally. That figure does not take into account U.S. citizens who originally came here illegally or are the American-born children of illegals.[19] As with other groups, their descendants tend to do considerably better economically than Latino immigrants themselves. In 2000, for example, first-generation Latino Americans earned an average of $457 per week, whereas the second generation averaged $535 per week, and those in subsequent generations, $550. Only 46 percent of the adult immigrants had earned a high school diploma, compared with 77 percent of their children, and 75 percent of subsequent generations.

As illustrated in table A.2, however, the picture varies a good deal among Latinos of different national origins. Regardless of how many generations removed they are from immigrant ancestors, Americans of Cuban, Central American, and South American origin tend to be better off economically and to be better educated than Puerto Rican or Mexican Americans. Some of these gaps have to do with differences in socioeconomic background as well. Following the Cuban Revolution, for example, the first wave of immigrants in the late 1950s was made up almost entirely of middle-class professionals, business men, and their families; and it did not take long for them and their descendants to match the economic and educational attainments of just about any other ethnic group in this country. These days, eighteen- to twenty-four-year-old Cuban Americans are slightly *more* likely than whites to be enrolled in college. Ninety percent attend full-time—more than blacks, whites, Asian Americans, American Indians, or Latinos in general—and they are just as likely as whites to pursue graduate study.

Or should I say, just as likely as *other whites*? For in Latin America, as in the United States, race and socioeconomic status are often related. Despite centuries of intermarriage among whites, blacks, and the indigenous populations of Latin America, members of its upper and middle classes also tend to be "whiter" in skin tone and physiognomy, on the average, than those living in poverty. Nick deLeo, Greg Bogosian, and Peter Galoszy may have been somewhat self-conscious about their failure to conform to the Celtic/Teutonic norm of "whiteness" (spending four years in Fargo, North Dakota, I often felt that way myself)—but the very span of skin tones and facial features that now comprise white America have made it much easier for a great many Cuban Americans to, as Greg put it, simply "blend into the culture." A great many South Americans have little aboriginal *or* Spanish ancestry and, in terms of physical appearance at least, would blend seamlessly into a white Anglo-Saxon Protestant family or community.

Even when they do not, however—even when a Latino is the spitting image of some Aztec or Taino or Incan ancestor—Latinos simply don't encounter the same degree of resistance, of race hatred, of primal fear that blacks are still up against. As for attitudes toward white-Latino intimacy and marriage, we need look no further than our popular media. Well before Sidney Poitier and Katharine Houghton caused a stir in *Guess Who's Coming to Dinner*—at a time when liaisons between whites and Asians were sufficiently controversial to take center stage in the Broadway musical *South Pacific*—white-Latina liaisons were a staple of westerns; in *Bye, Bye Birdie*, Chita Rivera was simply Dick Van Dyke's "Spanish Rose," and Desi Arnaz costarred with his Anglo wife Lucille Ball in what may be this country's all-time favorite sitcom.

Beyond the glitter of Hollywood, on the other hand, a disproportionate number of Mexican Americans, Central Americans, and other Latinos *are* victims of prejudice and economic exploitation, not just in border states but also in the furthest reaches of the Midwest and Northeast. Puerto Rican Americans, who by definition have never been illegal immigrants to this country, nonetheless continue to form a substantial portion of the inner-city underclass in New York, Chicago, and other cities. One strike against them, however, is that in contrast to Miami's first post-Castro Cubans, a great many Puerto Ricans "look" black and have been treated as such by whites, their Spanish accents, surnames, or cultural coloration notwithstanding. And even Latinos who don't "look black" are much more likely than whites to grow up poor, live in "rough" neighborhoods, and attend lower-quality public schools. All of this helps to explain why, even among the second generation and beyond, Latinos are significantly less likely than whites to graduate from high school or from a four-year college.

So any changes in admissions policies that help focus attention to the needs of *these* Latinos may be all to the good. Whether on their behalf or that of blacks, however, adding socioeconomic background to the mix of admissions criteria may be an especially problematic aspect of holistic assessment.

Through a Glass, Darkly: *How shall the burdens of poverty and discrimination be weighed?*

All things considered, background-conscious admissions is arguably *more*, not less meritocratic than race-blind, class-blind alternatives: For by taking into account not just what admissions candidates have already achieved, but also any psychosocial or socioeconomic constraints on those achievements, we can better estimate how much they are likely to achieve in the future, once those obstacles to achievement have been put aside.

There are some big problems, however, with turning this principle into practice. One concern some very high-profile minority academics and policy-makers share with most of the men I interviewed is that excessive attention to various forms of hardship may promote what African American linguist and former Berkeley professor John McWhorter has referred to as a "culture of victimization . . . of excuse-making" that would get in the way of future achievement.[20] A bigger difficulty for most whites, however, is that our everyday notion of fair *ends*—in this case, the allocation of scarce opportunities on the basis of merit—are tightly intertwined with everyday notions about fair *means*, embracing not just marginal equality but the kind of procedural transparency and consistency that was so important to Peter Galoszy and Pat Gaheogan.

One virtue of race or ethnicity per se as selection criteria is that, for the great majority of applicants, it is much easier to make categorical distinctions between members of different racial/ethnic groups than to draw the line between rich and poor, or between "comfortable" and "struggling." An accurate calculation of each student's social and economic background—taking into account not just current but past household income, family size, property values, marital and health histories, parents' and grandparents' educational and occupational profiles, and so forth—and the degree of advantage or disadvantage these imply is no simple task. Quantification of such factors at some University of California campuses can yield tallies worthy of George Orwell or Franz Kafka. "A student claiming disadvantage because of divorce would have to make a convincing case that it created a specific hardship—say, sudden loss of income. Getting the full 500 points [available to applicants on the basis of disadvantage] would take a life-altering event, such as being forced into foster care."[21]

As discussed earlier in this book, however, resisting quantification as Berkeley has will hardly satisfy the opposition, either in the case of race-conscious admissions or of California-style, nominally race-neutral comprehensive review. In the future as in the past, we can expect private institutions to be given more leeway, and a good many of the most selective have taken steps in the past few years to expand on the extremely small number of low-income students of any race that they have customarily enrolled.[22] But public college and universities are held to a stricter standard; so it should not surprise us when people like Harold Johnson of the Pacific Legal Foundation[23] question whether "inherently subjective factors like over-coming obstacles, squishy stuff like that, can ever be made to achieve the consistency, objectivity, and predictability that ought to be the hallmark of a taxpayer funded educational institution."[24]

Among opponents of explicitly race-conscious admissions generally, however, the biggest downside to the "squishier" aspects of holistic assessment is that considerable reliance on relatively subjective comparisons makes it that much easier to get away with a *degree* of race consciousness that the Supreme Court has never officially condoned.

Certainly, there was something disingenuous in the claim of Dennis Shields, Michigan's Law School's director of admissions at the time Barbara Grutter applied, that his frequent checks of admissions statistics to see if a "critical mass" of each racial/ethnic group had been selected yet did *not* mean that he had any particular target figures in mind, or that admissions reviewers were under any pressure to admit any particular percentage of minority students. As Justice Ruth Bader Ginsburg noted in her dissenting opinion on *Gratz*, "If honesty is the best policy, surely Michigan's accurately described, fully disclosed [undergraduate] affirmative action program is preferable to achieving similar numbers through winks, nods, and disguises."[25]

A penchant for winks and nods at Michigan may help to explain why, two months after the *Grutter* decision, the University of Michigan announced that its liberal arts college had abandoned its points system altogether, in favor of an individual review of each and every application, for which it was hiring and training additional staff.[26] Implementation of this policy would certainly consume much more time and money than undergraduate admissions ordinarily requires; and since the Court appears to have ruled out points systems only with respect to race, why wouldn't Michigan continue to assign points for students' academic records, establish cut scores for definite rejects, and *then* review holistically all of the remaining applicants? The answer, one can speculate, is that the latter approach might make it much easier for observers (like the watchdog groups mentioned in the introduction to this book) to compare the percentages of eventual admits of various ethnicities from that minimally admissible pool and perhaps find evidence of greater marginal preferences for blacks, Latinos, and American Indians than Michigan wishes to reveal.

Their suspicions are not misplaced: For however much Michigan or other schools argue that their motives are consistent with the Court's decisions—that they've gone no further than is needed to balance the distortions of biased measures, and that race and ethnicity come into play only to the degree that this helps ensure *every* student the best possible education—it is hard to believe them. Because everyone knows that their real motives—and those of the Court, the military, corporate America, and other defenders of affirmative action—are much broader, and dictate more attention to race and ethnicity, than educational quality alone would require.

Ballet Ruse: *Getting past the song and dance about classroom diversity*

Defending affirmative action admissions on the grounds that it enriches the educational experience of whites and Asians is a little like telling someone you read *Playboy* magazine for the articles. Certainly, Hugh Hefner's ground-breaking publication has given us some insightful journalism and cutting-edge commentary; but neither fans nor foes of the magazine would seriously argue that its popularity is based on anything other than its enticing photos of young women. In similar fashion, it is unlikely that many Americans take seriously the claim that a quest for diverse points of view is enough of a reason to violate conventional, meritocratic norms regarding the allocation of opportunities.

Certainly, the men I interviewed had some good things to say about diverse classrooms and the radically multiethnic campus they attended. But that was never their principle motive for advocating affirmative action admissions—nor the reason that opponents were reluctant to reject *all* race-conscious policies, or to give them the lowest possible rating. Strong or faint, ambivalent or un-equivocal, support for race-conscious policies and for greater student body diversity was invariably linked to a sense that colleges and universities had a duty to help correct for the social, political, and economic constraints on minority achievement *outside* the academy.

Likewise, those defending the University of Michigan before the Court made quite clear the centrality of that larger mission to its diversity agenda. The law school's counsel tied diversity to merit—but seemed to construct merit in relation to the needs of a diverse society still riddled with racism. What the school looked for, they argued, was "a strong likelihood of succeed-ing in the practice of law and *contributing* in diverse ways *to the well-being of others*." Therefore, the school sought "a mix of students with varying back-grounds and experiences who will *respect* and learn from *each other*" (italics added).[27] A report submitted to the court by Kent Syverud, who had served on Michigan's faculty before becoming dean of Vanderbilt Law School, defended Michigan's pursuit of a "critical mass" of each underrepresented minority group not just because greater numbers would expose fellow students to more diverse opinions generally, but also because it would help offset racial stereo-typing through exposure to diversity within each minority group. Former Law School Admissions Director Erica Munzel's claim that critical mass "encour-ages underrepresented minorities to participate in the classroom and not feel isolated"[28] once again links the school's admissions policy to its interest in com-bating the consequences of racism.

In similar fashion, the friend-of-court briefs filed by the U.S. government, by our military academies, and by several large corporations all emphasized the needs of the nation's public and private sectors for more diverse leadership, and for the *appearance* of genuine equality of opportunity as well. "Ensuring that public institutions are open and available to all segments of American society, including people of all races and ethnicities, represents a paramount government objective. . . . Nowhere is the importance of such openness more acute than in the context of higher education."[29]

Justice O'Connor's majority opinion on *Grutter* likewise seems to reflect a concern for the legacy of racism. She refers without objection, for example, to the law school's arguments for "critical mass."[30] Citing American Association of Law Schools data on the number of attorneys serving as governors and federal legislators—and the disproportionate number of graduates from a "handful" of selective schools among our senators and federal judges[31]—O'Connor observes,

> In order to cultivate a set of leaders with legitimacy in the eyes of the citizenry, it is necessary that the path to leadership be visibly open to talented and qualified individuals of every race and ethnicity. All members of our heterogeneous society must have confidence in the openness and integrity of the educational institutions that provide this training.[32]

Even when Justice Powell argued for the educative functions of diversity in *Bakke,* his assertion that "the nation's future depends upon leaders trained through wide exposure to the ideas and mores of *students as diverse as this Nation of many peoples*" (italics added)[33] suggests that the benefits of ethnic diversity in the classroom followed from, and were subordinate to, the social realities outside it.

But if the benefits of classroom diversity per se carry so little weight, either with the American people or with their highest court—while much more compelling arguments for the good of the larger society do not seem to jibe with our Constitution—this does not leave a very solid line of defense for a set of policies under constant siege from opponents.

Advocates can continue to advance their objectives, however, if they watch their step, send the right message, and keep in mind the larger goal of a country where affirmative action is no longer needed.

THE ROAD AHEAD

Having survived the courts, can affirmative action also survive public resistance? For the next twenty years, at least, private universities should remain free to consider each applicant's race or ethnicity along with other factors, and for this reason, may increase their ethnic diversity more than they otherwise would have, as able blacks and Latinos find it harder to gain admission to selective public institutions. As for the latter, the backlash against affirmative action could take several forms. More states could mandate that race no longer be considered in the admissions process. Alternatively, the Supreme Court's approval of race-conscious admissions could lead state legislators representing disgruntled whites to underfund public higher education, or to shift that funding from schools to students, who could then take their tuition vouchers to those private schools that they saw as less hamstrung by "political correctness."

Avoiding this kind of backlash may require some rethinking of the particular forms that affirmative action takes. Advocates also need to press the case that percentage plans are *not* a suitable alternative to race-conscious admissions, and to work toward the sorts of changes in public policy that will help to obviate the *need* for affirmative action twenty years hence.

Do the Right Things: *Enforcing common standards and some common ground*

At this point, the greatest threat to race-conscious admissions may be the spread of percentage plans to additional states. Battling this trend on the grounds that not enough blacks and Latinos are admitted under such plans, however, may be counterproductive. A more ecumenical argument may be that under percentage plans, state schools may actually be more likely to admit the "wrong" minorities: A black or Latino student with low test scores and no exceptional talents who graduates in the top fifth from a very low-performing high school, for example, might end up taking a spot that, under a race-conscious policy, would go instead to a black or Latino graduating in the second fifth of his class from an extremely competitive high school who is in fact much better prepared to succeed in college.

Like race-norming, moreover, percentage plans put exceptional weight on performance *relative to* one's most immediate peers, in place of a common scale of measurement. Along with standardized test scores, even competitive cheerleading or a significant role in community organizations may be much more comparable across communities than one's academic rank in class. It might also be helpful to point out to those who have railed against quotas that *absolute quotas are exactly what you get* when a certain percentage of each and every high school class is guaranteed admission to a state's top school or group of schools, regardless of their grades, test scores, or other attributes.

Like Gil Jarreaux, moreover, middle-class white parents may wish to protect high school students from the sort of cutthroat competition common in our economic life. By all accounts, it is *their* kids who are, on the average, most anxious about which colleges they get into. Do they really want to add more fuel to adolescent angst, and perhaps undercut valuable cooperative learning, with a college admissions system that heats up academic competition with the boy or girl across the aisle in their teenager's honors class? Percentage plans might also harm morale on campus, as woefully underprepared students of any race are essentially encouraged to get in over their heads, and blacks and Latinos are further stigmatized by some very evident inequalities.

That is, of course, one of the problems with race-conscious admissions as well. Ask any white advocate what the downside of affirmative action is, and they are likely to respond as several of my subjects did, that it is often most harmful to those it is designed to help, leading others—and sometimes blacks and Latinos themselves—to question whether they really deserve to be where they are. This was probably the most powerful argument in Supreme Court Justice Clarence Thomas's dissenting opinion on *Grutter*, where he quotes an 1865 speech by Frederick Douglas.

> "All I ask is, give [the black man] a chance to stand on his own legs. Let him alone! . . . Your interference is doing positive injury!" It is uncontested that each year, the Law School admits a handful of blacks who would [not] be admitted in the absence of racial discrimination. . . . Who can differentiate between those who belong and those who do not? . . . When blacks take positions in the highest places of government, industry, or academia, it is an open question today whether their skin color played a part in their advancement.[34]

It does no good to say people *shouldn't* feel like that: That's like saying that kids shouldn't need positive role models of their own background, or that they shouldn't allow themselves to be distracted by family problems or gang warfare in their neighborhoods. *Get real: It's human nature.* It is even more natural to suspect the qualifications of those who have been given special consideration without *first* having been subjected to a common test of minimal eligibility. My own survey of 1,600 undergraduates at the school where my interviews were conducted found significantly greater support for modified quotas on the part of graduate professional schools when those quotas were applied in conjunction with some minimum standard, in terms of grades and/or test scores, that everyone admitted, regardless of race or ethnicity, would have to meet.[35] Such an approach would work at the undergraduate level as well— demanding, perhaps, some minimum grade point average *or* rank in class *or* standardized test score, could go a long way toward convincing the general public that affirmative action was never intended to negate the significance of merit as it has traditionally been conceived and measured.

At the same time, advocates of affirmative action would do well to promote greater public discussion of what standardized tests can and cannot tell us about the relative potential of different applicants. In place of hard-to-prove assertions that a given test is racially biased, it might be more useful to emphasize the *class* bias in the tests, which may be a little easier to demonstrate and explain. The public also needs a better grasp of the relationship between the magnitude of test score differences and their usefulness in differentiating one person's potential from another's. This helps to explain why there is often so little relationship between admissions test scores and subsequent performance of students at a single institution, whose scores are more likely to cluster more tightly than scores in general at the high end, low end, or middle of a given test's entire span.

As for race-conscious campus programming, pressure from both public agencies and private organizations has already encouraged colleges and universities to move away from exclusively minority academic support programs, internships, mentorships, and so forth. Consistent with my findings, however, ethnic-specific social and cultural offerings—including "theme" housing, peer mentoring programs, student media, and minority student centers—have so far weathered protests against them, although they might easily fall prey to budget cutters or legal challenges. One thing in these programs' favor is that they are less likely than other forms of affirmative action to be viewed as giving minorities *more* of something that whites or Asians get less of than they want or need. And it is not difficult to appreciate the value of such programming as "homes away from home" to the great many minority students who are "at risk" academically or are vastly outnumbered by white classmates.

But in the end, a supportive campus enclave and remedial education may add up to too little, too late; and blaming test scores or their interpretation for unequal access is just killing the messenger. When affirmative action's critics argue that members of some minority groups are just not ready for the challenges of our most competitive campuses, the most productive response may be to agree with them—and to insist that more be done to ensure that blacks and Latinos actually have what it takes to compete more successfully at every level of schooling.

Do the Right Marginal Equality: *Enhancing opportunity for schoolchildren*

How can we make sure that more black and Latino youth can hit the ground running at our best colleges? A number of policy changes could lighten the impact of the culture of poverty on minority youth. Coupled with less extreme interpretations of Americans' right to bear arms, for example, more humane, more sensible policies on the use of marijuana and harder drugs might seriously constrain the cash flow of street gangs, their allure for a great many inner-city youth, and the threats they pose to inner-city families.

Better prospects for Latino youth—either in the United States or their countries of origin—will also require some serious retooling of U.S. immigration policies and of our role in Latin American politics and economic development. More judicious tax, trade, and job-creation policies generally might help to convince minority youth (and a great many whites as well) that a tight job market still leaves plenty of room for upward mobility.

Most important, however, we need to convince opponents of affirmative action that their professed commitment to marginal equality is simply not compatible with our current system of public education.

There are of course perennial complaints regarding inequitable differences in funding levels between richer and poorer school districts. Reinforcing these arguments, advocates of racial equity need to highlight the disproportionate percentages of inner-city schools' budgets devoted to security and maintenance—both more expensive in urban schools—and to special education, often in relation to disabilities especially prevalent among disadvantaged children, due in part to malnutrition and inadequate prenatal care. If we compared districts solely on the basis of the dollars spent educating the "average" student—her textbooks, his teachers' salaries, classroom technology, field trips, and so forth—the gap between upper-middle-class, mostly white school districts and low-income, mostly minority urban schools would be even more striking.

As to class size, research findings have been mixed on the question of whether schoolchildren retain more facts or master more formulae in smaller classes. Clearly, though, smaller classes allow each child more direct attention from the teacher, make it easier to keep students engaged, and provide more opportunities for each child to express herself and participate as fully and fruitfully as possible in classroom activities. If we're going to "teach to the test," the tests to aim for are the GMAT, the LSAT, and the MCAT, wherein the advantage lies with those who have had the best chance to develop their capacities for critical thinking—something harder to do in overcrowded, underfunded classrooms.

But if equalizing opportunity requires political conservatives to open their pockets a little wider and rethink their views on "cultural literacy," it may also require some rethinking among liberals. Legitimate qualms about the classist or racist consequences of ability grouping may, as Mel Gibran pointed out, often have the perverse effect of denying talented, motivated inner-city youth the best possible opportunity for overcoming myriad obstacles to achieving their full potential. Liberals may also need to rethink their support for aspects of special education regulations that sometimes make it more difficult than it ought to be to keep dangerous or disruptive students out of regular schools and classrooms.[36]

Liberals and conservatives alike, moreover, may want to rethink their common fear of "offensive" classroom discourse[37] and their intense commitment to district-by-district home rule. The latter makes it too easy to set a lower standard for inner-city schools and to underfund classroom teaching and learning. Excessive censorship of classroom discourse and learning materials, on the other hand, may deprive low-income minority youth of the sort of intellectual stimulation they may already be less likely to receive at home.

But we'll never policy-plan our way to full equality unless we find better ways to neutralize the persistent fears, distrust, and resentment that divide us.

Color and Community: *Educating for diversity, racial equality, and the common good*

Lurking behind the front lines of American race relations are the larger questions this book has touched on. What is college for? To the degree that we can accurately identify the most gifted, most dedicated, and most productive among us, just how much more wealth, power, influence, and opportunities than the average citizen do they deserve? What *is* the proper balance between individual autonomy and collective accountability, between our ties to families, neighborhoods, and regions, our ethnic and civic identity, and our obligations as members of an increasingly interdependent community of peoples around the globe?

These are fundamental questions of values that no laboratory research, no anthropological fieldwork, no philosophical paradigm or political theory can answer for us. Through their scholarship, classroom teaching, community involvement, and sponsorship of extracurricular activities, academics can continue to play an important role in elucidating the inherent conflicts such questions raise among the several "traditional values" competing for our allegiance and the influence of diverse cultural, religious, and historical backgrounds on how these questions are answered.

At the same time, however, academics and the schools they work for need to address racial antagonisms more directly. All of my experience as a student, teacher, and social scientist have convinced me that, as Steve Clayburgh put it, affirmative action will not "work" unless whites have a better grasp of "why we're doing this"—that is, of the historical, economic, social, and cultural dynamics of inequality.

Interviewing advocates as well as opponents of affirmative action, I was often shocked at how little they knew about Africa and Asia and Latin America and the islands of the Pacific. Perhaps every bachelor's degree ought to require some significant exposure to the indigenous cultures of these parts of the world, and of U.S. involvement in their economic and political evolution, as well as an understanding of slavery, Jim Crow, and the struggle for civil rights in the United States, of whites' seduction and betrayal of American Indians, and of the wholesale mistreatment of Asians and Chicanos. Somewhere along the line, college students also need to learn that most poor people are not black or Latino, and that not all blacks and Latinos are poor. They could certainly benefit from some exposure to the substantial research, in recent years, on affirmative action's short-term and long-term outcomes.[38] It does no good, moreover, to simply ignore whatever methodologically flawed, poorly argued, racist science or historiography comes down the pike. Refusing to examine in the classroom Charles Murray's theory of blacks' genetic inferiority,[39] for example, will not take those theories out of circulation but simply leave impressionable whites that much more vulnerable to his arguments, still readily available in this information age to anyone looking for scientific validation of whatever prejudices they already have.

At the same time, Americans of every background need to know something about the experience of poverty, prejudice, workplace exploitation, unclean living conditions, test bias, and condescending social policies experienced by successive waves of white immigrants. This is not to make the argument that whites, or even *some* whites, had it just as bad as any other racial group, or to deny distinctive features of white-on-minority discrimination. Quite the contrary: A proper accounting of the American experience of various white ethnic groups would also point up some decided advantages "white ethnics" enjoyed with respect to gaining social acceptance and improving their economic status (for example, substantial support from the relatively affluent descendants of smaller, earlier waves of Jewish and Roman Catholic immigrants).

Human nature being what it is, moreover, giving whites their due as victims should make them more, not less receptive to the notion that nonwhites had it *worse*. Exploring the parallels between different groups' experience—not excluding white Anglo-Saxon Protestants and their economic and religious conflicts with each other—could also help students of every racial and ethnic background grasp the larger historical, geographical, philosophical, psychological, and economic contexts of interethnic rivalries generally. Both in the courses they offer and the public forums they provide, American colleges and universities can continue to celebrate America's unparalleled achievement of a continent-spanning, radically multiethnic, free market democracy without blocking our view of numerous past and present lapses from a standard of social and economic justice that Americans continue to sacrifice their lives for overseas.

Can this kind of education really be delivered in a manner that avoids confrontation, that does not provoke anger and resentment among whites and minorities alike, and does not sully Americans' pride in our history and civic virtue? *No, it can't.* Whether between lovers or family members or among blacks and browns and whites, however, open confrontation may be the surest first step toward mutual understanding, reconciliation, and a strengthening of the tenuous bonds of identity and community. Done right, multicultural education may be our best hope for advancing a stronger sense of fellow feeling across racial and ethnic lines, and hence a sense of mutual obligation and mutual trust deep enough and broad enough to demand public policies to match.

Indeed, one powerful argument against race-conscious admissions or race-conscious anything is that it gets in the way of just the sort of fellow feeling necessary to achieve its ultimate objectives. There was ample evidence in my interviews, certainly, of the sort of hostility toward blacks or Latinos that affirmative action can engender. Among advocates as well as opponents, affirmative action admissions could throw a monkey wrench into interracial friendships—think of Mel Gibran—or dictate fundamentally unequal relationships between someone like Larry Dobbs and his much less well-prepared African American classmate. There is also the danger that the very availability of ethnic-specific campus programs may end up segregating minorities and balkanizing campus life just as surely as Jim Crow laws did half a century ago. There is something hypocritical about defending affirmative action on the grounds of the advantages of a diverse classroom, or lamenting the "white bubble" in which most whites' lives are spent and their perspectives shaped,[40] and then structuring campus life in a manner that helps to keep *every* student locked inside whatever ethnic bubble he or she may have arrived in. Vigorous give and take in the classroom is no substitute for the sort of unstudied, unselfconscious camaraderie out of which lifelong, life-changing friendships are built.

But is it fair to assign "fellow feeling" such an important role in the furtherance of racial equity? Cannot whites be enlisted in the fight against racism simply on the strength of an everyday sense of justice, reinforced by an acknowledgment of their own complicity with discriminatory practices that virtually every white American has arguably benefited from?

Yes and no. Whites *do* need to understand the myriad ways in which a white-dominated social, political, and economic order has oppressed members of other races, and the advantages conferred on *all* members of the dominant racial group in a multiracial society. They need to become much more aware, for example, of how much our economic growth and our cherished "American way of life" owe to black slaves and Latin American agricultural workers, both in this country and abroad. But "whiteness studies" seems to demand much more than that. Eileen O'Brien, for example, cites approvingly some minority activists' dissatisfaction with even actively antiracist whites:

"Humility is something that white people need big-time, because even in this antiracist organization I have found that many of them develop this notion that . . . they

are better than the average white." . . . Those white antiracists who struggle for em-
pathic relationships with people of color [must] not only strive to reduce personal
prejudice and discrimination but humble themselves to alternative interpretations
of their actions, understanding that they occupy a privileged position in white supremacy that has little to do with their individual convictions.[41]

In similar fashion, Christine Clark characterizes the best white allies in the
struggle for equality as "antiracist racists" who

> know that even in the practice of the confrontation of injustice, they are still
> racist. . . . [Antiracist racism] embodies an honest experience of the complexities
> of racism occupying one's psyche mediated with [sic] a profound commitment to
> the lifelong confrontation and attempted eradication of it from one's psyche.[42]

In other words, how *dare* whites imagine that they might ever cleanse themselves of the taint of what Hal Voorhees referred to ironically as "white original sin"?

On one hand, "in your face" confrontations with white complacency force
whites to look more closely at our own lives, attitudes, and behavior in relation
to the perpetuation of a racist society. Repeatedly, my interviews illustrate the
considerable percentage of white Americans who are a little too comfortable
with the notion that since they are *not* "racists" in the traditional sense of the
word, the furtherance of racial equity should require nothing more from them
than color-blind egalitarianism. On the other hand, if we paint *all* whites with
the same brush and portray racism as the sort of chronic ailment that, like her-
pes or alcoholism, simply *cannot* be overcome, this is more likely to sour
whites on the antiracist agenda than to win their allegiance. Indeed, whites'
alienation *from other whites*—Jack Uberhof's frustration with his parents,
Greg Bogosian's discomfort with his employer's double standard, the North-
erner's sense of superiority over Southern "rednecks," the American Jew's
anger at ordinary Germans who did nothing to stop Adolph Hitler—has probably energized American whites to battle racism at least as much as any sense
of their own individual culpability.

What did seem to make a difference to the affirmative action advocates I interviewed, rather, was a sense of themselves as party to a *collective* shame, or at
least a collective liability, for an economic, political, and social system that had
failed to live up to its principles (hence the crucial importance of a more thor-
ough understanding of America's history) coupled with an understanding that
we had no right to blame the victim for acting *just as whites would* in the face
of similar economic and social pressures: This is how *I, too*, might very well respond to bad schools, absent fathers, gang-ridden neighborhoods, or the challenges of immigrant life. "They" are, after all, pretty much like the rest of *us*.

That is not to suggest that the price of racial equity is a denial, a "white-washing" of cultural differences. But it may be dangerous to exaggerate those differences in the manner that many minority educators and activists seem to encourage. For one thing, allusions to differences in "culture"—whether in attitudes, beliefs, customs, behavior, interpersonal expression, what have you—often seem to imply greater homogeneity *within* the black, Latino, American Indian, Asian American, or white "communities" respectively than history or lived experience supports. On the contrary, differences in region, history, national origin, religious faith, educational levels, and especially economic status have helped to create cultural differences *within* the white, black, and Latino communities at least as great as the differences between them. We should also bear in mind that assimilation toward a *common* culture has not only been inevitable but multidirectional—that this country's language and politics and religious traditions are exquisite hybrids, no less than its menus, architecture, and performing arts.

We need to recognize, moreover, that exaggerated notions of cultural difference are not simply harmless conceits but barriers to minority advancement, to the degree that they actually encourage racial stereotypes and hence help to maintain the social, political, and economic status quo. Think of Gil Jarreaux's assertion that, "Certain cultures just do not . . . tend to go to college . . . [or] get on track," or Tom Sorbo's aside that his high school friend in upper-middle-class suburbia was "not *really* black." How many whites have steered clear of black or Latino neighbors, lawyers, psychologists, or investment counselors on the grounds that, "They're just different from us, *they say so themselves*"? How many activists and social scientists have inadvertently encouraged some minority youth to honor, as legitimate cultural differences, aspects of behavior common in economically marginalized communities—of any race—that tend to discourage academic achievement?

All in all, there is nothing wrong with celebrating ethnic diversity, and the unique character and traditions of one's own ethnic group, as long as it does not divert too much attention from *economic* issues that have more to do with inequality than any cultural mismatch in our communities or our schools; and as long as the notion of cultural differences does not help to fuel the worst kind of ethnic chauvinism *among whites*, which remains a convenient salve for economic insecurity. Teachers, scholars, and political leaders need to find better ways to counter the widespread assumption that it is affirmative action itself and minorities' failure to "adapt," as Tom Sorbo put it—not new technology, or undue corporate influence, or a globalized market for goods and labor, or ill-advised diplomatic and military ventures—that is cheating whites out of good jobs or their fair share of government largesse. Only through a stronger sense of community among *all* Americans can we mount the strongest possible defense against common threats to our physical safety, our political liberty, and every American's fair shot at a better life.

NOTES

1. This may be especially true for American men, socialized to "hang tough" in the face of difficulties, to "take care of themselves" when faced down by opponents, to focus a great deal of attention on athletic contests that are as much about individual endurance and playing through one's pain as they are about teamwork. What we demand of ourselves, however, we are more likely to demand of others; so it should not surprise us that American men are significantly less likely than American women to endorse progressive policies designed to help bridge the gap between other people's wants or needs and what those people can actually achieve on their own. Very likely, were one to conduct similar interviews with a sample of women, the tension between the self-reliance and collective accountability would not have been quite so obvious or so acute.

2. Making the rounds among disgruntled Democrats this year is cognitive scientist George Lakoff's *Don't Think of An Elephant* (White River Junction, Vermont: Chelsea Green, 2004) which, among other things, argues that conflicts between progressives and conservatives reflect competing commitments to "nurturant parent" and "strict father" models of family life, as these translate into prescriptions for public policy. What my findings suggest, however, is that most conservatives may be quite nurturing to members of their *actual* families, and others near and dear to them, reserving the strict father model to those outside their inner circles.

3. See, for example, transcripts of interviews with whites in Eduardo Bonilla-Silva's *Racism without Racists*, or in "White Views of Civil Rights: Color-Blindness and Equality of Opportunity," by Nancy DiTomaso, Rochelle Parks-Yancy, and Corinne Post, pp. 189–98 in *White Out: The Continuing Significance of Racism*, ed. Ashley W. Doane and Eduardo Bonilla-Silva, New York: Routledge, 2003.

4. P. 67, Sigmund Freud, *Group Psychology and the Analysis of the Ego*, New York: Bantam, 1960, translated by J. Strachey from *Massenpsychologie und Ich-Analyse*. Leipzig, Vienna, and Zurich: Internationaler Psychoanlytischer Verlag, 1921.

5. Excerpted in "Editorial Pages and Columnists Weigh In on High Court's Rulings," *The Chronicle of Higher Education*, July 4, 2003, p. S9.

6. *Grutter v. Bollinger et al.*, 539 U.S., 2003, p. 28.

7. Appellant's brief quoted in *Grutter* v. *Bollinger*, p. 18.

8. John Moores, *A Preliminary Report on University of California, Berkeley Admission Process for 2002*, Oakland: University of California, 2003, p. 3.

9. Information on the SAT, GMAT, LSAT, and MCAT, respectively, is available at www.collegeboard.com, www.mba.com/mba, www.lsac.org, and www.aamc.org/students/mcat. Depending on what information is sought, visitors to these sites may need to register, but most of the information cited is available free of charge and can be accessed without signing up for the tests themselves.

10. *Grutter* v. *Bollinger*, U.S. District Court, Eastern District of Michigan, Southern Division, trial transcript, February 6, 2002, pp. 88–156.

11. One of the most recent reviews of pertinent research findings is George Farkas's "The Black-White Test Score Gap," *Contexts* 3:2, Spring 2004, pp. 12–19. The issue of racial differences in standardized test scores is also addressed in the March 2000 (6:1) issue of *Psychology, Public Policy, and Law*; see especially Linda F. Wightman, "The Role of Standardized Admission

Tests in the Debate about Merit, Academic Standards, and Affirmative Action," pp. 90–100, Cecil R. Reynolds, "Why Is Psychometric Research on Bias in Mental Testing So Often Ignored?" pp. 144–50, and John E. Hunter and Frank L. Schmidt, "Racial and Gender Bias in Ability and Achievement Tests: Resolving the Apparent Paradox," pp. 151–58.

12. Hillary Rodham Clinton, *It Takes a Village: And Other Lessons Children Teach Us*, New York: Simon and Schuster, 1996.

13. One recent study of the top 10 percent of four-year colleges, in terms of selectivity, found that 74 percent of their student bodies, in aggregate, came from the wealthiest quarter of American households, while just 3 percent came from the least wealthy quarter. See Richard D. Kahlenberg, ed., *America's Untapped Resource: Low-Income Students in Higher Education*, New York, Century Foundation Press, 2004.

14. Along with *botanical, marionette, palette, putrefaction, reciprocate,* and *superficial,* all of these words appeared in the fourteen-item verbal analogies section of the "Diagnostic Mini-SAT," one of the test-preparation materials that could be downloaded free of charge in 2004 from www.collegeboard.com.

15. Italicized adjectives and the singular forms of italicized nouns are taken from some of the practice exercises provided by the College Board for the reading comprehension and sentence completion portions of the 2006 SAT Reasoning Test.

16. Tamar Lewin, "New SAT Writing Test Is Planned," *The New York Times*, June 23, 2002.

17. See, for example, Robert J. Sternberg et al., "Theory-Based University Admissions Testing for a New Millennium." *Educational Psychology*, 39:3, 185–98, 2004; and Robert J. Sternberg, "Accomplishing the Goals of Affirmative Action—with or without Affirmative Action," *Change* 37:1, 6–13, 2005.

18. Some examples: One of the items used to measure creativity asks test-takers to write two short stories, each based on one of the selection of unusual titles, such as "2983," "It's Moving Backwards," and "The Octopus' Sneakers" (Sternberg et al., "Theory-Based University Admissions Testing for a New Millennium," p. 3). Some of the "practical intelligence" items involve rating on a seven-point scale each of several options for responding to "problems encountered in everyday life," such as being "asked to write a letter of recommendation for someone one does not know particularly well" (p. 19 of the same article).

19. These and other statistics on Latinos in this section are drawn from or based on figures provided in four recent studies by the Pew Hispanic Center in Washington, D.C.: *Estimated Numbers of Unauthorized Migrants Residing in the United States: The Total, Mexican, and Non-Mexican Central American Unauthorized Populations in Mid-2001*, by Frank D. Bean, Jennifer Van Hook, Karen Woodrow-Lafield, 2001; *Counting the "Other Hispanics": How Many Colombians, Dominicans, Ecuadorians, Guatemalans and Salvadorans Are There in the United States?* by Roberto Suro, 2002; *Latinos in Higher Education: Many Enroll, Too Few Graduate*, by Richard Fry, 2002; and *The Rise of the Second Generation: Changing Patterns in Hispanic Population Growth*, by Roberto Suro and Jeffrey Passell, 2003.

20. John McWhorter, "Victims Hed [*sic*] Here," *The Washington Post*, August 4, 2002.

21. Michelle Locke, "California Colleges Say Hardships Help Pick Good Students," Associated Press, July 28, 2002.

22. The issue of expanding opportunities for students of modest socioeconomic backgrounds is discussed at length in *Equity and Excellence in American Higher Education*, a new book by William G. Bowen, Martin A. Kurzweil, Eugene M. Tobin, and Susanne Pichler (Charlottesville, VA: University of Virginia Press, 2005), and in a recent article by the first three authors, "From 'Bastions of Privilege' to 'Engines of Opportunity,'" in the *Chronicle of Higher Education* 51:25 (February 5), B18.

23. A public-interest law firm based in Sacramento, California, the Pacific Legal Foundation continues to oppose what it views as a continuation of racial preferences on the part of the University of California.

24. Michelle Locke, "California Colleges Say Hardships Help Pick Good Students," Associated Press, July 28, 2002.

25. *Gratz v. Bollinger et al.*, 516 U.S., 2003, Justice Ginsburg dissenting, Part II.

26. Peter Schmidt, "Foes of Affirmative Action Push Colleges to Reveal Policies on Race-Conscious Admissions." *Chronicle of Higher Education*, March 26, 2004.

27. *Gratz v. Bollinger, et al.*, 516 U.S., 2003, p. 6, quoting Appellant's Brief 110.

28. *Gratz v. Bollinger et al.*, 516 U.S., 2003, p. 6, quoting Appellant's Brief 110.

29. *Gratz v. Bollinger, et al.*, 516 U.S., 2003, pp. 11–12, quoting Brief for the United States as *Amicus Curiae*.

30. "We are satisfied that the Law School adequately considered race-neutral alternatives currently capable of producing a critical mass without forcing the Law School to abandon the academic selectivity that is the cornerstone of its educational mission." *Grutter v. Bollinger*, pp. 28–29.

31. "Individuals with law degrees occupy roughly half the state governorships, more than half the seats in the United States Senate, and more than a third of the seats in the United States House of Representatives. . . . [moreover] A handful of [highly selective] law schools accounts for 25 of 100 United States Senators, 74 United States Courts of Appeals judges, and nearly 200 of the more than 600 United States District Court judges." Brief for Association of American Law Schools, p. 6, cited in *Grutter v. Bollinger et al.*, 539 U.S., 2003, p. 20.

32. *Grutter v. Bollinger et al.*, 539 U.S., 2003, p. 20.

33. *Regents of Univ. of Cal. v. Bakke*, 438 U.S., 1978, p. 49, quoting from *Keyishian v. Board of Regents of Univ. of State of N.Y.*, 385 U.S., 1967.

34. *Grutter v. Bollinger et al.*, 539 U.S., 2003, Justice Thomas, dissenting, p. 1, quoting from *What the Black Man Wants: An Address Delivered in Boston, Massachusetts, on 26 January 1865*, reprinted in *The Frederick Douglass Papers, Book 4*, J. Blassingame and J. McKivigan, eds., New Haven: Yale University Press, 1991.

35. Lipson, Helen D. Undergraduates' Perspectives on Professional Schools' Affirmative Action Policies, presented at the annual meeting of the Midwest Sociological Society, Chicago, 1993.

36. An excellent illustration is provided in the April 11, 2004, *Los Angeles Times* editorial on the L.A. school district's de facto policy of assigning students to schools partly on the basis of where a particular student from a particular neighborhood is least likely to be attacked. Superintendent Roy Romer explains, "We have to run this institution so that every kid has a right to come in this door and get an education." Special education laws dictate placement in the "least restrictive setting" in which a given student can succeed—which does not necessarily provide the best environment for success to his or her classmates. Without knowing all the details, it is nonetheless difficult to disagree with the editorialist: "Officials say they are boxed in by competing agendas: the need to maintain campus safety and the responsibility to give gang members a chance at education. . . . Yes—but what kind of message do the district's tactics convey to hardworking students asked to accept the omnipotence of gangs in order to get an education?"

37. On this topic, Diane Ravitch really says it all in *The Language Police: How Pressure Groups Restrict What Students Learn*, New York: Alfred A. Knopf, 2003.

38. See, for example, William Bowen and Derek Bok's *The Shape of the River: Long-term Consequences of Considering Race in University Admissions*, Princeton, NJ: Princeton University Press, 2000; Richard Sander's "A Systemic Analysis of Affirmative Action in American Law Schools," *Stanford Law Review*, 57:2, 2005; and Thomas J. Espenshade and Chuang Y. Chung's

"The Opportunity Cost of Admissions Preferences at Elite Universities," *Social Science Quarterly*, 86:2 (June, 2005), 293–305.

39. The fullest elaboration of this theory may be found in Richard Herrnstein and Charles Murray, *The Bell Curve: Intelligence and Class Structure in American Life*, New York: Free Press, 1994.

40. Joe Feagin and Eileen O'Brien employ this term in *White Men on Race: Power, Privilege, and the Shaping of Cultural Consciousness*, Boston: Beacon Press, 2003, noting, "Unless more whites . . . break off the social isolation that generally characterizes their entire lives, we can expect [a] serious lack of empathy across the color line to continue, and the blindness to much racial discrimination to persist."

41. Pp. 262–63, 267, "The Political Is Personal: The Influence of White Supremacy on White Antiracists' Personal Relationships," pp. 253–67 in *White Out: The Continuing Significance of Racism*, ed. Ashley W. Doane and Eduardo Bonilla-Silva, New York: Routledge, 2003.

42. P. 93, "The Secret: White Lies Are Never Little," pp. 92–110 in *Becoming and Unbecoming White: Owning and Disowning a Racial Identity*, ed. Christine Clark and James O'Donnell, Westport, CT: Bergin and Garvey, 1999.

APPENDIX

Table A.1. Interview Subjects and Policy Preferences,* Alphabetically by (Pseudonymous) First Names

Pseudonym	Age	Under-graduate Major(s)	Anticipated Graduate Professional Degree(s)	Approves Absolute Quotas?	Quotas w/ Race-Norming?	Quotas w/ Race-Neutral Cut Scores?	Reweighted Criteria?	Racially-Targeted Recruiting?	College-Level Racially-Targeted Programs?	Pre-College Racially-Targeted Interventions?
Bill Sajak	25	business	MBA	—	—	—	●	—	●	●
Doug Peruggia	22	humanities	JD	—	—	—	●	●	●	—
Charlie Kilgallen	34	business	MBA or JD	—	●	●	●	●	●	—
Chris Feraios	21	business	MBA	—	—	—	—	—	—	—
Dan Lysenko	22	social science	MBA or JD	—	—	—	●	●	●	●
Dave Zaluba	26	natural science	MD	—	●	●	●	●	●	●
Mike Benedetto	21	natural science	MD	—	●	—	●	●	●	●
Drew Kazinski	21	business	JD & MBA	—	—	—	●	—	—	—
Gil Jarreaux	22	business	MBA	—	—	—	●	●	●	●
Greg Bogosian	20	business	JD	—	—	—	●	●	—	—
Hal Voorhees	21	humanities	JD	—	●	●*	●	—	●	●
Isaac Fedelovich	21	natural science	MD	—	—	—	●	●	●	●
Jack Uberhof	25	business	MBA	—	—	—	●	—	—	●
Jeff McEwen	23	social science	JD	—	—	—	●	●	—	—
Joe Murtaugh	23	arts & business	MBA	—	—	—	●	●	—	—
Larry Dobbs	29	business	MBA	—	●	●	—	—	●	●
Len Hellstrom	35	health professions	MD	—	●	●	●	●	●	●

Name	Age	Field	Degree						
Marc Huston	21	natural science	MD	—	—	•	•	—	—
Matt Vigoda	20	humanities	JD	•	•	•	•	•	•
Mel Gibran	21	engineering	MBA	•	•	•	•	•	•
Nick deLeo	22	natural science	MD	—	—	•	•	—	•
Pat Gaheogan	20	social science	JD	—	—	•	•	—	•
Peter Galoszy	25	business	MBA	—	—	•	—	—	—
Phil Zeckman	26	social science	JD	•	•	•	•	•	—
Rick Skilling	23	natural science	MBA	—	—	•	•	—	•
Rob Ingraham	20	natural science	MD	—	—	•	•	—	•
Sam Turner	25	education	MD	—	—	•	•	—	—
Sean Hanna	20	natural science	MD	•	•	•	•	•	•
Steve Clayburgh	23	business	JD & MBA	•	•	•	•	•	•
Tim Kovacs	26	humanities & natural science	MD	—	—	•	•	—	—
Tom Sorbo	24	social science	JD	•	•	•	—	—	—
Zack Pritchard	23	natural science	MD	—	—	•	•	•	•

* Bullets indicate that the subject gave an "acceptable" or "very acceptable" rating (4 or 5 on a five-point scale) to the policy in question. More details on each policy are provided in the introduction. Not listed here is the lottery option, which no one endorsed.

** Isaac did not actually endorse any of the quota options, but assigned a rating of '3' to modified quotas with race-neutral cut scores because he felt that race should be taken into account to some degree. Tim Kovacs assigned the same score to the same policy, but elsewhere made it clear that he did not approve considerations of race in the admissions process. For purposes of comparison, then, Isaac was grouped with the advocates and Tim with the opponents of race-conscious admissions to graduate professional schools.

Table A.2. 2004 SAT, GMAT, LSAT, and MCAT Mean Scores By Self-Identified Racial/Ethnic/National Origins[a]

	SAT Verbal		SAT Math		GMAT		LSAT		MCAT Verbal Reasoning	MCAT Physical Sciences	MCAT Biological Sciences
	M	F	M	F	M	F	M	F			
Range of possible scores	200–800		200–800		200–800		100–200		1–15	1–15	1–15
American Indian or Alaskan Native[b]	488	480	508	470	502	462	150.7	148.9	7.9	7.6	8.1
Asian or Pacific Islander[b]	509	505	592	563	562	544	154.6	153.9	8.8	9.7	9.8
Black/African American	428	432	438	420	446	415	144.0	143.4	7.0	6.9	7.3
Cuban[c]	—	—	—	—	—	—	—	—	8.7	8.8	9.2
Mexican/Chicano	457	446	477	444	481	442	149.7	148.6	8.3	8.0	8.7
Puerto Rican	462	454	470	439	478	437	141.2	139.6	6.7	6.8	7.5
Other Latin American Designation[d]	469	456	487	448	500	457	149.6	147.5	8.1	8.2	8.6
White/Caucasian	531	525	550	514	549	509	154.8	153.7	9.4	9.2	9.7

[a]SAT averages are taken from 2004 Profile of College Bound Seniors, issued by the College Entrance Examination Board, 2004. GMAT averages are taken from Profile of GMAT Candidates, issued by the Graduate Management Admissions Council, 2004. LSAT scores were provided by Robert Carr, senior statistician, Law School Admission Council, and are based on the scores of everyone who applied to at least one law school in 2004, most of whom also took the LSAT in that year. MCAT averages are drawn from Facts: Applicants, Matriculants, and Graduates, issued by the American Association of Medical Colleges in 2004.

[b]In contrast to the other tests, GMAT scores for those of Pacific-Islander origins are included with those for American Indians and Alaskan natives.

[c]Separate SAT, GMAT, and LSAT averages for Cuban Americans were not available.

[d]This may include those with origins in other nations of Latin America, those with mixed Latin American heritage (e.g., Mexican and Puerto Rican), and those who listed themselves simply as "Latino" or "Hispanic."

BIBLIOGRAPHY

Alba, Manual, Margaret Butler, Monique Dennis-Elmore, Wanda Johnson, Sock-Foon MacDougal, Eileen Rudert, and Mireille Zieseniss. 2002. *Beyond Percentage Plans: The Challenge of Equal Opportunity in Higher Education.* Washington, D.C.: U.S. Commission on Civil Rights.

Allen, Walter R. 1985. "Black Student, White Campus: Structural, Interpersonal, and Psychological Correlates of Success." *Journal of Negro Students* 54, 134–37.

Association of American Medical Colleges. 2000. *Characteristics of 1999 MCAT Examinees.* Chicago.

Attinasi, L. C., Jr. 1989. "Getting In: Mexican-Americans' Perceptions of University Attendance and the Implications for Freshman Year Persistence." *Journal of Higher Education* 60:3 (May–June), 247–77.

Bean, Frank D., Jennifer Van Hook, and Karen Woodrow-Lafield. 2001. *Estimates of Numbers of Unauthorized Migrants Residing in the United States: The Total, Mexican, and Non-Mexican Central American Unauthorized Populations in Mid-2001.* Washington, D.C.: Pew Hispanic Center.

Bonilla-Silva, Eduardo. 2003. *Racism without Racists: Color-Blind Racism and the Persistence of Racial Inequality in the United States.* New York: Rowman and Littlefield.

Bowen, William, and Derek Bok. 2000. *The Shape of the River: Long-term Consequences of Considering Race in University Admissions.* Princeton, NJ: Princeton University Press.

Bowen, William G., Martin A. Kurzweil, Eugene M. Tobin, and Susanne Pichler. 2005. *Equity and Excellence in American Higher Education.* Charlottesville, VA: University of Virginia Press.

Calvin, Allen. 2000. "Use of Standardized Tests in Admissions in Postsecondary Institutions of Higher Education." *Psychology, Public Policy, and Law* 6:1 (March), 20–32.

Ceci, Stephen J. 2000. "So Near and Yet So Far: Lingering Questions About the Use of Measures of General Intelligence for College Admissions and Employment Screening." *Psychology, Public Policy, and Law* 6:1 (March), 233–52.

Chavez, Linda. 2002. "California Still Uses Outlawed Policy." *Chicago Sun Times*, August 10.

Chronicle of Higher Education. 2003. "Editorial Pages and Columnists Weigh In on High Court's Rulings." July 4, S9.

Clark, Christine, and James O'Donnell, eds. 1999. *Becoming and Unbecoming White: Owning and Disowning a Racial Identity.* Westport, CT: Bergin and Garvey.

Clegg, Roger. 2005. "Time Has Not Favored Racial Preferences," *Chronicle of Higher Education* 51:19, January 14, B10.

College Entrance Examination Board. 2005. "*About SAT.*" www.collegeboard.com/student/testing/sat/about/SATI.html, 2005. Princeton, NJ.

———. 2005. *College-Bound Seniors: A Profile of SAT Program Test-Takers.* Princeton, NJ.

Costantini, E., and J. King. 1985. "Affirmative Action: The Configuration, Concomitants, and Antecedents of Student Opinion." *Youth and Society* 16:4, 499–525.

Crosby, Faye J. 2004. *Affirmative Action Is Dead: Long Live Affirmative Action.* New Haven: Yale University Press.

Doane, Ashley W., and Eduardo Bonilla-Silva. 2003. *White Out: The Continuing Significance of Racism.* New York: Routledge.

Douglass, Frederick. 1865. *What the Black Man Wants: An Address Delivered in Boston, Massachusetts, on 26 January 1865.* Reprinted in J. Blassingame and J. McKivigan, eds., *The Frederick Douglass Papers, Book 4,* New Haven: Yale University Press, 1991. Dovidio, John F., and Samuel L. Gaertner, eds. 1986. *Prejudice, Discrimination and Racism.* Orlando, FL: Academic Press.

Espenshade, Thomas J., and Chuang Y. Chung. 2005. "The Opportunity Cost of Admissions Preferences at Elite Universities," *Social Science Quarterly,* 86:2 (June), 293–305. Farkas, George. 2004. "The Black-White Test Score Gap." *Contexts* 3:2 (Spring), 12–19.

Feagin, Joseph, and Eileen O'Brien. 2003. *White Men on Race: Power, Privilege, and the Shaping of Cultural Consciousness.* Boston: Beacon Press.

Fleming, Jacqueline. 1984. *Blacks in College: A Comparative Study of Students' Success in Black and White Institutions.* San Francisco: Jossey-Bass.

Freud, Sigmund. 1921. *Massenpsychologie und Ich-Analyse.* Leipzig, Vienna, and Zurich: Internationaler Psychoanlytischer Verlag. Translation by J. Strachey as *Group Psychology and the Analysis of the Ego,* New York: Bantam, 1960.

Fry, Richard. 2002. *Latinos in Higher Education: Many Enroll, Too Few Graduate.* Washington, D.C.: Pew Hispanic Center.

Gilbert, W. S., and Arthur Sullivan. 1999. *The Mikado in Full Score.* Dover, England: Dover Publications.

Golden, Daniel. 2002. "Extra Credit: To Get into UCLA, It Helps to Face 'Life Challenges.'" *Wall Street Journal,* August 4. *Gratz v. Bollinger et al.,* 516 U.S., 2003.

Grutter v. Bollinger et al., 539 U.S., 2003.

Halpern, Diane F. 2000. "Validity, Fairness, and Group Differences." *Psychology, Public Policy, and Law* 6:1 (March), 56–62.

Heinz, John P., and Edward O. Lauerman. 1983. *Chicago Lawyers: The Social Structure of the Bar.* Chicago: Russell Sage Foundation and the American Bar Association.

Herrnstein, Richard, and Charles Murray. 1984. *The Bell Curve: Intelligence and Class Structure in American Life.* New York: Free Press.

Hezlett, S., N. Kuncel, A. Vey, D. Ones, J. Campbell, and W. J. Camara. The effectiveness of the SAT in predicting success early and late in college: A comprehensive meta-analysis. Paper presented at the annual meeting of the National Council of Measurement in Education, Seattle, WA.

Hopwood et al. v. State of Texas et al., United States Court of Appeals for the Fifth Circuit, 94-50569, 1996.

Hunter, John E., and Frank L. Schmidt. 2000. "Racial and Gender Bias in Ability and Achievement Tests: Resolving the Apparent Paradox." *Psychology, Public Policy, and Law* 6:1 (March), 151–58.

Jackman, Mary R., and M. J. Muha. 1984. "Education and Intergroup Attitudes: Moral Enlightenment, Superficial Democratic Commitment, or Ideological Refinement?" *American Sociological Review* 49, 751–69.

Jensen, Arthur R. 2000. "Testing: The Dilemma of Group Differences." *Psychology, Public Policy, and Law* 6:1 (March), 121–27.

Johnson, Lyndon Baines. 1965. "Howard University Commencement Address." June 4, 1965.

Kahlenberg, Richard D., ed. 2004. *America's Untapped Resource: Low-Income Students in Higher Education.* New York: Century Foundation Press.

Keyishian v. Board of Regents of Univ. of State of N.Y., 385 U.S., 1967.

Kinder, D. R., and D. O. Sears. 1981. "Prejudice and Politics: Symbolic Racism versus Racial Threats to the Good Life." *Journal of Personality and Social Psychology* 40, 414–31.

Kluegel, James R., and Eliot R. Smith. 1986. *Beliefs About Inequality: Americans' Views of What Is and What Ought to Be.* Hawthorne, NY: Aldine de Gruyter.

Lewin, Tamar. 2003. "New SAT Writing Test Is Planned." *The New York Times*, June 23.

Lakoff, George. 2004. *Don't Think of An Elephant.* White River Junction, Vermont: Chelsea Green.

Lipset, S. M., and W. Schneider. 1978. "The Bakke Case: How Would It Be Decided at the Bar of Public Opinion?" *Public Opinion*, March/April, 38–44.

Lipson, Helen D. 1993. Undergraduates' perspectives on professional schools' affirmative action policies. Paper presented at the annual meeting of the Midwest Sociological Society, Chicago.

Locke, Michelle. 2002. "California Colleges Say Hardships Help Pick Good Students." Associated Press, July 28.

———. 2002. "Faculty Gives New UC Admissions Process Passing Grade." Associated Press, November 7.

McClelland, K. E., and C. J. Auster. 1990. "Public Platitudes and Hidden Tensions: Racial Climates at Predominantly White Liberal Arts Colleges." *Journal of Higher Education* 61:6 (November/December), 607–42.

McConahay, John B. 1986. "Modern Racism, Ambivalence, and the Modern Racism Scale." Pp. 91–125 in John F. Dovidio and Samuel L. Gaertner, eds., *Prejudice, Discrimination, and Racism.* Orlando, FL: Academic Press.

McConahay, John B., B. B. Hardee, and V. Batts. 1997. "Has Racism Declined in America? It Depends on Who Is Asking and What Is Asked." *Journal of Conflict Resolution* 25, 563–79.

McWhorter, John. 2002. "Victims Hed [sic] Here." *The Washington Post*, August 4.

Moores, John. 2003. *A Preliminary Report on University of California, Berkeley Admission Process for 2002.* Oakland, CA: University of California.

Oberlin College Deans' Research Group. 1988. Black Student Persistence to Graduation at Oberlin College: Summary and Recommendation. Oberlin, OH: Oberlin College.

Oliver, M. L., C. J. Rodriguez, and R. A. Mickelson. 1985. "Brown and Black and White: The Social Adjustment and Academic Performance of Chicano and Black Students in a Predominantly White University." *Urban Review* 17, 3–23.

Orr, Amy J. 2003. "Black-White Differences in Achievement: The Importance of Wealth." *Sociology of Education* 76 (October), 281–304.

Powers, John R. 1982. *Do Black Patent Leather Shoes Really Reflect Up?* New York: Samuel French.

Regents of Univ. of Cal. v. Bakke, 438 U.S., 1978.

Ravitch, Diane. 2003. *The Language Police: How Pressure Groups Restrict What Students Learn.* New York: Alfred A. Knopf.

Reynolds, Cecil R. 2000. "Why Is Psychometric Research on Bias in Mental Testing So Often Ignored?" *Psychology, Public Policy, and Law* 6:1 (March), pp. 144–50.

Rosenfeld, Michel. 1991. *Affirmative Action and Justice: A Philosophical and Constitutional Inquiry.* New Haven: Yale University Press.

Sander, Richard. 2005. "A Systemic Analysis of Affirmative Action in American Law Schools," *Stanford Law Review* 57:2, 2005.

Schuman, Howard, Charlotte Steeh, and Lawrence Bobo. 1985. *Racial Attitudes in America: Trends and Interpretations.* Cambridge, MA: Harvard University Press.

Sedlacek, W. E. 1987. "Black Students on White Campuses: 20 Years of Research." *Journal of College Student Personnel 28* (November), 484–95.

Shaw, George Bernard. 1916. *Pygmalion.* In *Androcles and the Lion; Overruled; Pygmalion.* London: Constable.

Schmidt, Peter. 2004. "Foes of Affirmative Action Push Colleges to Reveal Policies on Race-Conscious Admissions." *Chronicle of Higher Education,* March 26.

Sears, David O., Lawrence Bobo, and James Sidanius, eds. 1999. *Racialized Politics: The Debate About Racism in America.* Chicago: University of Chicago Press.

Sowell, Thomas. 1990. *Preferential Policies: An International Perspective.* New York: William Morrow.

Sternberg, Robert J., the Rainbow Project Collaborators, and the University of Michigan Business School Project Collaborators. 2004. "Theory-Based University Admissions Testing for a New Millennium." *Educational Psychology* 39:3, 185–98.

Sternberg, Robert J. 2005. "Accomplishing the Goals of Affirmative Action—with or without Affirmative Action." *Change* 37:1, 6–13.

Suro, Roberto. 2002. *Counting the "Other Hispanics": How Many Colombians, Dominicans, Ecuadorians, Guatemalans and Salvadorans Are There in the United States?* Washington, D.C.: Pew Hispanic Center.

Suro, Roberto, and Jeffrey Passell. 2003. *The Rise of the Second Generation: Changing Patterns in Hispanic Population Growth.* Washington, D.C.: Pew Hispanic Center.

Sweezy v. New Hampshire, 354 U.S., 1957.

Tienda, Marta. 2003. *Affirmative Action and its Discontents: Lessons from the Texas Top 10% Plan.* Ann Arbor: University of Michigan.

University of Michigan, *2004-2005 Application for Undergraduate Admission.*

U.S. Commission on Civil Rights. 2002. *Beyond Percentage Plans: The Challenge of Equal Opportunity in Higher Education.* Washington, D.C.

Vargas, Jose. 1992. "Fraternity Skit Revives Racial Tensions." *Chicago Flame,* April 14, 4:30, 1, 9.

Warde, Cardinal, and Karl W. Reid. 2003. *Minority Introduction to Engineering, Entrepreneurship and Science Program (MITE²S) 2003 Final Report.* Cambridge, MA: Massachusetts Institute of Technology.

Wightman, Linda F. 2000. "The Role of Standardized Admission Tests in the Debate about Merit, Academic Standards, and Affirmative Action." *Psychology, Public Policy, and Law* 6:1 (March), 90–100.

Williams, W. M. 2000. "Perspectives on Intelligence Testing, Affirmative Action, and Educational Policy." *Psychology, Public Policy, and Law* 6, 5–19.

Wolff, Edward N. 2002. *Top Heavy: The Increasing Inequality of Wealth in America and What Can Be Done About It.* New York: New Press, W. W. Norton, 2002.

INDEX

ACT, 52. *See also* tests
affirmative action: definition of, 2;
   examples of, 2, 5; models of, presented
   to interview subjects, 16–18; public
   opinion regarding, 1–2, 3–4, 22n12,
   182, 184. *See also* benefits/legitimacy
   of affirmative action; costs/negatives/
   illegitimacy of affirmative action;
   criteria for admissions decisions;
   programming and outreach; race-
   conscious admissions; recruiting *qua*
   advertising and promotion
African Americans. *See* blacks
American Association of Law Schools,
   182
American Civil Rights Institute, 11, 14
American Indians: academic and
   economic attainments of, 5, 177;
   affirmative action on behalf of, 2, 8,
   10, 11, 12, 16, 188; designation as,
   20n2; history of white violence
   against and betrayal of, 178, 188;
   value of traditional medicines of,
   54–55. *See also* racism
American Negro College Fund, 146

Arabs and Arab-Americans, 148. *See also*
   Palestinians and Palestinian
   Americans; Middle-Easterners and
   Middle-Eastern Americans
Armenian Americans, 74, 103, 117
Arnaz, Desi, 178
Asians and Asian Americans: affirmative
   action on behalf of, 21n9, 46;
   definition of, 21n2; discrimination
   against and exploitation of, 99, 178;
   explanations for academic,
   occupational, and economic
   attainment among, 5, 18, 58, 59, 61,
   74–75, 129, 135, 147, 150, 163; extent
   of academic, professional, and
   economic attainment among, 5, 18,
   75, 156, 177. *See also* Chinese and
   Chinese-Americans; families; race-
   conscious admissions; self-help
athletic performance, 149; consideration
   of, in admissions decisions, 9, 10, 39,
   52, 169, 192n1; hereditary basis of,
   59, 61, 83; prestige value of, 54, 72
Austin neighborhood, Chicago, 109
Autobiology of Malcolm X, The, 94

ABOUT THE AUTHOR

A Philadelphia native, **Helen D. Lipson** spent most of her adult life in Chicago, where the research for *Talking Affirmative Action* was conducted. She earned her Ph.D. in public policy analysis from the University of Illinois at Chicago and worked as a teacher, editor, program evaluator, and institutional researcher at UIC, Roosevelt University, the City College of Chicago, and other schools.

Heading west, she spent four years in Fargo, ND, crossing the Red River to work with at-risk students at Minnesota State University Moorhead's New Center for Multidisciplinary Studies. Dr. Lipson now lives in Oregon, where she has been involved in public opinion research at Portland State University, Oregon State University, and the Oregon State Public Interest Research Group. Among her current projects is a group of short stories tentatively titled *Degrees of Freedom.*